AF538545

EVOLUTION-MECHANISM AND PROCESSES

EVOLUTION-MECHANISM AND PROCESSES

By
Dr. M. Prakash
Dept. of Zoology
M.M.H. Post Graduate College
Ghaziabad (U.P.)
(India)

DISCOVERY PUBLISHING HOUSE PVT. LTD.
NEW DELHI-110 002

Published by:
Tilak Wasan
DISCOVERY PUBLISHING HOUSE PVT. LTD.
4383/4A, Ansari Road, Darya Ganj
New Delhi-110 002 (India)
Phone : +91-11-23279245, 43596064-65
Fax : +91-11-23253475
E-mail : parul.wasan@gmail.com
discoverypublishinghouse@gmail.com
web : www.discoverypublishinggroup.com

***First Edition:* 2012**

ISBN: 978-93-5056-083-9

Evolution-Mechanism and Processes

Printed at:
Shree Balaji Art Press
Delhi

Preface

Evolution is the process of change in all forms of life over generations, and evolutionary biology is the study of how evolution occurs.

The biodiversity of life evolves by means of natural selection, mutations and genetic drift. The process of natural selection is based on three conditions. *First*, every individual is supplied with hereditary material in the form of genes that are received from their parents; then, passed on to their offspring. *Second*, organisms tend to produce more offspring than the environment can support. *Third*, there are variations among offspring as a consequence of either the random introduction of new genes via mutations or reshuffling of existing genes during sexual reproduction.

Natural selection will occur when these facts of nature (heredity, overproduction of offspring, and variation) hold true. Natural selection means individuals do not have equal chances of reproductive success. As a consequence, some individuals produce more offspring and thus have a higher degree of fitness. Traits that ensure organisms are better adapted to their living conditions become more common in descendant populations. For this reason, populations will never remain exactly the same over successive generations. The forces of evolution are most evident when populations become isolated, either through geographic distance or by mechanisms that prevent genetic exchange. Over time, isolated populations can branch off into new species.

Random genetic drift describes another natural process that regulates the evolution of minor mutations in the genes, leading to changes in allele frequencies over time. These smaller mutations occur with regular frequency in and among populations. The vast majority of genetic mutations neither assist, change the appearance of, nor bring harm to individuals. These mutated genes are neutrally sorted among populations and survive across generations by chance alone. When species migrate they carry different genetic varieties to different places. When organisms mate they exchange genetic material and new individuals are born.

The outward expression of each unique genetic mixture in different environments, the phenotype, comprises a diversity of traits that can be measured and observed as individuals grow and develop. In contrast to genetic drift, natural selection is not a random process because it acts on traits that become adaptive for their functional utilities that are necessary for survival. Natural selection and random genetic drift are forever constant and dynamic parts of life. More than 99.9 per cent of all species have become extinct since life began over 3.5 billion years ago. Evolution is more death than survival and over time this has shaped the branching structure in the tree of life.

Author

Contents

1 Introduction

Evolution is the process of change in all forms of life over generations, and evolutionary biology is the study of how evolution occurs.

The biodiversity of life evolves by means of natural selection, mutations and genetic drift. The process of natural selection is based on three conditions. *First*, every individual is supplied with hereditary material in the form of genes that are received from their parents; then, passed on to their offspring. *Second*, organisms tend to produce more offspring than the environment can support. *Third*, there are variations among offspring as a consequence of either the random introduction of new genes via mutations or reshuffling of existing genes during sexual reproduction.

Natural selection will occur when these facts of nature (heredity, overproduction of offspring, and variation) hold true. Natural selection means individuals do not have equal chances of reproductive success. As a consequence, some individuals produce more offspring and thus have a higher degree of fitness. Traits that ensure organisms are better adapted to their living conditions become more common in descendant populations. For this reason, populations will never remain exactly the same over successive generations. The forces of evolution are most evident when populations become isolated, either through geographic distance or by mechanisms that prevent genetic exchange. Over time, isolated populations can branch off into new species.

Random genetic drift describes another natural process that regulates the evolution of minor mutations in the genes, leading to changes in allele frequencies over time. These smaller mutations occur with regular frequency in and among populations. The vast majority of genetic mutations neither assist, change the appearance of, nor bring harm to individuals. These mutated genes are neutrally sorted among populations and survive across generations by chance alone. When species migrate they carry different genetic varieties to different places. When organisms mate they exchange genetic material and new individuals are born.

The outward expression of each unique genetic mixture in different environments, the phenotype, comprises a diversity of traits that can be measured and observed as individuals grow and develop. In contrast to genetic drift, natural selection is not a random process because it acts on traits that become adaptive for their functional utilities that are necessary for survival. Natural selection and random genetic drift are forever constant and dynamic parts of life. More than 99.9 per cent of all species have become extinct since life began over 3.5 billion years ago. Evolution is more death than survival and over time this has shaped the branching structure in the tree of life.

The modern understanding of evolution began with the 1859 publication of Charles Darwin's *'On the Origin of Species'*. In addition, Gregor Mendel's work with plants helped to explain the hereditary patterns of genetics. Fossil discoveries in paleontology, advances in population genetics and a global network of scientific research have provided further details into the mechanisms of evolution. Scientists now have a good understanding of the origin of new species (speciation) and have observed the speciation process in the laboratory and in the wild. Evolution is the principal theory that biologists use to understand life and is used in many disciplines, including medicine, psychology, conservation biology, anthropology, forensics, agriculture and other social-cultural applications.

In the 19th century, natural history collections and museums were a popular pastime. The European expansion and naval expeditions employed naturalists and curators of grand museums showcasing preserved and live specimens of the varieties of life. Charles Darwin was an English graduate who was educated and trained in the disciplines of natural history science. Such natural historians would collect, catalogue, describe and study the vast collections of specimens stored and managed by curators at these museums. Charles Darwin served as a ship's naturalist on board the HMS Beagle, assigned to a five-year research expedition around the world. During his voyage, Darwin observed and collected an abundance of organisms, being very interested in the diverse forms of life along the coasts of South America and the neighbouring Galapagos Islands.

Charles Darwin gained extensive experience as he collected and studied the natural history of life forms from distant places. Through his studies, Darwin formulated the idea that each species had developed from ancestors with similar features. In 1838, he described how a process he called natural selection would make this happen.

Darwin's idea of how evolution works relied on the following observations:

- ❖ If all the individuals of a species reproduced successfully, the population of that species would increase uncontrollably;
- ❖ Populations tend to remain about the same size from year to year;
- ❖ Environmental resources are limited;
- ❖ No two individuals in a given species are exactly alike;
- ❖ Much of this variation in a population can be passed on to offspring.

Darwin deduced that since organisms produce more offspring than their environment could possibly support, there must be a competitive struggle for survival—only a few individuals can survive out of each generation. Darwin realized that it was not chance alone that determined survival. Instead, survival depends on the traits of each individual and if these traits aid or hinder survival and reproduction. Well-adapted, or 'fit'; individuals are likely to leave more offspring than their less well-adapted competitors. Darwin realized that the unequal ability of individuals to survive and reproduce could cause gradual changes in the population. Traits that help an organism survive and reproduce would accumulate over generations. On the other hand, traits that hinder survival and reproduction would disappear. Darwin used the term *natural selection* to describe this process.

Natural selection is commonly equated with *survival of the fittest*, but this expression originated in Herbert Spencer's *Principles of Biology* in 1864, after Charles Darwin published his original works. *Survival of the fittest* describes the process of natural selection incorrectly, because natural selection is not only about survival and it is not always the fittest that survives.

Observations of variations in animals and plants formed the basis of the theory of natural selection. For example, Darwin observed that orchids and insects have a close relationship that allows the pollination of the plants. He noted that orchids have a variety of structures that attract insects, so that pollen from the flowers gets stuck to the insects' bodies. In this way, insects transport the pollen from a male to a female orchid. In spite of the elaborate appearance of orchids, these specialized parts are made from the same basic structures that make up other flowers. In *Fertilisation of Orchids* Darwin proposed that the orchid flowers did not represent the work of an ideal engineer, but were adapted from pre-existing parts, through natural selection.

Darwin was still researching and experimenting with his ideas on natural selection when he received a letter from Alfred Wallace describing a theory very similar to his own. This led to an immediate joint publication of both theories. Both Wallace and Darwin saw the history of life like a family tree, with each fork in the tree's limbs being a common ancestor. The tips of the limbs represented modern species and the branches represented the common ancestors that are shared amongst many different species. To explain these relationships, Darwin said that all living things were related, and this meant that all life must be descended from a few forms, or even from a single common ancestor. He called this process *descent with modification*.

Darwin published his theory of evolution by natural selection in *On the Origin of Species* in 1859. His theory means that all life, including humanity, is a product of continuing natural processes. The implication that all life on Earth has a common ancestor has met with objections from some religious groups who believe even today that the different types of life are due to special creation. Their objections are in contrast to the level of support for the theory by more than 99 per cent of those within the scientific community today.

Darwin's theory of natural selection laid the groundwork for modern evolutionary theory, and his experiments and observations showed that the organisms in populations varied from each other, that some of these variations were inherited, and that these differences could be acted on by natural selection. However, he could not explain the source of these variations. Like many of his predecessors, Darwin mistakenly thought that heritable traits were a product of use and disuse, and that features acquired during an organism's lifetime could be passed on to its offspring. He looked for examples, such as large ground feeding birds getting stronger legs through exercise, and weaker wings from not flying until, like the ostrich, they could not fly at all. This misunderstanding was called the inheritance of acquired characters and was part of the theory of transmutation of species put forward in 1809 by Jean-Baptiste Lamarck. In the late 19th century this theory became known as Lamarckism. Darwin produced an unsuccessful theory he called pangenesis to try to explain how acquired characteristics could be inherited. In the 1880s August Weismann's experiments indicated that changes from use and disuse could not be inherited, and Lamarckism gradually fell from favour.

The missing information needed to help explain how new features could pass from a parent to its offspring was provided by the pioneering genetics work of Gregor Mendel. Mendel's experiments with several generations of pea plants demonstrated that inheritance works by separating and reshuffling hereditary information during the formation of sex cells and recombining that information during fertilization. This is like mixing different hands of cards, with an organism getting a random mix of half of the cards from one parent, and half of the cards from the other. Mendel called the information *factors*; however, they later became known as genes. Genes are the basic units of heredity in living organisms. They contain the information that directs the physical development and behaviour of organisms.

Genes are made of DNA, a long molecule that carries information. This information is encoded in the sequence of nucleotides in the DNA, just as the sequence of the letters in words carries information on a page. The genes are like short instructions built up of the 'letters' of the DNA alphabet. Put together, the entire set of these genes gives enough information to serve as an 'instruction manual' of how to build and run an organism. The instructions spelled out by this DNA alphabet can be changed, however, by mutations, and this may alter the instructions carried within the genes. Within the cell, the genes are carried in chromosomes, which are packages for carrying the DNA, with the genes arranged along them like beads on a string. It is the reshuffling of the chromosomes that results in unique combinations of genes in offspring.

Although such mutations in DNA are random, natural selection is not a process of chance: the environment determines the probability of reproductive success. The end products of natural selection are organisms that are adapted to their present environments. Natural selection does not involve progress towards an ultimate goal. Evolution does not necessarily strive for more advanced, more intelligent, or more sophisticated life forms. For example, fleas (wingless parasites) are descended from a winged, ancestral scorpionfly, and snakes are lizards that no longer require limbs — although pythons still grow tiny structures that are the remains of their ancestor's hind legs. Organisms are merely the outcome of variations that succeed or fail, dependent upon the environmental conditions at the time.

Rapid environmental changes typically cause extinctions. Of all species that have existed on Earth, 99.9 per cent are now extinct. Since life began on Earth, five major mass extinctions have led to large and sudden drops in the variety of species. The most recent, the Cretaceous—Tertiary extinction event, occurred 65 million years ago, and has attracted more attention than all others because it killed the dinosaurs.

Modern Synthesis

The modern evolutionary synthesis was the outcome of a merger of several different scientific fields into a cohesive understanding of evolutionary theory. In the 1930s and 1940s, efforts were made to merge

Darwin's theory of natural selection, research in heredity, and understandings of the fossil records into a unified explanatory model. The application of the principles of genetics to naturally occurring populations, by scientists such as Theodosius Dobzhansky and Ernst Mayr, advanced understanding of the processes of evolution. Dobzhansky's 1937 work *Genetics and the Origin of Species* was an important step in bridging the gap between genetics and field biology. Mayr, on the basis of an understanding of genes and direct observations of evolutionary processes from field research, introduced the biological species concept, which defined a species as a group of interbreeding or potentially interbreeding populations that are reproductively isolated from all other populations. The paleontologist George Gaylord Simpson helped to incorporate fossil research, which showed a pattern consistent with the branching and non-directional pathway of evolution of organisms predicted by the modern synthesis.

The modern synthesis emphasizes the importance of populations as the unit of evolution, the central role of natural selection as the most important mechanism of evolution, and the idea of gradualism to explain how large changes evolve as an accumulation of small changes over long periods of time.

Research in the field of paleontology, the study of fossils, supports the idea that all living organisms are related. Fossils provide evidence that accumulated changes in organisms over long periods of time have led to the diverse forms of life we see today. A fossil itself reveals the organism's structure and the relationships between present and extinct species, allowing paleontologists to construct a family tree for all of the life forms on Earth.

Modern paleontology began with the work of Georges Cuvier (1769-1832). Cuvier noted that, in sedimentary rock, each layer contained a specific group of fossils. The deeper layers, which he proposed to be older, contained simpler life forms. He noted that many forms of life from the past are no longer present today. One of Cuvier's successful contributions to the understanding of the fossil record was establishing extinction as a fact. In an attempt to explain extinction, Cuvier proposed the idea of 'revolutions' or catastrophism in which he speculated that geological catastrophes had occurred throughout the Earth's history, wiping out large numbers of species. Cuvier's theory of revolutions was later replaced by uniformitarian theories, notably those of James Hutton and Charles Lyell who proposed that the Earth's geological changes were gradual and consistent. However, current evidence in the fossil record supports the concept of mass extinctions. As a result, the general idea of catastrophism has re-emerged as a valid hypothesis for at least some of the rapid changes in life forms that appear in the fossil records.

A very large number of fossils have now been discovered and identified. These fossils serve as a chronological record of evolution. The fossil record provides examples of transitional species that demonstrate ancestral links between past and present life forms. One such transitional fossil is *Archaeopteryx*, an ancient organism that had the distinct characteristics of a reptile (such as a long, bony tail and conical teeth) yet also had characteristics of birds (such as feathers and a wishbone). The implication from such a find is that modern reptiles and birds arose from a common ancestor.

Comparative Anatomy

The comparison of similarities between organisms of their form or appearance of parts, called their morphology, has long been a way to classify life into closely related groups. This can be done by comparing the structure of adult organisms in different species or by comparing the patterns of how cells grow, divide and even migrate during an organism's development.

Taxonomy

Taxonomy is the branch of biology that names and classifies all living things. Scientists use morphological and genetic similarities to assist them in categorizing life forms based on ancestral relationships. For example, orangutans, gorillas, chimpanzees, and humans all belong to the same taxonomic grouping referred to as a family — in this case the family called *Hominidae*. These animals are grouped together because of similarities in morphology that come from common ancestry (called *homology*).

Strong evidence for evolution comes from the analysis of *homologous* structures: structures in different species that no longer perform the same task but which share a similar structure. Such is the case of the forelimbs of mammals. The forelimbs of a human, cat, whale, and bat all have strikingly similar bone structures. However, each of these four species' forelimbs performs a different task. The same bones that construct a bat's wings, which are used for flight, also construct a whale's flippers, which are used for swimming. Such a 'design' makes little sense if they are unrelated and uniquely constructed for their particular tasks. The theory of evolution explains these homologous structures: all four animals shared a common ancestor, and each has undergone change over many generations. These changes in structure have produced forelimbs adapted for different tasks.

In some cases, anatomical comparison of structures in the embryos of two or more species provides evidence for a shared ancestor that may not be obvious in the adult forms. As the embryo develops, these homologies can be lost to view, and the structures can take on different functions. Part of the basis of classifying the vertebrate group (which includes humans), is the presence of a tail (extending beyond the anus) and pharyngeal slits. Both structures appear during some stage of embryonic development but are not always obvious in the adult form.

Because of the morphological similarities present in embryos of different species during development, it was once assumed that organisms re-enact their evolutionary history as an embryo. It was thought that human embryos passed through an amphibian then a reptilian stage before completing their development as mammals. Such a re-enactment, (often called *Recapitulation theory*), is not supported by scientific evidence. What does occur, however, is that the first stages of development are similar in broad groups of organisms. At very early stages, for instance, all vertebrates appear extremely similar, but do not exactly resemble any ancestral species. As development continues, specific features emerge from this basic pattern.

Vestigial Structures

Homology includes a unique group of shared structures referred to as *vestigial structures*. *Vestigial* refers to anatomical parts that are of minimal, if any, value to the organism that possesses them. These apparently illogical structures are remnants of organs that played an important role in ancestral forms. Such is the case in whales, which have small vestigial bones that appear to be remnants of the leg bones of their ancestors which walked on land. Humans also have vestigial structures, including the ear muscles, the wisdom teeth, the appendix, the tail bone, body hair (including goose bumps), and the semilunar fold in the corner of the eye.

Anatomical comparisons can be misleading, as not all anatomical similarities indicate a close relationship. Organisms that share similar environments will often develop similar physical features, a process known as *convergent evolution*. Both sharks and dolphins have similar body forms, yet are only distantly related — sharks are fish and dolphins are mammals. Such similarities are a result of both populations being exposed to the same selective pressures. Within both groups, changes that aid swimming have been favoured. Thus, over time, they developed similar appearances (morphology), even though they are not closely related.

Every living organism (with the possible exception of RNA viruses) contains molecules of DNA, which carries genetic information. Genes are the pieces of DNA that carry this information, and they influence the properties of an organism. Genes determine an individual's general appearance and to some extent their behaviour. If two organisms are closely related, their DNA will be very similar. On the other hand, the more distantly related two organisms are, the more differences they will have. For example, brothers are closely related and have very similar DNA, while cousins share a more distant relationship and have far more differences in their DNA. Similarities in DNA are used to determine the relationships between species in much the same manner as they are used to show relationships between individuals. For example, comparing chimpanzees with gorillas and humans shows that there is as much as a 96 per cent similarity between the DNA of humans and chimps. Comparisons of DNA indicate that humans and chimpanzees are more closely related to each other than either species is to gorillas.

The field of molecular systematics focuses on measuring the similarities in these molecules and using this information to work out how different types of organisms are related through evolution. These comparisons have allowed biologists to build a *relationship tree* of the evolution of life on Earth. They have even allowed scientists to unravel the relationships between organisms whose common ancestors lived such a long time ago that no real similarities remain in the appearance of the organisms.

Co-evolution is a process in which two or more species influence the evolution of each other. All organisms are influenced by life around them; however, in co-evolution there is evidence that genetically determined traits in each species directly resulted from the interaction between the two organisms.

An extensively documented case of co-evolution is the relationship between *Pseudomyrmex*, a type of ant, and the acacia, a plant that the ant uses for food and shelter. The relationship between the two is so intimate that it has led to the evolution of special structures and behaviours in both organisms. The ant defends the acacia against herbivores and clears the forest floor of the seeds from competing plants. In response, the plant has evolved swollen thorns that the ants use as shelter and special flower parts that the ants eat. Such co-evolution does not imply that the ants and the tree choose to behave in an altruistic manner. Rather, across a population small genetic changes in both ant and tree benefited each. The benefit gave a slightly higher chance of the characteristic being passed on to the next generation. Over time, successive mutations created the relationship we observe today.

Artificial selection is the controlled breeding of domestic plants and animals. Humans determine which animal or plant will reproduce and which of the offspring will survive; thus, they determine which genes will be passed on to future generations. The process of artificial selection has had a significant impact on the evolution of domestic animals. For example, people have produced different types of dogs by controlled breeding. The differences in size between the Chihuahua and the Great Dane are the result of artificial selection. Despite their dramatically different physical appearance, they and all other dogs evolved from a few wolves domesticated by humans in what is now China less than 15,000 years ago.

Artificial selection has produced a wide variety of plants. In the case of maize (corn), recent genetic evidence suggests that domestication occurred 10,000 years ago in central Mexico. Prior to domestication, the edible portion of the wild form was small and difficult to collect. Today *The Maize Genetics Cooperation Stock Centre* maintains a collection of more than 10,000 genetic variations of maize that have arisen by random mutations and chromosomal variations from the original wild type.

In artificial selection the new breed or variety that emerges is the one with random mutations attractive to humans, while in natural selection the surviving species is the one with random mutations useful to it in its non-human environment. In both natural and artificial selection the variations are a result of random mutations, and the underlying genetic processes are essentially the same. Darwin carefully observed the outcomes of artificial selection in animals and plants to form many of his arguments in support of natural selection. Much of his book *On the Origin of Species* was based on these observations of the many varieties of domestic pigeons arising from artificial selection. Darwin proposed that if humans could achieve dramatic changes in domestic animals in short periods, then natural selection, given millions of years, could produce the differences seen in living things today.

Given the right circumstances, and enough time, evolution leads to the emergence of new species. Scientists have struggled to find a precise and all-inclusive definition of *species*. Ernst Mayr (1904–2005) defined a species as a population or group of populations whose members have the potential to interbreed naturally with one another to produce viable, fertile offspring. (The members of a species cannot produce viable, fertile offspring with members of *other* species). Mayr's definition has gained wide acceptance among biologists, but does not apply to organisms such as bacteria, which reproduce asexually.

Speciation is the lineage-splitting event that results in two separate species forming from a single common ancestral population. A widely accepted method of speciation is called *allopatric speciation*. Allopatric speciation begins when a population becomes geographically separated. Geological processes, such as the emergence of mountain ranges, the formation of canyons, or the flooding of land bridges by changes in sea level may result in separate populations. For speciation to occur, separation must be substantial, so that genetic exchange between the two populations is completely disrupted. In their separate environments, the genetically isolated groups follow their own unique evolutionary pathways. Each group will accumulate different mutations as well as be subjected to different selective pressures. The accumulated genetic changes may result in separated populations that can no longer interbreed if they are reunited. Barriers that prevent interbreeding are either *prezygotic* (prevent mating or fertilization) or *postzygotic* (barriers that occur after fertilization). If interbreeding is no longer possible, then they will be considered different species.

Usually the process of speciation is slow, occurring over very long time spans; thus direct observations within human life-spans are rare. However speciation has been observed in present day organisms, and past speciation events are recorded in fossils. Scientists have documented the formation of five new species of cichlid fishes from a single common ancestor that was isolated fewer than 5000 years ago from the parent stock in Lake Nagubago. The evidence for speciation in this case was morphology (physical appearance) and lack of natural interbreeding. These fish have complex mating rituals and a variety of colourations; the slight modifications introduced in the new species have changed the mate selection process and the five forms that arose could not be convinced to interbreed.

The theory of evolution is widely accepted among the scientific community, serving to link the diverse specialty areas of biology. Evolution provides the field of biology with a solid scientific base. The significance of evolutionary theory is best described by the title of a paper by Theodosius Dobzhansky (1900-1975), published in *American Biology Teacher*; 'Nothing in Biology Makes Sense Except in the Light of Evolution'. Nevertheless, the theory of evolution is not static. There is much discussion within the scientific community concerning the mechanisms behind the evolutionary process. For example, the rate at which evolution occurs is still under discussion. In addition, there are conflicting opinions as to which is the primary unit of evolutionary change — the organism or the gene.

Two views exist concerning the rate of evolutionary change. Darwin and his contemporaries viewed evolution as a slow and gradual process. Evolutionary trees are based on the idea that profound differences in species are the result of many small changes that accumulate over long periods.

The view that evolution is gradual had its basis in the works of the geologist James Hutton (1726-1797) and his theory called 'gradualism'.

Hutton's theory suggests that profound geological change was the cumulative product of a relatively slow continuing operation of processes which can still be seen in operation today, as opposed to catastrophism which promoted the idea that sudden changes had causes which can no longer be seen at work. A uniformitarian perspective was adopted for biological changes. Such a view can seem to contradict the fossil record, which shows evidence of new species appearing suddenly, then persisting in that form for long periods. The paleontologist Stephen Jay Gould (1941-2002) developed a model that suggests that evolution, although a slow process in human terms, undergoes periods of relatively rapid change over only a few thousand or million years, alternating with long periods of relative stability, a model called 'punctuated equilibrium' which explains the fossil record without contradicting Darwin's ideas.

A common unit of selection in evolution is the organism. Natural selection occurs when the reproductive success of an individual is improved or reduced by an inherited characteristic, and reproductive success is measured by the number of an individual's surviving offspring. The organism view has been challenged by a variety of biologists as well as philosophers. Richard Dawkins (born 1941) proposes that much insight can be gained if we look at evolution from the gene's point of view; that is, that natural selection operates as an evolutionary mechanism on genes as well as organisms. In his 1976 book *'The Selfish Gene'*, he explains:

> "Individuals are not stable things, they are fleeting. Chromosomes too are shuffled to oblivion, like hands of cards soon after they are dealt. But the cards themselves survive the shuffling. The cards are the genes. The genes are not destroyed by crossing-over; they merely change partners and march on. Of course they march on. That is their business. They are the replicators and we are their survival machines. When we have served our purpose we are cast aside. But genes are denizens of geological time: genes are forever".

Others view selection working on many levels, not just at a single level of organism or gene; for example, Stephen Jay Gould called for a hierarchical perspective on selection.

Several basic observations establish the theory of evolution, which explains the variety and relationship of all living things. There are genetic variations within a population of individuals. Some individuals, by chance, have features that allow them to survive and thrive better than their kind. The individuals that survive will be more likely to have offspring of their own. The offspring might inherit the useful feature.

Evolution is not a random process. While mutations are random, natural selection is not. Evolution is an inevitable result of imperfectly copying, self-replicating organisms reproducing over billions of years under the selective pressure of the environment. The outcome of evolution is not a perfectly designed organism. The outcome is simply an individual that can survive better and reproduce more successfully than its neighbours in a particular environment. Fossils, the genetic code, and the peculiar distribution of life on Earth provide a record of evolution and demonstrate the common ancestry of all organisms, both living and long dead. Evolution can be directly observed in artificial selection, the selective breeding for certain traits of domestic animals and plants. The diverse breeds of cats, dogs, horses, and agricultural plants serve as examples of evolution.

2 The Mechanism of Evolution

Evolution (also known as biological, genetic or organic evolution) is the change in the inherited traits of a population of organisms through successive generations. This change results from interactions between processes that introduce variation into a population, and other processes that remove it. As a result, variants with particular traits become more, or less, common. A trait is a particular characteristic—anatomical, biochemical or behavioural—that is the result of gene—environment interaction.

The main source of variation is mutation, which introduces genetic changes. These changes are heritable (can be passed on through reproduction), and may give rise to alternative traits in organisms. Another source of variation is genetic recombination, which shuffles the genes into new combinations which can result in organisms exhibiting different traits. Under certain circumstances, variation can also be increased by the transfer of genes between species, and by the extremely rare, but significant, wholesale incorporation of genomes through endosymbiosis.

Two main processes cause variants to become more common or rarer in a population. One is natural selection, through which traits that aid survival and reproduction become more common, while traits that hinder survival and reproduction become rarer. Natural selection occurs because only a small proportion of individuals in each generation will survive and reproduce, since resources are limited and organisms produce many more offspring than their environment can support. Over many generations, heritable variation in traits is filtered by natural selection and the beneficial changes are successively retained through differential survival and reproduction. This iterative process adjusts traits so they become better suited to an organism's environment: these adjustments are called adaptations.

However, not all changes are adaptive. Another cause of evolution is genetic drift, which leads to random changes in how common traits are in a population. Genetic drift is most important when traits do not strongly influence survival—particularly so in small populations, in which chance plays a disproportionate role in the frequency of traits passed on to the next generation. Genetic drift is important in the neutral theory of molecular evolution, and plays a role in the molecular clocks that are used in phylogenetic studies.

A key process in evolution is speciation, in which a single ancestral species splits and diversifies into multiple new species. There are several modes through which this occurs. Ultimately, all living (and extinct) species are descended from a common ancestor via a long series of speciation events. These events stretch back in a diverse 'tree of life' which has grown over the 3.5 billion years during which life has existed on Earth. This is visible in anatomical, genetic and other similarities between groups of organisms, geographical distribution of related species, the fossil record and the recorded genetic changes in living organisms over many generations.

Evolutionary biologists document the fact that evolution occurs, and also develop and test theories which explain its causes. The study of evolutionary biology began in the mid-nineteenth century, when research into the fossil record and the diversity of living organisms convinced most scientists that species changed over time. The mechanism driving these changes remained unclear until the theory of natural selection was independently proposed by Charles Darwin and Alfred Wallace. In 1859, Darwin's seminal work *On the Origin of Species* brought the new theory of evolution by natural selection to a wide audience, leading to the overwhelming acceptance of evolution among scientists. In the 1930s, Darwinian natural selection became understood in combination with Mendelian inheritance, forming the modern evolutionary synthesis, which connected the substrate of evolution (inherited genetics) and the mechanism of evolution (natural selection). This powerful explanatory and predictive theory has become the central organizing principle of modern biology, directing research and providing a unifying explanation for the history and diversity of life on Earth. Evolution is applied and studied in fields as diverse as agriculture, anthropology, conservation biology, ecology, medicine, paleontology, philosophy, and psychology along with other specific topics in the previous listed fields.

The roots of naturalistic thinking on biology can be dated to at least the 6th century BCE, with the Greek philosopher Anaximander. However, the growth of modern biology out of natural history is fairly recent. The word *evolution* (from the Latin *evolutio*, meaning 'to unroll like a scroll') appeared in English in the 17th century. As biological knowledge grew in the 18th century, proto-evolutionary ideas were set out by a few natural philosophers such as Pierre Maupertuis in 1745 and Erasmus Darwin in 1796. The ideas of the biologist Jean-Baptiste Lamarck about transmutation of species influenced radicals, but were rejected by mainstream scientists. Charles Darwin formulated his idea of natural selection in 1838 and was still developing his theory in 1858 when Alfred Russel Wallace sent him a similar theory, and both were presented to the Linnean Society of London in separate papers. At the end of 1859, Darwin's publication of *On the Origin of Species* explained natural selection in detail and presented evidence leading to increasingly wide acceptance of the occurrence of evolution.

Debate about the mechanisms of evolution continued, and Darwin could not explain the source of the heritable variations which would be acted on by natural selection. Like Lamarck, he still thought that parents passed on adaptations acquired during their lifetimes, a theory which was subsequently dubbed Lamarckism. In the 1880s, August Weismann's experiments indicated that changes from use and disuse were not heritable, and Lamarckism gradually fell from favour. More significantly, Darwin could not account for how traits were passed down from generation to generation. In 1865 Gregor Mendel found that traits were inherited in a predictable manner. When Mendel's work was rediscovered in 1900s, disagreements over the rate of evolution predicted by early geneticists and biometricians led to a rift between the Mendelian and Darwinian models of evolution.

Yet it was the rediscovery of Gregor Mendel's pioneering work on the fundamentals of genetics (of which Darwin and Wallace were unaware) by Hugo de Vries and others in the early 1900s that provided the impetus for a better understanding of how variation occurs in plant and animal traits. That variation is the main fuel used by natural selection to shape the wide variety of adaptive traits observed in organic life. Even though Hugo de Vries and other early geneticists rejected gradual natural selection, their rediscovery of and subsequent work on genetics eventually provided a solid basis on which the theory of evolution stood even more convincingly than when it was originally proposed.

The apparent contradiction between Darwin's theory of evolution by natural selection and Mendel's work was reconciled in the 1920s and 1930s by evolutionary biologists such as J.B.S. Haldane, Sewall Wright, and particularly Ronald Fisher, who set the foundations for the establishment of the field of population genetics. The end result was a combination of evolution by natural selection and Mendelian inheritance, the modern evolutionary synthesis. In the 1940s, the identification of DNA as the genetic material by Oswald Avery and colleagues and the subsequent publication of the structure of DNA by James Watson and Francis Crick in 1953, demonstrated the physical basis for inheritance. Since then, genetics and molecular biology have become core parts of evolutionary biology and have revolutionised the field of phylogenetics.

In its early history, evolutionary biology primarily drew in scientists from traditional taxonomically oriented disciplines, whose specialist training in particular organisms addressed general questions in evolution. As evolutionary biology expanded as an academic discipline, particularly after the development of the modern evolutionary synthesis, it began to draw more widely from the biological sciences. Currently the study of evolutionary biology involves scientists from fields as diverse as biochemistry, ecology, genetics and physiology, and evolutionary concepts are used in even more distant disciplines such as psychology, medicine, philosophy and computer science. In the 21st century, current research in evolutionary biology deals with several areas where the modern evolutionary synthesis may need modification or extension, such as assessing the relative importance of various ideas on the unit of selection and evolvability and how to fully incorporate the findings of evolutionary developmental biology.

Evolution in organisms occurs through changes in heritable traits — particular characteristics of an organism. In humans, for example, eye colour is an inherited characteristic and an individual might inherit the 'brown-eye trait' from one of their parents. Inherited traits are controlled by genes and the complete set of genes within an organism's genome is called its genotype.

The complete set of observable traits that make up the structure and behaviour of an organism is called its phenotype. These traits come from the interaction of its genotype with the environment. As a result, many aspects of an organism's phenotype are not inherited. For example, suntanned skin comes from the interaction between a person's genotype and sunlight; thus, suntans are not passed on to people's children. However, some people tan more easily than others, due to differences in their genotype; a striking example are people with the inherited trait of albinism, who do not tan at all and are very sensitive to sunburn.

Heritable traits are passed from one generation to the next via DNA, a molecule that encodes genetic information. DNA is a long polymer composed of four types of bases. The sequence of bases along a particular DNA molecule specify the genetic information, in a manner similar to a sequence of letters spelling out a sentence. Before a cell divides, the DNA is copied, so that each of the resulting two cells will inherit the DNA sequence.

Portions of a DNA molecule that specify a single functional unit are called genes; different genes have different sequences of bases. Within cells, the long strands of DNA form condensed structures called chromosomes. The specific location of a DNA sequence within a chromosome is known as a locus. If the DNA sequence at a locus varies between individuals, the different forms of this sequence are called alleles. DNA sequences can change through mutations, producing new alleles. If a mutation occurs within a gene, the new allele may affect the trait that the gene controls, altering the phenotype of the organism.

However, while this simple correspondence between an allele and a trait works in some cases, most traits are more complex and are controlled by multiple interacting genes. The study of such complex traits is a major area of current genetic research. Another unsolved question in genetics is whether or not epigenetics is important in evolution. Epigenetics is when a trait is inherited without there being any change in gene sequences.

Variation

An individual organism's phenotype results from both its genotype and the influence from the environment it has lived in. A substantial part of the variation in phenotypes in a population is caused by the differences between their genotypes. The modern evolutionary synthesis defines evolution as the change over time in this genetic variation. The frequency of one particular allele will fluctuate, becoming more or less prevalent relative to other forms of that gene. Evolutionary forces act by driving these changes in allele frequency in one direction or another. Variation disappears when a new allele reaches the point of fixation — when it either disappears from the population or replaces the ancestral allele entirely.

Variation comes from mutations in genetic material, migration between populations (gene flow), and the reshuffling of genes through sexual reproduction. Variation also comes from exchanges of genes between different species; for example, through horizontal gene transfer in bacteria, and hybridization in plants. Despite the constant introduction of variation through these processes, most of the genome of a species is identical in all individuals of that species. However, even relatively small changes in genotype can lead to dramatic changes in phenotype: for example, chimpanzees and humans differ in only about 5 per cent of their genomes.

Random mutations constantly occur in the genomes of organisms; these mutations create genetic variation. Mutations are changes in the DNA sequence of a cell's genome and are caused by radiation, viruses, transposons and mutagenic chemicals, as well as errors that occur during meiosis or DNA replication. These mutations involve several different types of change in DNA sequences; these can either have no effect, alter the product of a gene, or prevent the gene from functioning. Studies in the fly *Drosophila melanogaster* suggest that if a mutation changes a protein produced by a gene, this will probably be harmful, with about 70 per cent of these mutations having damaging effects, and the remainder being either neutral or weakly beneficial. Due to the damaging effects that mutations can have on cells, organisms have evolved mechanisms such as DNA repair to remove mutations. Therefore, the optimal mutation rate for a species is a trade-off between costs of a high mutation rate, such as deleterious mutations, and the metabolic costs of maintaining systems to reduce the mutation rate, such as DNA repair enzymes. Viruses that use RNA as their genetic material have rapid mutation rates, which can be an advantage since these viruses will evolve constantly and rapidly, and thus evade the defensive responses of e.g. the human immune system.

Mutations can involve large sections of a chromosome becoming duplicated (usually by genetic recombination), which can introduce extra copies of a gene into a genome. Extra copies of genes are a major source of the raw material needed for new genes to evolve. This is important because most new genes evolve within gene families from pre-existing genes that share common ancestors. For example, the human eye uses four genes to make structures that sense light: three for colour vision and one for night vision; all four are descended from a single ancestral gene. New genes can be created from an ancestral gene when a duplicate copy mutates and acquires a new function. This process is easier once a gene has been duplicated because it increases the redundancy of the system; one gene in the pair can acquire a new function while the other copy continues to perform its original function. Other types of mutation can even create entirely new genes from previously noncoding DNA. The creation of new genes can also involve small parts of several genes being duplicated, with these fragments then recombining to form new combinations with new functions. When new genes are assembled from shuffling pre-existing parts, domains act as modules with simple independent functions, which can be mixed together creating new combinations with new and complex functions. For example, polyketide synthases are large enzymes that make antibiotics; they contain up to one hundred independent domains that each catalyze one step in the overall process, like a step in an assembly line.

Changes in chromosome number may involve even larger mutations, where segments of the DNA within chromosomes break and then rearrange. For example, two chromosomes in the *Homo* genus fused to produce human chromosome 2; this fusion did not occur in the lineage of the other apes, and they retain these separate chromosomes. In evolution, the most important role of such chromosomal rearrangements may be to accelerate the divergence of a population into new species by making populations less likely to interbreed, and thereby preserving genetic differences between these populations.

Sequences of DNA that can move about the genome, such as transposons, make up a major fraction of the genetic material of plants and animals, and may have been important in the evolution of genomes. For example, more than a million copies of the Alu sequence are present in the human genome, and these sequences have now been recruited to perform functions such as regulating gene expression. Another effect of these mobile DNA sequences is that when they move within a genome, they can mutate or delete existing genes and thereby produce genetic diversity.

In asexual organisms, genes are inherited together, or *linked*, as they cannot mix with genes of other organisms during reproduction. In contrast, the offspring of sexual organisms contain random mixtures of their parents' chromosomes that are produced through independent assortment. In a related process called homologous recombination, sexual organisms exchange DNA between two matching chromosomes. Recombination and reassortment do not alter allele frequencies, but instead change which alleles are associated with each other, producing offspring with new combinations of alleles. Sex usually increases genetic variation and may increase the rate of evolution. However, asexuality is advantageous in some environments as it can evolve in previously sexual animals. Here, asexuality might allow the two sets of alleles in their genome to diverge and gain different functions.

Recombination allows even alleles that are close together in a strand of DNA to be inherited independently. However, the rate of recombination is low (approximately two events per chromosome per generation). As a result, genes close together on a chromosome may not always be shuffled away from each other, and genes that are close together tend to be inherited together, a phenomenon known as linkage. This tendency is measured by finding how often two alleles occur together on a single chromosome, which is called their linkage disequilibrium. A set of alleles that is usually inherited in a group is called a haplotype. This can be important when one allele in a particular haplotype is strongly beneficial:

natural selection can drive a selective sweep that will also cause the other alleles in the haplotype to become more common in the population; this effect is called genetic hitchhiking.

From a genetic viewpoint, evolution is a *generation-to-generation change in the frequencies of alleles within a population that shares a common gene pool.* A population is a localised group of individuals belonging to the same species. For example, all of the moths of the same species living in an isolated forest represent a population. A single gene in this population may have several alternate forms, which account for variations between the phenotypes of the organisms. An example might be a gene for colouration in moths that has two alleles: black and white. A gene pool is the complete set of alleles for a gene in a single population; the allele frequency measures the fraction of the gene pool composed of a single allele (for example, what fraction of moth colouration genes are the black allele). Evolution occurs when there are changes in the frequencies of alleles within a population of interbreeding organisms; for example, the allele for black colour in a population of moths becoming more common.

To understand the mechanisms that cause a population to evolve, it is useful to consider what conditions are required for a population not to evolve. The *Hardy-Weinberg principle* states that the frequencies of alleles (variations in a gene) in a sufficiently large population will remain constant if the only forces acting on that population are the random reshuffling of alleles during the formation of the sperm or egg, and the random combination of the alleles in these sex cells during fertilization. Such a population is said to be in *Hardy-Weinberg equilibrium*; it is not evolving.

When alleles cannot be separated by recombination — such as in mammalian *Y* chromosomes, which pass intact from fathers to sons — harmful mutations accumulate. By breaking up allele combinations, sexual reproduction allows the removal of harmful mutations and the retention of beneficial mutations. In addition, recombination and reassortment can produce individuals with new and advantageous gene combinations. These positive effects are balanced by the fact that sex reduces an organism's reproductive rate, can cause mutations and may separate beneficial combinations of genes. The reasons for the evolution of sexual reproduction are therefore unclear and this question is still an active area of research in evolutionary biology, that has prompted ideas such as the Red Queen hypothesis.

Gene flow is the exchange of genes between populations, which are usually of the same species. Examples of gene flow within a species include the migration and then breeding of organisms, or the exchange of pollen. Gene transfer between species includes the formation of hybrid organisms and horizontal gene transfer.

Migration into or out of a population can change allele frequencies, as well as introducing genetic variation into a population. Immigration may add new genetic material to the established gene pool of a population. Conversely, emigration may remove genetic material. As barriers to reproduction between two diverging populations are required for the populations to become new species, gene flow may slow this process by spreading genetic differences between the populations. Gene flow is hindered by mountain ranges, oceans and deserts or even man-made structures such as the Great Wall of China, which has hindered the flow of plant genes.

Depending on how far two species have diverged since their most recent common ancestor, it may still be possible for them to produce offspring, as with horses and donkeys mating to produce mules. Such hybrids are generally infertile, due to the two different sets of chromosomes being unable to pair up during meiosis. In this case, closely related species may regularly interbreed, but hybrids will be selected against and the species will remain distinct. However, viable hybrids are occasionally formed and these new species can either have properties intermediate between their parent species, or possess a totally new phenotype. The importance of hybridization in creating new species of animals is unclear, although cases have been seen in many types of animals, with the gray tree frog being a particularly well-studied example.

Hybridization is, however, an important means of speciation in plants, since polyploidy (having more than two copies of each chromosome) is tolerated in plants more readily than in animals. Polyploidy is important in hybrids as it allows reproduction, with the two different sets of chromosomes each being able to pair with an identical partner during meiosis. Polyploids also have more genetic diversity, which allows them to avoid inbreeding depression in small populations.

Horizontal gene transfer is the transfer of genetic material from one organism to another organism that is not its offspring; this is most common among bacteria. In medicine, this contributes to the spread of antibiotic resistance, as when one bacteria acquires resistance genes it can rapidly transfer them to other species. Horizontal transfer of genes from bacteria to eukaryotes such as the yeast *Saccharomyces cerevisiae* and the adzuki bean beetle *Callosobruchus chinensis* may also have occurred. An example of larger-scale transfers are the eukaryotic bdelloid rotifers, which appear to have received a range of genes from bacteria, fungi, and plants. Viruses can also carry DNA between organisms, allowing transfer of genes even across biological domains. Large-scale gene transfer has also occurred between the ancestors of eukaryotic cells and prokaryotes, during the acquisition of chloroplasts and mitochondria.

The two main mechanisms that produce evolution are natural selection and genetic drift. Natural selection is the process which favours genes that aid survival and reproduction. Genetic drift is the random change in the frequency of alleles, caused by the random sampling of a generation's genes during reproduction. The relative importance of natural selection and genetic drift in a population varies depending on the strength of the selection and the effective population size, which is the number of individuals capable of breeding. Natural selection usually predominates in large populations, whereas genetic drift dominates in small populations. The dominance of genetic drift in small populations can even lead to the fixation of slightly deleterious mutations. As a result, changing population size can dramatically influence the course of evolution. Population bottlenecks, where the population shrinks temporarily and therefore loses genetic variation, result in a more uniform population.

Natural Selection

Natural selection is the process by which genetic mutations that enhance reproduction become, and remain, more common in successive generations of a population. It has often been called a 'self-evident' mechanism because it necessarily follows from three simple facts:

- ❖ Heritable variation exists within populations of organisms.
- ❖ Organisms produce more offspring than can survive.
- ❖ These offspring vary in their ability to survive and reproduce.

These conditions produce competition between organisms for survival and reproduction. Consequently, organisms with traits that give them an advantage over their competitors pass these advantageous traits on, while traits that do not confer an advantage are not passed on to the next generation.

The central concept of natural selection is the evolutionary fitness of an organism. Fitness is measured by an organism's ability to survive and reproduce, which determines the size of its genetic contribution to the next generation. However, fitness is not the same as the total number of offspring: instead fitness is indicated by the proportion of subsequent generations that carry an organism's genes. For example, if an organism could survive well and reproduce rapidly, but its offspring were all too small and weak to survive, this organism would make little genetic contribution to future generations and would thus have low fitness.

If an allele increases fitness more than the other alleles of that gene, then with each generation this allele will become more common within the population. These traits are said to be 'selected *for*'. Examples of traits that can increase fitness are enhanced survival, and increased fecundity. Conversely, the lower fitness caused by having a less beneficial or deleterious allele results in this allele becoming rarer — they are 'selected *against*'. Importantly, the fitness of an allele is not a fixed characteristic; if the environment changes, previously neutral or harmful traits may become beneficial and previously beneficial traits become harmful. However, even if the direction of selection does reverse in this way, traits that were lost in the past may not re-evolve in an identical form.

Natural selection within a population for a trait that can vary across a range of values, such as height, can be categorised into three different types. The first is directional selection, which is a shift in the average value of a trait over time — for example organisms slowly getting taller. Secondly, disruptive selection is selection for extreme trait values and often results in two different values becoming most common, with selection against the average value. This would be when either short or tall organisms had an advantage, but not those of medium height. Finally, in stabilizing selection there is selection against extreme trait values on both ends, which causes a decrease in variance around the average value and less diversity. This would, for example, cause organisms to slowly become all the same height.

A special case of natural selection is sexual selection, which is selection for any trait that increases mating success by increasing the attractiveness of an organism to potential mates. Traits that evolved through sexual selection are particularly prominent in males of some animal species, despite traits such as cumbersome antlers, mating calls or bright colours that attract predators, decreasing the survival of individual males. This survival disadvantage is balanced by higher reproductive success in males that show these hard to fake, sexually selected traits.

Natural selection most generally makes nature the measure against which individuals, and individual traits, are more or less likely to survive. 'Nature' in this sense refers to an ecosystem, that is, a system in which organisms interact with every other element, physical as well as biological, in their local environment. Eugene Odum, a founder of ecology, defined an ecosystem as: "Any unit that includes all of the organisms . . . in a given area interacting with the physical environment so that a flow of energy leads to clearly defined trophic structure, biotic diversity, and material cycles (i.e.: exchange of materials between living and non-living parts) within the system". Each population within an ecosystem occupies a distinct niche, or position, with distinct relationships to other parts of the system. These relationships involve the life history of the organism, its position in the food chain, and its geographic range. This broad understanding of nature enables scientists to delineate specific forces which, together, comprise natural selection.

An active area of research is the unit of selection, with natural selection being proposed to work at the level of genes, cells, individual organisms, groups of organisms and species. None of these are mutually exclusive and selection can act on multiple levels simultaneously. An example of selection occurring below the level of the individual organism are genes called transposons, which can replicate and spread throughout a genome. Selection at a level above the individual, such as group selection, may allow the evolution of co-operation, as discussed below.

Genetic Drift

Genetic drift is the change in allele frequency from one generation to the next that occurs because alleles in offspring are a random sample of those in the parents, as well as from the role that chance plays in determining whether a given individual will survive and reproduce. In mathematical terms, alleles are subject to sampling error. As a result, when selective forces are absent or relatively weak, allele frequencies tend to "drift" upward or downward randomly (in a random walk). This drift halts when an allele eventually becomes fixed, either by disappearing from the population, or replacing the other alleles entirely. Genetic drift may therefore eliminate some alleles from a population due to chance alone. Even in the absence of selective forces, genetic drift can cause two separate populations that began with the same genetic structure to drift apart into two divergent populations with different sets of alleles.

The time for an allele to become fixed by genetic drift depends on population size, with fixation occurring more rapidly in smaller populations. The precise measure of population that is important is called the effective population size. The effective population is always smaller than the total population since it takes into account factors such as the level of inbreeding, the number of animals that are too old or young to breed, and the lower probability of animals that live far apart managing to mate with each other.

An example when genetic drift is probably of central importance in determining a trait is the loss of pigments from animals that live in caves, a change that produces no obvious advantage or disadvantage in complete darkness. However, it is usually difficult to measure the relative importance of selection and drift, so the comparative importance of these two forces in driving evolutionary change is an area of current research. These investigations were prompted by the neutral theory of molecular evolution, which proposed that most evolutionary changes are the result of the fixation of neutral mutations that do not have any immediate effects on the fitness of an organism. Hence, in this model, most genetic changes in a population are the result of constant mutation pressure and genetic drift.

This form of the neutral theory is now largely abandoned, since it does not seem to fit the genetic variation seen in nature. However, a more recent and better-supported version of this model is the nearly neutral theory, where most mutations only have small effects on fitness.

Evolution influences every aspect of the form and behaviour of organisms. Most prominent are the specific behavioural and physical adaptations that are the outcome of natural selection. These adaptations increase fitness by aiding activities such as finding food, avoiding predators or attracting mates. Organisms can also respond to selection by co-operating with each other, usually by aiding their relatives or engaging in mutually beneficial symbiosis. In the longer term, evolution produces new species through splitting ancestral populations of organisms into new groups that cannot or will not interbreed.

These outcomes of evolution are sometimes divided into macroevolution, which is evolution that occurs at or above the level of species, such as extinction and speciation, and microevolution, which is smaller evolutionary changes, such as adaptations, within a species or population. In general, macroevolution is regarded as the outcome of long periods of microevolution. Thus, the distinction between micro- and macroevolution is not a fundamental one — the difference is simply the time involved. However, in macroevolution, the traits of the entire species may be important. For instance, a large amount of variation among individuals allows a species to rapidly adapt to new habitats, lessening the chance of it going extinct, while a wide geographic range increases the chance of speciation, by making it more likely that part of the population will become isolated. In this sense, microevolution and macroevolution might involve selection at different levels — with microevolution acting on genes and organisms, *vs.* macroevolutionary processes such as species selection acting on entire species and affecting their rates of speciation and extinction.

A common misconception is that evolution has goals or long-term plans; realistically however, evolution has no long-term goal and does not necessarily produce greater complexity. Although complex species have evolved, they occur as a side effect of the overall number of organisms increasing, and simple forms of life still remain more common in the biosphere. For example, the overwhelming majority of species are microscopic prokaryotes, which form about half the world's biomass despite their small size, and constitute the vast majority of Earth's biodiversity. Simple organisms have therefore been the dominant form of life on Earth throughout its history and continue to be the main form of life up to the present day, with complex life only appearing more diverse because it is more noticeable. Indeed, the evolution of microorganisms is particularly important to modern evolutionary research, since their rapid reproduction allows the study of experimental evolution and the observation of evolution and adaptation in real time.

Adaptation

Adaptation is one of the basic phenomena of biology, and is the *process* whereby an organism becomes better suited to its habitat. Also, the term adaptation may refer to a trait that is important for an organism's survival. For example, the adaptation of horses' teeth to the grinding of grass, or the ability of horses to run fast and escape predators. By using the term *adaptation* for the evolutionary process, and *adaptive trait* for the product (the bodily part or function), the two senses of the word may be distinguished. Adaptations are produced by natural selection. The following definitions are due to Theodosius Dobzhansky.

1. *Adaptation* is the evolutionary process whereby an organism becomes better able to live in its habitat or habitats.
2. *Adaptedness* is the state of being adapted: the degree to which an organism is able to live and reproduce in a given set of habitats.
3. An *adaptive trait* is an aspect of the developmental pattern of the organism which enables or enhances the probability of that organism surviving and reproducing.

Adaptation may cause either the gain of a new feature, or the loss of an ancestral feature. An example that shows both types of change is bacterial adaptation to antibiotic selection, with genetic changes causing antibiotic resistance by both modifying the target of the drug, or increasing the activity of transporters that pump the drug out of the cell. Other striking examples are the bacteria *Escherichia coli* evolving the ability to use citric acid as a nutrient in a long-term laboratory experiment, *Flavobacterium* evolving a novel enzyme that allows these bacteria to grow on the by-products of nylon manufacturing, and the soil bacterium *Sphingobium* evolving an entirely new metabolic pathway that degrades the synthetic pesticide pentachlorophenol. An interesting but still controversial idea is that some adaptations might increase the ability of organisms to generate genetic diversity and adapt by natural selection (increasing organisms' evolvability).

A baleen whale skeleton, *a* and *b* label flipper bones, which were adapted from front leg bones: while *c* indicates vestigial leg bones, suggesting an adaptation from land to sea.

Adaptation occurs through the gradual modification of existing structures. Consequently, structures with similar internal organization may have different functions in related organisms. This is the result of a single ancestral structure being adapted to function in different ways. The bones within bat wings, for example, are very similar to those in mice feet and primate hands, due to the descent of all these structures from a common mammalian ancestor. However, since all living organisms are related to some extent, even organs that appear to have little or no structural similarity, such as arthropod, squid and vertebrate eyes, or the limbs and wings of arthropods and vertebrates, can depend on a common set of homologous genes that control their assembly and function; this is called deep homology.

During adaptation, some structures may lose their original function and become vestigial structures. Such structures may have little or no function in a current species, yet have a clear function in ancestral species, or other closely related species. Examples include pseudogenes, the non-functional remains of eyes in blind cave-dwelling fish, wings in flightless birds, nd the presence of hip bones in whales and snakes. Examples of vestigial structures in humans include wisdom teeth, the coccyx, the vermiform appendix, and other behavioural vestiges such as goose bumps, and primitive reflexes.

However, many traits that appear to be simple adaptations are in fact exaptations: structures originally adapted for one function, but which coincidentally became somewhat useful for some other function in the process. One example is the African lizard *Holaspis guentheri*, which developed an extremely flat head for hiding in crevices, as can be seen by looking at its near relatives. However, in this species, the head has become so flattened that it assists in gliding from tree to tree—an exaptation. Within cells, molecular machines such as the bacterial flagella and protein sorting machinery evolved by the recruitment of several pre-existing proteins that previously had different functions. Another example is the recruitment of enzymes from glycolysis and xenobiotic metabolism to serve as structural proteins called crystallins within the lenses of organisms' eyes.

A critical principle of ecology is that of competitive exclusion: no two species can occupy the same niche in the same environment for a long time. Consequently, natural selection will tend to force species to adapt to different ecological niches. This may mean that, for example, two species of cichlid fish adapt to live in different habitats, which will minimise the competition between them for food.

An area of current investigation in evolutionary developmental biology is the developmental basis of adaptations and exaptations. This research addresses the origin and evolution of embryonic development and how modifications of development and developmental processes produce novel features. These studies have shown that evolution can alter development to create new structures, such as embryonic bone structures that develop into the jaw in other animals instead forming part of the middle ear in mammals. It is also possible for structures that have been lost in evolution to reappear due to changes in developmental genes, such as a mutation in chickens causing embryos to grow teeth similar to those of crocodiles. It is now becoming clear that most alterations in the form of organisms are due to changes in a small set of conserved genes.

Co-evolution

Common garter snake (*Thamnophis sirtalis sirtalis*) which has evolved resistance to tetrodotoxin in its amphibian prey.

Interactions between organisms can produce both conflict and co-operation. When the interaction is between pairs of species, such as a pathogen and a host, or a predator and its prey, these species can develop matched sets of adaptations. Here, the evolution of one species causes adaptations in a second species. These changes in the second species then, in turn, cause new adaptations in the first species. This cycle of selection and response is called co-evolution. An example is the production of tetrodotoxin in the rough-skinned newt and the evolution of tetrodotoxin resistance in its predator, the common garter snake. In this predator-prey pair, an evolutionary arms race has produced high levels of toxin in the newt and correspondingly high levels of toxin resistance in the snake.

Co-operation

However, not all interactions between species involve conflict. Many cases of mutually beneficial interactions have evolved. For instance, an extreme cooperation exists between plants and the mycorrhizal fungi that grow on their roots and aid the plant in absorbing nutrients from the soil. This is a reciprocal relationship as the plants provide the fungi with sugars from photosynthesis. Here, the fungi actually grow inside plant cells, allowing them to exchange nutrients with their hosts, while sending signals that suppress the plant immune system.

Coalitions between organisms of the same species have also evolved. An extreme case is the eusociality found in social insects, such as bees, termites and ants, where sterile insects feed and guard the small number of organisms in a colony that are able to reproduce. On an even smaller scale, the somatic cells that make up the body of an animal limit their reproduction so they can maintain a stable organism, which then supports a small number of the animal's germ cells to produce offspring. Here, somatic cells respond to specific signals that instruct them whether to grow, remain as they are, or die. If cells ignore these signals and multiply inappropriately, their uncontrolled growth causes cancer.

Such cooperation within species may have evolved through the process of kin selection, which is where one organism acts to help raise a relative's offspring. This activity is selected for because if the *helping* individual contains alleles which promote the helping activity, it is likely that its kin will *also* contain these alleles and thus those alleles will be passed on. Other processes that may promote cooperation include group selection, where cooperation provides benefits to a group of organisms.

Speciation

Speciation is the process where a species diverges into two or more descendant species. Evolutionary biologists view species as statistical phenomena and not categories or types. This view is counterintuitive since the classical idea of species is still widely held, with a species seen as a class of organisms exemplified by a 'type specimen' that bears all the traits common to this species. Instead, a species is now defined as a separately evolving lineage that forms a single gene pool. Although properties such as genetics and morphology are used to help separate closely related lineages, this definition has fuzzy boundaries. Indeed, the exact definition of the term 'species' is still controversial, particularly in prokaryotes, and this is called the species problem. Biologists have proposed a range of more precise definitions, but the definition used is a pragmatic choice that depends on the particularities of the species concerned. Typically the actual focus on biological study is the population, an observable *interacting* group of organisms, rather than a species, an observable *similar* group of individuals.

Speciation has been observed multiple times under both controlled laboratory conditions and in nature. In sexually reproducing organisms, speciation results from reproductive isolation followed by genealogical divergence. There are four mechanisms for speciation. The most common in animals is allopatric speciation, which occurs in populations initially isolated geographically, such as by habitat fragmentation or migration. Selection under these conditions can produce very rapid changes in the appearance and behaviour of organisms. As selection and drift act independently on populations isolated from the rest of their species, separation may eventually produce organisms that cannot interbreed.

The second mechanism of speciation is peripatric speciation, which occurs when small populations of organisms become isolated in a new environment. This differs from allopatric speciation in that the isolated populations are numerically much smaller than the parental population. Here, the founder effect causes rapid speciation through both rapid genetic drift and selection on a small gene pool.

The third mechanism of speciation is parapatric speciation. This is similar to peripatric speciation in that a small population enters a new habitat, but differs in that there is no physical separation between these two populations. Instead, speciation results from the evolution of mechanisms that reduce gene flow between the two populations. Generally this occurs when there has been a drastic change in the environment within the parental species' habitat. One example is the grass *Anthoxanthum odoratum*, which can undergo parapatric speciation in response to localised metal pollution from mines. Here, plants evolve that have resistance to high levels of metals in the soil. Selection against interbreeding with the metal-sensitive parental population produced a gradual change in the flowering time of the metal-resistant plants, which eventually produced complete reproductive isolation. Selection against hybrids between the two populations may cause *reinforcement*, which is the evolution of traits that promote mating within a species, as well as character displacement, which is when two species become more distinct in appearance.

Finally, in sympatric speciation species diverge without geographic isolation or changes in habitat. This form is rare since even a small amount of gene flow may remove genetic differences between parts of a population. Generally, sympatric speciation in animals requires the evolution of both genetic differences and non-random mating, to allow reproductive isolation to evolve.

One type of sympatric speciation involves cross-breeding of two related species to produce a new hybrid species. This is not common in animals as animal hybrids are usually sterile. This is because during meiosis the homologous chromosomes from each parent are from different species and cannot successfully pair. However, it is more common in plants because plants often double their number of chromosomes, to form polyploids. This allows the chromosomes from each parental species to form matching pairs during meiosis, since each parent's chromosomes are represented by a pair already. An example of such a speciation event is when the plant species *Arabidopsis thaliana* and *Arabidopsis arenosa* cross-bred to give the new species *Arabidopsis suecica*. This happened about 20,000 years ago, and the speciation process has been repeated in the laboratory, which allows the study of the genetic mechanisms involved in this process. Indeed, chromosome doubling within a species may be a common cause of reproductive isolation, as half the doubled chromosomes will be unmatched when breeding with undoubled organisms.

Speciation events are important in the theory of punctuated equilibrium, which accounts for the pattern in the fossil record of short 'bursts' of evolution interspersed with relatively long periods of stasis, where species remain relatively unchanged. In this theory, speciation and rapid evolution are linked, with natural selection and genetic drift acting most strongly on organisms undergoing speciation in novel habitats or small populations. As a result, the periods of stasis in the fossil record correspond to the parental population, and the organisms undergoing speciation and rapid evolution are found in small populations or geographically restricted habitats, and therefore rarely being preserved as fossils.

Origin of Life

The origin of life is a necessary precursor for biological evolution, but understanding that evolution occurred once organisms appeared and investigating how this happens does not depend on understanding exactly how life began. The current scientific consensus is that the complex biochemistry that makes up life came from simpler chemical reactions, but it is unclear how this occurred. Not much is certain about the earliest developments in life, the structure of the first living things, or the identity and nature of any last universal common ancestor or ancestral gene pool. Consequently, there is no scientific consensus on how life began, but proposals include self-replicating molecules such as RNA, and the assembly of simple cells.

Common Descent

All organisms on Earth are descended from a common ancestor or ancestral gene pool. Current species are a stage in the process of evolution, with their diversity the product of a long series of speciation and extinction events. The common descent of organisms was first deduced from four simple facts about organisms: *First,* they have geographic distributions that cannot be explained by local adaptation. *Second,* the diversity of life is not a set of completely unique organisms, but organisms that share morphological similarities. *Third,* vestigial traits with no clear purpose resemble functional ancestral traits, and *finally,* that organisms can be classified using these similarities into a hierarchy of nested groups — similar to a family tree. However, modern research has suggested that, due to horizontal gene transfer, this 'tree of life' may be more complicated than a simple branching tree since some genes have spread independently between distantly related species.

Past species have also left records of their evolutionary history. Fossils, along with the comparative anatomy of present-day organisms, constitute the morphological, or anatomical, record. By comparing the anatomies of both modern and extinct species, paleontologists can infer the lineages of those species. However, this approach is most successful for organisms that had hard body parts, such as shells, bones or teeth.

Further, as prokaryotes such as bacteria and archaea share a limited set of common morphologies, their fossils do not provide information on their ancestry.

More recently, evidence for common descent has come from the study of biochemical similarities between organisms. For example, all living cells use the same basic set of nucleotides and amino acids. The development of molecular genetics has revealed the record of evolution left in organisms' genomes: dating when species diverged through the molecular clock produced by mutations. For example, these DNA sequence comparisons have revealed that humans and chimpanzees share 96 per cent of their genomes and analyzing the few areas where they differ helps shed light on when the common ancestor of these species existed.

Despite the uncertainty on how life began, it is generally accepted that prokaryotes inhabited the Earth from approximately 3-4 billion years ago. No obvious changes in morphology or cellular organization occurred in these organisms over the next few billion years.

The eukaryotes were the next major change in cell structure. These came from ancient bacteria being engulfed by the ancestors of eukaryotic cells, in a cooperative association called endosymbiosis. The engulfed bacteria and the host cell then underwent co-evolution, with the bacteria evolving into either mitochondria or hydrogenosomes. An independent second engulfment of cyanobacterial-like organisms led to the formation of chloroplasts in algae and plants. It is unknown when the first eukaryotic cells appeared though they first emerged between 1.6–2.7 billion years ago.

The history of life was that of the unicellular eukaryotes, prokaryotes, and archaea until about 610 million years ago when multicellular organisms began to appear in the oceans in the Ediacaran period. The evolution of multicellularity occurred in multiple independent events, in organisms as diverse as sponges, brown algae, cyanobacteria, slime moulds and myxobacteria.

Soon after the emergence of these first multicellular organisms, a remarkable amount of biological diversity appeared over approximately 10 million years, in an event called the Cambrian explosion. Here, the majority of types of modern animals appeared in the fossil record, as well as unique lineages that subsequently became extinct. Various triggers for the Cambrian explosion have been proposed, including the accumulation of oxygen in the atmosphere from photosynthesis. About 500 million years ago, plants and fungi colonised the land, and were soon followed by arthropods and other animals. Insects were particularly successful and even today make up the majority of animal species. Amphibians first appeared around 300 million years ago, followed by early amniotes, then mammals around 200 million years ago and birds around 100 million years ago (both from 'reptile'–like lineages). However, despite the evolution of these large animals, smaller organisms similar to the types that evolved early in this process continue to be highly successful and dominate the Earth, with the majority of both biomass and species being prokaryotes.

Evolutionary biology, and in particular the understanding of how organisms evolve through natural selection, is an area of science with many practical applications. A major technological application of evolution is artificial selection, which is the intentional selection of certain traits in a population of organisms. Humans have used artificial selection for thousands of years in the domestication of plants and animals. More recently, such selection has become a vital part of genetic engineering, with selectable markers such as antibiotic resistance genes being used to manipulate DNA in molecular biology. It is also possible to use repeated rounds of mutation and selection to evolve proteins with particular properties, such as modified enzymes or new antibodies, in a process called directed evolution.

Understanding the changes that have occurred during organism's evolution can reveal the genes needed to construct parts of the body, genes which may be involved in human genetic disorders. For example, the Mexican tetra is an albino cavefish that lost its eyesight during evolution. Breeding together different populations of this blind fish produced some offspring with functional eyes, since different mutations had occurred in the isolated populations that had evolved in different caves. This helped identify genes required for vision and pigmentation, such as crystallins and the melanocortin 1 receptor. Similarly, comparing the genome of the Antarctic icefish, which lacks red blood cells, to close relatives such as the Antarctic rockcod revealed genes needed to make these blood cells.

As evolution can produce highly optimised processes and networks, it has many applications in computer science. Here, simulations of evolution using evolutionary algorithms and artificial life started with the work of Nils Aall Barricelli in the 1960s, and was extended by Alex Fraser, who published a series of papers on simulation of artificial selection. Artificial evolution became a widely recognised optimization method as a result of the work of Ingo Rechenberg in the 1960s and early 1970s, who used evolution strategies to solve complex engineering problems. Genetic algorithms in particular became popular through the writing of John Holland. As academic interest grew, dramatic increases in the power of computers allowed practical applications, including the automatic evolution of computer programmes. Evolutionary algorithms are now used to solve multi-dimensional problems more efficiently than software produced by human designers, and also to optimise the design of systems.

In the 19th century, particularly after the publication of *On the Origin of Species* in 1859, the idea that life had evolved was an active source of academic debate centred on the philosophical, social and religious implications of evolution. Nowadays, the fact that organisms evolve is uncontested in the scientific literature and the modern evolutionary synthesis is widely accepted by scientists. However, evolution remains a contentious concept for some theists.

While various religions and denominations have reconciled their beliefs with evolution through concepts such as theistic evolution, there are creationists who believe that evolution is contradicted by the creation myths found in their respective religions and who raise various objections to evolution. As had been demonstrated by responses to the publication of *Vestiges of the Natural History of Creation* in 1844, the most controversial aspect of evolutionary biology is the implication of human evolution that human mental and moral faculties, which had been thought purely spiritual, are not distinctly separated from those of other animals. In some countries—notably the United States—these tensions between science and religion have fueled the current creation-evolution controversy, a religious conflict focussing on politics and public education. While other scientific fields such as cosmology and Earth science also conflict with literal interpretations of many religious texts, evolutionary biology experiences significantly more opposition from religious literalists.

The teaching of evolution in American secondary school biology classes was uncommon in most of the first half of the 20th century. The Scopes Trial decision of 1925 caused the subject to become very rare in American secondary biology textbooks for a generation, but it was gradually re-introduced about a generation later and legally protected with the 1968 *Epperson vs. Arkansas* decision. Since then, the competing religious belief of creationism was legally disallowed in secondary school curricula in various decisions in the 1970s and 1980s, but it returned in the form of intelligent design, to be excluded once again in the 2005 *Kitzmiller vs. Dover Area School District* case.

Another example somewhat associated with evolutionary theory that is now widely regarded as unwarranted is 'Social Darwinism', a derogatory term associated with the 19th century Malthusian theory developed by Whig philosopher Herbert Spencer. It was later expanded by others into ideas about 'survival of the fittest' in commerce and human societies as a whole, and led to claims that social inequality, sexism, racism, and imperialism were justified. However, these ideas contradict Darwin's own views, and contemporary scientists and philosophers consider these ideas to be neither mandated by evolutionary theory nor supported by data.

3 Evolutionary Thought

Evolutionary thought, the conception that species change over time, has roots in antiquity, in the ideas of the ancient Greeks, Romans and Chinese as well as in mediaeval Islamic science. However, until the 18th century, Western biological thinking was dominated by essentialism, the belief that every species has essential characteristics that are unalterable. This began to change during the Enlightenment when evolutionary cosmology and the mechanical philosophy spread from the physical sciences to natural history. Naturalists began to focus on the variability of species; the emergence of paleontology with the concept of extinction further undermined the static view of nature. In the early 19th century, Jean-Baptiste Lamarck proposed his theory of the transmutation of species, the first fully formed scientific theory of evolution.

In 1858, Charles Darwin and Alfred Russel Wallace published a new evolutionary theory that was explained in detail in Darwin's *On the Origin of Species* (1859). Unlike Lamarck, Darwin proposed common descent and a branching tree of life. The theory was based on the idea of natural selection, and it synthesized a broad range of evidence from animal husbandry, biogeography, geology, morphology and embryology.

The debate over Darwin's work led to the rapid acceptance of the general concept of evolution, but the specific mechanism he proposed, natural selection, was not widely accepted until it was revived by developments in biology that occurred during 1920s through the 1940s. Before that time most biologists argued that other factors were responsible for evolution. Alternatives to natural selection suggested during the eclipse of Darwinism included inheritance of acquired characteristics (neo-Lamarckism), an innate drive for change (orthogenesis), and sudden large mutations (saltationism). The synthesis of natural selection with Mendelian genetics during the 1920s and 1930s founded the new discipline of population genetics. Throughout the 1930s and 1940s, population genetics became integrated with other biological fields, resulting in a widely applicable theory of evolution that encompassed much of biology—the modern evolutionary synthesis.

Following the establishment of evolutionary biology, studies of mutation and variation in natural populations, combined with biogeography and systematics, led to sophisticated mathematical and causal models of evolution. Paleontology and comparative anatomy allowed more detailed reconstructions of the history of life. After the rise of molecular genetics in the 1950s, the field of molecular evolution developed, based on protein sequences and immunological tests, and later incorporating RNA and DNA studies. The gene-centred view of evolution rose to prominence in the 1960s, followed by the neutral theory of molecular evolution, sparking debates over adaptationism, the units of selection, and the relative importance of genetic drift *versus* natural selection. In the late 20th century, DNA sequencing led to molecular phylogenetics and the reorganization of the tree of life into the three-domain system. In addition, the newly recognized factors of symbiogenesis and horizontal gene transfer introduced yet more complexity into evolutionary history.

Several ancient Greek philosophers discussed ideas that involved change in living organisms over time. Anaximander (c.610-546 BC) proposed that the first animals lived in water and animals that live on land were generated from them. Empedocles (c. 490-430 BC) wrote of a non-supernatural origin for living things, suggesting that adaptation did not require an organizer or final cause. Aristotle summarized his idea: "Wherever then all the parts came about just what they would have been if they had come to be for an end, such things survived, being organized spontaneously in a fitting way; whereas those which grew otherwise perished and continue to perish . . ." although Aristotle himself rejected this view.

Plato (c. 428-348 BC) was, in the words of biologist and historian Ernst Mayr, 'the great antihero of evolutionism', as he established the philosophy of essentialism, which he called the Theory of Forms. This theory holds that objects observed in the real world are only *reflections* of a limited number of essences (*eide*). Variation merely results from an imperfect reflection of these constant essences. In his *Timaeus*, Plato set forth the idea that the Demiurge had created the cosmos and everything in it because, being good, and hence, ". . . free from jealousy, He desired that all things should be as like Himself as they could be". The creator created all conceivable forms of life, since ". . . without them the universe will be incomplete, for it will not contain every kind of animal which it ought to contain, if it is to be perfect". This 'plenitude principle' — the idea that all potential forms of life are essential to a perfect creation—greatly influenced Christian thought.

Aristotle (384-322 BC), one of the most influential of the Greek philosophers, is the earliest natural historian whose work has been preserved in any real detail. His writings on biology resulted from his research into natural history on and around the isle of Lesbos, and have survived in the form of four books, usually known by their Latin names, *De anima* (on the essence of life), *Historia animalium* (inquiries about animals), *De generatione animalium* (reproduction), and *De partibus animalium* (anatomy). Aristotle's works contain some remarkably astute observations and interpretations—along with sundry myths and mistakes—reflecting the uneven state of knowledge during his time. However, for Charles Singer, "Nothing is more remarkable than [Aristotle's] efforts to [exhibit] the relationships of living things as a *scala naturæ*." This *scala naturæ*, described in *Historia animalium*, classified organisms in relation to a hierarchical 'Ladder of Life' or 'Chain of Being', placing them according to their complexity of structure and function, with organisms that showed greater vitality and ability to move described as 'higher organisms'.

Chinese

Ideas on changing biologic species were expressed by ancient Chinese thinkers such as Zhuangzi (Chuang Tzu), a Taoist philosopher who lived around the 4th century BC. According to Joseph Needham, Taoism explicitly denies the fixity of biological species and Taoist philosophers speculated that species had developed differing attributes in response to differing environments. Humans, nature and the heavens are seen as existing in a state of 'constant transformation' known as the Tao, in contrast with the more static view of nature typical of Western thought.

Romans

Titus Lucretius Carus (d. 50 BC), the Roman philosopher and atomist, wrote the poem *On the Nature of Things* (*De rerum natura*), which provides the best surviving explanation of the ideas of the Greek Epicurean philosophers. It describes the development of the cosmos, the Earth, living things, and human society through purely naturalistic mechanisms, without any reference to supernatural involvement. *On the Nature of Things* would influence the cosmological and evolutionary speculations of philosophers and scientists during and after the Renaissance.

Augustine of Hippo

In line with earlier Greek thought, the 4th century bishop and theologian, St. Augustine of Hippo, wrote that the creation story in Genesis should not be read too literally. In his book *De Genesi ad litteram* ('On The Literal Interpretation of Genesis'), he stated that in some cases new creatures may have come about through the 'decomposition' of earlier forms of life. For Augustine, "plant, fowl and animal life are not perfect ... but created in a state of potentiality", unlike what he considered the theologically perfect forms of angels, the firmament and the human soul. Augustine's idea 'that forms of life had been transformed 'slowly over time' prompted Father Giuseppe Tanzella-Nitti, Professor of Theology at the Pontifical Santa Croce University in Rome, to claim that Augustine had suggested a form of evolution.

Although Greek and Roman evolutionary ideas died out in Europe after the fall of the Roman Empire, they were not lost to Islamic philosophers and scientists. In the Islamic Golden Age of the 8th to the 13th centuries, philosophers explored ideas about natural history. These ideas included transmutation from non-living to living: "from mineral to plant, from plant to animal and from animal to man".

The first Muslim biologist and philosopher to publish detailed speculations about natural history, the Afro-Arab writer al-Jahiz, wrote in the 9th century. In the *Book of Animals,* he considered the effects of the environment on an animal's chances for survival, and described the struggle for existence. Al-Jahiz also wrote descriptions of food chains. Al-Jahiz speculated on the influence of the environment on animals and considered the effects of the environment on the likelihood of an animal to survive. For example, Al-Jahiz's wrote in his *Book of Animals*: "All animals, in short, cannot exist without food, neither can the hunting animal escape being hunted in his turn. Every weak animal devours those weaker than itself. Strong animals cannot escape being devoured by other animals stronger than they".

During the Early Middle Ages, Greek classical learning was all but lost to the West. However, contact with the Islamic world, where Greek manuscripts were preserved and expanded, soon led to a massive spate of Latin translations in the 12th century. Europeans were re-introduced to the works of Plato and Aristotle, as well as to Islamic thought. Christian thinkers of the scholastic school, in particular Abelard and Thomas Aquinas, combined Aristotelian classification with Plato's ideas of the goodness of God, and of all potential life forms being present in a perfect creation, to organize all inanimate, animate, and spiritual beings into a huge interconnected system: the *scala naturœ*, or great chain of being.

Within this system, everything that existed could be placed in order, from 'lowest' to 'highest', with Hell at the bottom and God at the top–below God, an angelic hierarchy marked by the orbits of the planets, mankind in an intermediate position, and worms the lowest of the animals. As the universe was ultimately perfect, the great chain was also perfect. There were no empty links in the chain, and no link was represented by more than one species. Therefore no species could ever move from one position to another. Thus, in this Christianized version of Plato's perfect universe, species could never change, but remained forever fixed, in accordance with the text of *Genesis*. For humans to forget their position was seen as sinful, whether they behaved like lower animals or aspired to a higher station than was given them by their Creator.

Creatures on adjacent steps were expected to closely resemble each other, an idea expressed in the saying: *natura non facit saltum* ("nature does not make leaps"). This basic concept of the great chain of being greatly influenced the thinking of Western civilization for centuries (and still has an influence today). It formed a part of the argument from design presented by natural theology. As a classification system, it became the major organizing principle and foundation of the emerging science of biology in the 17th and 18th centuries.

While the development of the great chain of being and the argument from design by Christian theologians contributed to the view that the natural world fit into an unchanging designed hierarchy, some theologians were more open to the possibility that the world might have developed through natural processes. Thomas Aquinas went even farther than Augustine of Hippo in arguing that scriptural texts like Genesis should not be interpreted in a literal way that conflicted with or constrained what natural philosophers learned about the workings of the natural world. He felt that the autonomy of nature was a sign of God's goodness and that there was no conflict between the concept of a divinely created universe, and the idea that the universe may have evolved over time through natural mechanisms. However, Aquinas disputed the views of those like the ancient Greek philosopher Empodocles who held that such natural processes showed that the universe could have developed without an underlying purpose. Rather holding that: "Hence, it is clear that nature is nothing but a certain kind of art, i.e., the divine art, impressed upon things, by which these things are moved to a determinate end. It is as if the shipbuilder were able to give to timbers that by which they would move themselves to take the form of a ship".

In the first half of the 17th century, René Descartes's mechanical philosophy encouraged the use of the metaphor of the universe as a machine, a concept that would come to characterise the scientific revolution. Between 1650 and 1800, some evolutionist theories supported the view that the universe, including life on Earth, had developed mechanically, entirely without divine guidance. In contrast, most contemporary theories of evolution, such of those of Gottfried Leibniz and J. G. Herder, held that evolution was a fundamentally *spiritual* process. In 1751, Pierre Louis Maupertuis veered toward more materialist ground. He wrote of natural modifications occurring during reproduction and accumulating over the course of many generations, producing races and even new species, a description that anticipated in general terms the concept of natural selection.

In 1796, Georges Cuvier published his findings on the differences between living elephants and those found in the fossil record. His analysis demonstrated that mammoths and mastodons were distinct species, different from any living animal, effectively ending a long-running debate over whether the extinction of a species was possible. In 1788, James Hutton described gradual geological processes operating continuously over deep time. In the 1790s William Smith began the process of ordering rock strata by examining fossils in the layers while he worked on his geologic map of England. Independently, in 1811, Georges Cuvier and Alexandre Brongniart published an influential study of the geologic history of the region around Paris, based on the stratigraphic succession of rock layers. These works helped establish the antiquity of the Earth. Cuvier advocated catastrophism to explain the patterns of extinction and faunal succession revealed by the fossil record.

Knowledge of the fossil record continued to advance rapidly during the first few decades of the 19th century. By the 1840s, the outlines of the geologic timescale were becoming clear, and in 1841 John Phillips named three major eras, based on the predominant fauna of each: the Paleozoic, dominated by marine invertebrates and fish, the Mesozoic, the age of reptiles, and the current Cenozoic age of mammals. This progressive picture of the history of life was accepted even by conservative English geologists like Adam Sedgwick and William Buckland; however, like Cuvier, they attributed the progression to repeated catastrophic episodes of extinction followed by new episodes of creation. Unlike Cuvier, Buckland and some other advocates of natural theology among British geologists made efforts to explicitly link the last catastrophic episode proposed by Cuvier to the biblical flood.

From 1830 to 1833, Charles Lyell published his multi-volume work *Principles of Geology*, which, building on Hutton's ideas, advocated a uniformitarian alternative to the catastrophic theory of geology. Lyell claimed that, rather than being the products of cataclysmic (and possibly supernatural) events, the geologic features of the Earth are better explained as the result of the same gradual geologic forces observable in the present day—but acting over immensely long periods of time. Although Lyell opposed evolutionary ideas (even questioning the consensus that the fossil record demonstrates a true progression), his concept that the Earth was shaped by forces working gradually over an extended period, and the immense age of the Earth assumed by his theories, would strongly influence future evolutionary thinkers such as Charles Darwin.

Transmutation of Species

Jean-Baptiste Lamarck proposed, in his *Philosophie Zoologique* of 1809, a theory of the transmutation of species. Lamarck did not believe that all living things shared a common ancestor but rather that simple forms of life were created continuously by spontaneous generation. He also believed that an innate life force drove species to become more complex over time, advancing up a linear ladder of complexity that was related to the great chain of being. Lamarck recognized that species were adapted to their environment. He explained this by saying that the same innate force driving increasing complexity caused the organs of an animal (or a plant) to change based on the use or disuse of those organs, just as muscles are affected by exercise. He argued that these changes would be inherited by the next generation and produce slow adaptation to the environment. It was this secondary mechanism of adaptation through the inheritance of acquired characteristics that would become known as Lamarckism and would influence discussions of evolution into the 20th century.

A radical British school of comparative anatomy that included the anatomist Robert Grant was closely in touch with Lamarck's French school of *Transformationism*. One of the French scientists who influenced Grant was the anatomist Étienne Geoffroy Saint-Hilaire, whose ideas on the unity of various animal body plans and the homology of certain anatomical structures would be widely influential and lead to intense debate with his colleague Georges Cuvier. Grant became an authority on the anatomy and reproduction of marine invertebrates. He developed Lamarck's and Erasmus Darwin's ideas of transmutation and evolutionism, and investigated homology, even proposing that plants and animals had a common evolutionary starting point. As a young student Charles Darwin joined Grant in investigations of the life cycle of marine animals. In 1826 an anonymous paper, probably written by Robert Jameson, praised Lamarck for explaining how higher animals had 'evolved' from the simplest worms; this was the first use of the word 'evolved' in a modern sense.

In 1844, the Scottish publisher Robert Chambers anonymously published an extremely controversial but widely read book entitled *Vestiges of the Natural History of Creation*. This book proposed an evolutionary scenario for the origins of the Solar System and life on Earth. It claimed that the fossil record showed a progressive ascent of animals with current animals being branches off a main line that leads progressively to humanity. It implied that the transmutations lead to the unfolding of a preordained plan that had been woven into the laws that governed the universe. In this sense it was less completely materialistic than the ideas of radicals like Robert Grant, but its implication that humans were only the last step in the ascent of animal life incensed many conservative thinkers. The high profile of the public debate over *Vestiges*, with its depiction of evolution as a progressive process, would greatly influence the perception of Darwin's theory a decade later.

Ideas about the transmutation of species were associated with the radical materialism of the Enlightenment and were attacked by more conservative thinkers. Georges Cuvier attacked the ideas of Lamarck and Geoffroy Saint-Hilaire, agreeing with Aristotle that species were immutable. Cuvier believed that the individual parts of an animal were too closely correlated with one another to allow for one part of the anatomy to change in isolation from the others and argued that the fossil record showed patterns of catastrophic extinctions followed by re-population, rather than gradual change over time. He also noted that drawings of animals and animal mummies from Egypt, which were thousands of years old, showed no signs of change when compared with modern animals. The strength of Cuvier's arguments and his scientific reputation helped keep transmutational ideas out of the mainstream for decades.

In Britain the philosophy of natural theology remained influential. William Paley's 1802 book *Natural Theology* with its famous watchmaker analogy had been written at least in part as a response to the transmutational ideas of Erasmus Darwin. Geologists influenced by natural theology, such as Buckland and Sedgwick, made a regular practice of attacking the evolutionary ideas of Lamarck, Grant, and *The Vestiges of the Natural History of Creation*. Although the geologist Charles Lyell opposed scriptural geology, he also believed in the immutability of species, and in his *Principles of Geology* (1830-1833), he criticized Lamarck's theories of development. Idealists such as Louis Agassiz and Richard Owen believed that each species was fixed and unchangeable because it represented an idea in the mind of the creator. They believed that relationships between species could be discerned from developmental patterns in embryology, as well as in the fossil record, but that these relationships represented an underlying pattern of divine thought, with progressive creation leading to increasing complexity and culminating in humanity. Owen developed the idea of 'archetypes' in the Divine mind that would produce a sequence of species related by anatomical homologies, such as vertebrate limbs. Owen led a public campaign that successfully marginalized Robert Grant in the scientific community. Darwin would make good use of the homologies analyzed by Owen in his own theory, but the harsh treatment of Grant, and the controversy surrounding *Vestiges*, showed him the need to ensure that his own ideas were scientifically sound.

Several writers anticipated aspects of Darwin's theory, and in the third edition of *On the Origin of Species* published in 1861 Darwin named those he knew about in an introductory appendix, *An Historical Sketch of the Recent Progress of Opinion on the Origin of Species*, which he expanded in later editions.

In 1813, William Charles Wells read before the Royal Society essays assuming that there had been evolution of humans, and recognising the principle of natural selection. Charles Darwin and Alfred Russel Wallace were unaware of this work when they jointly published the theory in 1858, but Darwin later acknowledged that Wells had recognised the principle before them, writing that the paper "An Account of a White Female, part of whose Skin resembles that of a Negro" was published in 1818, and "he distinctly recognises the principle of natural selection, and this is the first recognition which has been indicated; but he applies it only to the races of man, and to certain characters alone." When Darwin was developing his theory, he was influenced by Augustin de Candolle's *natural system* of classification, which laid emphasis on the war between competing species.

Patrick Matthew wrote in the obscure book *Naval Timber and Arboriculture* (1831) of "continual balancing of life to circumstance. . . . [The] progeny of the same parents, under great differences of circumstance, might, in several generations, even become distinct species, incapable of co-reproduction." Charles Darwin discovered this work after the initial publication of the *Origin*. In the brief historical sketch that Darwin included in the 3rd edition he says "Unfortunately the view was given by Mr. Matthew very briefly in an Appendix to a work on a different subject. . . . He clearly saw, however, the full force of the principle of natural selection".

It is possible to look through the history of biology from the ancient Greeks onwards and discover anticipations of almost all of Darwin's key ideas. However, as historian of science Peter J. Bowler says, "Through a combination of bold theorizing and comprehensive evaluation, Darwin came up with a concept of evolution that was unique for the time." Bowler goes on to say that simple priority alone is not enough to secure a place in the history of science; someone has to develop an idea and convince others of its importance to have a real impact.

T.H. Huxley said in his essay on the reception of the *Origin of Species*:

> The suggestion that new species may result from the selective action of external conditions upon the variations from their specific type which individuals present and which we call spontaneous because we are ignorant of their causation is as wholly unknown to the historian of scientific ideas as it was to biological specialists before 1858. But that suggestion is the central idea of the *Origin of Species*, and contains the quintessence of Darwinism.

Natural Selection

The biogeographical patterns Charles Darwin observed in places such as the Galapagos islands during the voyage of the Beagle caused him to doubt the fixity of species, and in 1837 Darwin started the first of a series of secret notebooks on transmutation. Darwin's observations led him to view transmutation as a process of divergence and branching, rather than the ladder-like progression envisioned by Lamarck and others. In 1838 he read the new 6th edition of *An Essay on the Principle of Population*, written in the late 18th century by Thomas Malthus. Malthus' idea of population growth leading to a struggle for survival combined with Darwin's knowledge on how breeders selected traits, led to the inception of Darwin's theory of natural selection. Darwin did not publish his ideas on evolution for 20 years. However he did share them with certain other naturalists and friends, starting with Joseph Hooker, with whom he discussed his unpublished 1844 essay on natural selection. During this period he used the time he could spare from his other scientific work to slowly refine his ideas and, aware of the intense controversy around transmutation, amass evidence to support them. In September 1854 he began full time work on writing his book on natural selection.

Unlike Darwin, Alfred Russel Wallace, influenced by the book *Vestiges of the Natural History of Creation*, already suspected that transmutation of species occurred when he began his career as a naturalist. By 1855 his biogeographical observations during his field work in South America and the Malay Archipelago made him confident enough in a branching pattern of evolution to publish a paper stating that every species originated in close proximity to an already existing closely allied species. Like Darwin, it was

Wallace's consideration of how the ideas of Malthus might apply to animal populations that led him to conclusions very similar to those reached by Darwin about the role of natural selection. In February 1858 Wallace, unaware of Darwin's unpublished ideas, composed his thoughts into an essay and mailed them to Darwin, asking for his opinion. The result was the joint publication in July of an extract from Darwin's 1844 essay along with Wallace's letter. Darwin also began work on a short abstract summarising his theory, which he would publish in 1859 as *On the Origin of Species*.

1859-1930s: Darwin and His Legacy

By the 1850s whether or not species evolved was a subject of intense debate, with prominent scientists arguing both sides of the issue. However, it was the publication of Charles Darwin's *On the Origin of Species* (1859) that fundamentally transformed the discussion over biological origins. Darwin argued that his branching version of evolution explained a wealth of facts in biogeography, anatomy, embryology, and other fields of biology. He also provided the first cogent mechanism by which evolutionary change could persist: his theory of natural selection.

One of the first and most important naturalists to be convinced by *Origin* of the reality of evolution was the British anatomist Thomas Henry Huxley. Huxley recognized that unlike the earlier transmutational ideas of Lamarck and *Vestiges*, Darwin's theory provided a mechanism for evolution without supernatural involvement, even if Huxley himself was not completely convinced that natural selection was the key evolutionary mechanism. Huxley would make advocacy of evolution a cornerstone of the programme of the X Club to reform and professionalise science by displacing natural theology with naturalism and to end the domination of British natural science by the clergy. By the early 1870s in English-speaking countries, thanks partly to these efforts, evolution had become the mainstream scientific explanation for the origin of species. In his campaign for public and scientific acceptance of Darwin's theory, Huxley made extensive use of new evidence for evolution from paleontology. This included evidence that birds had evolved from reptiles, including the discovery of *Archaeopteryx* in Europe, and a number of fossils of primitive birds with teeth found in North America. Another important line of evidence was the finding of fossils that helped trace the evolution of the horse from its small five-toed ancestors. However, acceptance of evolution among scientists in non-English speaking nations such as France, and the countries of southern Europe and Latin America was slower. An exception to this was Germany, where both August Weismann and Ernst Haeckel championed this idea: Haeckel used evolution to challenge the established tradition of metaphysical idealism in German biology, much as Huxley used it to challenge natural theology in Britain. Haeckel and other German scientists would take the lead in launching an ambitious programme to reconstruct the evolutionary history of life based on morphology and embryology.

Darwin's theory succeeded in profoundly altering scientific opinion regarding the development of life and in producing a small philosophical revolution. However, this theory could not explain several critical components of the evolutionary process. Specifically, Darwin was unable to explain the source of variation in traits within a species, and could not identify a mechanism that could pass traits faithfully from one generation to the next. Darwin's hypothesis of pangenesis, while relying in part on the inheritance of acquired characteristics, proved to be useful for statistical models of evolution that were developed by his cousin Francis Galton and the 'biometric' school of evolutionary thought. However, this idea proved to be of little use to other biologists.

Application to Humans

Charles Darwin was aware of the severe reaction in some parts of the scientific community against the suggestion made in *Vestiges of the Natural History of Creation* that humans had arisen from animals by a process of transmutation. Therefore he almost completely ignored the topic of human evolution in *The Origin of Species*. Despite this precaution, the issue featured prominently in the debate that followed the book's publication. For most of the first half of the 19th century, the scientific community believed that, although geology had shown that the Earth and life were very old, human beings had appeared suddenly just a few thousand years before the present. However, a series of archaeological discoveries in the 1840s and 1850s showed stone tools associated with the remains of extinct animals. By the early 1860s, as summarized in Charles Lyell's 1863 book *Geological Evidences of the Antiquity of Man*, it had become widely accepted that humans had existed during a prehistoric period — which stretched many thousands of years before the start of written history. This view of human history was more compatible with an evolutionary origin for humanity than was the older view. On the other hand, at that time there was no fossil evidence to demonstrate human evolution. The only human fossils found before the discovery of Java man in the 1890s were either of anatomically modern humans or of Neanderthals that were too close, especially in the critical characteristic of cranial capacity, to modern humans for them to be convincing intermediates between humans and other primates.

Therefore the debate that immediately followed the publication of *The Origin of Species* centred on the similarities and differences between humans and modern apes. Carolus Linnaeus had been criticised in the 18th century for grouping humans and apes together as primates in his ground breaking classification system. Richard Owen vigorously defended the classification suggested by Cuvier and Johann Friedrich Blumenbach that placed humans in a separate order from any of the other mammals, which by the early 19th century had become the orthodox view. On the other hand, Thomas Henry Huxley sought to demonstrate a close anatomical relationship between humans and apes. In one famous incident, Huxley showed that Owen was mistaken in claiming that the brains of gorillas lacked a structure present in human brains. Huxley summarized his argument in his highly influential 1863 book *Evidence as to Man's Place in Nature.* Another viewpoint was advocated by Charles Lyell and Alfred Russel Wallace. They agreed that humans shared a common ancestor with apes, but questioned whether any purely materialistic mechanism could account for all the differences between humans and apes, especially some aspects of the human mind.

In 1871, Darwin published *The Descent of Man, and Selection in Relation to Sex,* which contained his views on human evolution. Darwin argued that the differences between the human mind and the minds of the higher animals were a matter of degree rather than of kind. For example, he viewed morality as a natural outgrowth of instincts that were beneficial to animals living in social groups. He argued that all the differences between humans and apes were explained by a combination of the selective pressures that came from our ancestors moving from the trees to the plains, and sexual selection. The debate over human origins, and over the degree of human uniqueness continued well into the 20th century.

The concept of evolution was widely accepted in scientific circles within a few years of the publication of *Origin,* but the acceptance of natural selection as its driving mechanism was much less widespread. The four major alternatives to natural selection in the late 19th century were theistic evolution, neo-Lamarckism, orthogenesis, and saltationism. Theistic evolution (a term promoted by Darwin's greatest American advocate Asa Gray) was the idea that God intervened in the process of evolution to guide it in such a way that the living world could still be considered to be designed. However, this idea gradually fell out of favour among scientists, as they became more and more committed to the idea of methodological naturalism and came to believe that direct appeals to supernatural involvement were scientifically unproductive. By 1900, theistic evolution had largely disappeared from professional scientific discussions, although it retained a strong popular following.

In the late 19th century, the term neo-Lamarckism came to be associated with the position of naturalists who viewed the inheritance of acquired characteristics as the most important evolutionary mechanism. Advocates of this position included the British writer and Darwin critic Samuel Butler, the German biologist Ernst Haeckel, and the American paleontologist Edward Drinker Cope. They considered Lamarckism to be philosophically superior to Darwin's idea of selection acting on random variation. Cope looked for, and thought he found, patterns of linear progression in the fossil record. Inheritance of acquired characteristics was part of Haeckel's recapitulation theory of evolution, which held that the embryological development of an organism repeats its evolutionary history. Critics of neo-Lamarckism, such as the German biologist August Weismann and Alfred Russel Wallace, pointed out that no one had ever produced solid evidence for the inheritance of acquired characteristics. Despite these criticisms, neo-Lamarckism remained the most popular alternative to natural selection at the end of the 19th century, and would remain the position of some naturalists well into the 20th century.

Orthogenesis was the hypothesis that life has an innate tendency to change, in a unilinear fashion, towards ever-greater perfection. It had a significant following in the 19th century, and its proponents included the Russian biologist Leo Berg and the American paleontologist Henry Fairfield Osborn. Orthogenesis was popular among some paleontologists, who believed that the fossil record showed a gradual and constant unidirectional change. Saltationism was the idea that new species arise as a result of large mutations. It was seen as a much faster alternative to the Darwinian concept of a gradual process of small random variations being acted on by natural selection, and was popular with early geneticists such as Hugo de Vries, William Bateson, and early in his career, T.H. Morgan. It became the basis of the mutation theory of evolution.

Mendelian Genetics, Biometrics, and Mutation

The so-called rediscovery of Gregor Mendel's laws of inheritance in 1900 ignited a fierce debate between two camps of biologists. In one camp were the Mendelians, who were focussed on discrete variations and the laws of inheritance. They were led by William Bateson (who coined the word *genetics*) and Hugo de Vries (who coined the word *mutation*). Their opponents were the biometricians, who were interested in the continuous variation of characteristics within populations. Their leaders, Karl Pearson and Walter Frank Raphael Weldon, followed in the tradition of Francis Galton, who had focussed on measurement and statistical analysis of variation within a population. The biometricians rejected Mendelian genetics on the basis that discrete units of heredity, such as genes, could not explain the continuous range of variation seen in real populations. Weldon's work with crabs and snails provided evidence that selection pressure from the environment could shift the range of variation in wild populations, but the Mendelians maintained that the variations measured by biometricians were too insignificant to account for the evolution of new species.

When T.H. Morgan began experimenting with breeding the fruit fly *Drosophila melanogaster*, he was a saltationist who hoped to demonstrate that a new species could be created in the lab by mutation alone. Instead, the work at his lab between 1910 and 1915 reconfirmed Mendelian genetics and provided solid experimental evidence linking it to chromosomal inheritance. His work also demonstrated that most mutations had relatively small effects, such as a change in eye colour, and that rather than creating a new species in a single step, mutations served to increase variation within the existing population.

Population Genetics

The Mendelian and biometrician models were eventually reconciled with the development of population genetics. A key step was the work of the British biologist and statistician R.A. Fisher. In a series of papers starting in 1918 and culminating in his 1930 book *The Genetical Theory of Natural Selection*, Fisher showed that the continuous variation measured by the biometricians could be produced by the combined action of many discrete genes, and that natural selection could change gene frequencies in a population, resulting in evolution. In a series of papers beginning in 1924, another British geneticist, J.B.S. Haldane, applied statistical analysis to real-world examples of natural selection, such as the evolution of industrial melanism in peppered moths, and showed that natural selection worked at an even faster rate than Fisher assumed.

The American biologist Sewall Wright, who had a background in animal breeding experiments, focussed on combinations of interacting genes, and the effects of inbreeding on small, relatively isolated populations that exhibited genetic drift. In 1932, Wright introduced the concept of an adaptive landscape and argued that genetic drift and inbreeding could drive a small, isolated sub-population away from an adaptive peak, allowing natural selection to drive it towards different adaptive peaks. The work of Fisher, Haldane and Wright founded the discipline of population genetics. This integrated natural selection with Mendelian genetics, which was the critical first step in developing a unified theory of how evolution worked.

Modern Evolutionary Synthesis

In the first few decades of the 20th century, most field naturalists continued to believe that Lamarckian and orthogenic mechanisms of evolution provided the best explanation for the complexity they observed in the living world. But as the field of genetics continued to develop, those views became less tenable. Theodosius Dobzhansky, a postdoctoral worker in T.H. Morgan's lab, had been influenced by the work on genetic diversity by Russian geneticists such as Sergei Chetverikov. He helped to bridge the divide between the foundations of microevolution developed by the population geneticists and the patterns of macroevolution observed by field biologists, with his 1937 book *Genetics and the Origin of Species*. Dobzhansky examined the genetic diversity of wild populations and showed that, contrary to the assumptions of the population geneticists, these populations had large amounts of genetic diversity, with marked differences between sub-populations. The book also took the highly mathematical work of the population geneticists and put it into a more accessible form. In Great Britain E.B. Ford, the pioneer of ecological genetics, continued throughout the 1930s and 1940s to demonstrate the power of selection due to ecological factors including the ability to maintain genetic diversity through genetic polymorphisms such as human blood types. Ford's work would contribute to a shift in emphasis during the course of the modern synthesis towards natural selection over genetic drift.

Evolutionary biologist Ernst Mayr was influenced by the work of the German biologist Bernhard Rensch showing the influence of local environmental factors on the geographic distribution of sub-species and closely related species. Mayr followed up on Dobzhansky's work with the 1942 book *Systematics and the Origin of Species*, which emphasized the importance of allopatric speciation in the formation of new species. This form of speciation occurs when the geographical isolation of a sub-population is followed by the development of mechanisms for reproductive isolation. Mayr also formulated the biological species concept that defined a species as a group of interbreeding or potentially interbreeding populations that were reproductively isolated from all other populations.

In the 1944 book *Tempo and Mode in Evolution*, George Gaylord Simpson showed that the fossil record was consistent with the irregular non-directional pattern predicted by the developing evolutionary synthesis, and that the linear trends that earlier paleontologists had claimed supported orthogenesis and neo-Lamarckism did not hold up to closer examination. In 1950, G. Ledyard Stebbins published *Variation and Evolution in Plants*, which helped to integrate botany into the synthesis. The emerging cross-disciplinary consensus on the workings of evolution would be known as the modern evolutionary synthesis. It received its name from the book *Evolution: The Modern Synthesis* by Julian Huxley.

The evolutionary synthesis provided a conceptual core-in particular, natural selection and Mendelian population genetics — that tied together many, but not all, biological disciplines. It helped establish the legitimacy of evolutionary biology, a primarily historical science, in a scientific climate that favoured experimental methods over historical ones. The synthesis also resulted in a considerable narrowing of the range of mainstream evolutionary thought (what Stephen Jay Gould called the 'hardening of the synthesis'): by the 1950s, natural selection acting on genetic variation was virtually the only acceptable mechanism of evolutionary change (panselectionism), and macroevolution was simply considered the result of extensive microevolution.

The middle decades of the 20th century saw the rise of molecular biology, and with it an understanding of the chemical nature of genes as sequences of DNA and their relationship, through the genetic code, to protein sequences. At the same time, increasingly powerful techniques for analyzing proteins, such as protein electrophoresis and sequencing, brought biochemical phenomena into realm of the synthetic theory of evolution. In the early 1960s, biochemists Linus Pauling and Emile Zuckerkandl proposed the molecular clock hypothesis: that sequence differences between homologous proteins could be used to calculate the time since two species diverged. By 1969, Motoo Kimura and others provided a theoretical basis for the molecular clock, arguing that—at the molecular level at least–most genetic mutations are neither harmful nor helpful and that genetic drift, rather than natural selection, is responsible for a large portion of genetic change: the neutral theory of molecular evolution. Studies of protein differences *within* species also brought molecular data to bear on population genetics by providing estimates of the level of heterozygosity in natural populations.

From the early 1960s, molecular biology was increasingly seen as a threat to the traditional core of evolutionary biology. Established evolutionary biologists–particularly Ernst Mayr, Theodosius Dobzhansky and G.G. Simpson, three of the architects of the modern synthesis—were extremely skeptical of molecular approaches, especially when it came to the connection (or lack thereof) to natural selection. The molecular clock hypothesis and the neutral theory were particularly controversial, spawning the neutralist-selectionist debate over the relative importance of drift and selection, which continued into the 1980s without a clear resolution.

Gene-centred View

In the mid-1960s, George C. Williams strongly critiqued explanations of adaptations worded in terms of 'survival of the species' (group selection arguments). Such explanations were largely replaced by a gene-centered view of evolution, epitomized by the kin selection arguments of W.D. Hamilton, George R. Price and John Maynard Smith. This viewpoint would be summarized and popularized in the influential 1976 book *The Selfish Gene* by Richard Dawkins. Models of the period showed that group selection was severely limited in its strength; though newer models do admit the possibility of significant multi-level selection.

In 1973, Leigh Van Valen proposed the term 'Red Queen', which he took from *Through the Looking-Glass* by Lewis Carroll, to describe a scenario where a species involved in one or more evolutionary arms races would have to constantly change just to keep pace with the species with which it was co-evolving. Hamilton, Williams and others suggested that this idea might explain the evolution of sexual reproduction: the increased genetic diversity caused by sexual reproduction would help maintain resistance against rapidly evolving parasites, thus making sexual reproduction common, despite the tremendous cost from the gene-centric point of view of a system where only half of an organism's genome is passed on during reproduction. The gene-centric view has also led to an increased interest in Darwin's old idea of sexual selection, and more recently in topics such as sexual conflict and intragenomic conflict.

Sociobiology

W.D. Hamilton's work on kin selection contributed to the emergence of the discipline of sociobiology. The existence of altruistic behaviours has been a difficult problem for evolutionary theorists from the beginning. Significant progress was made in 1964 when Hamilton formulated the inequality in kin selection known as Hamilton's rule, which showed how eusociality in insects (the existence of sterile worker classes) and many other examples of altruistic behaviour could have evolved through kin selection. Other theories followed, some derived from game theory, such as reciprocal altruism. In 1975, E.O. Wilson published the influential and highly controversial book *Sociobiology: The New Synthesis* which claimed evolutionary theory could help explain many aspects of animal, including human, behaviour. Critics of sociobiology, including Stephen Jay Gould and Richard Lewontin, claimed that sociobiology greatly overstated the degree to which complex human behaviours could be determined by genetic factors. They also claimed that the theories of sociobiologists often reflected their own ideological biases. Despite these criticisms, work has continued in sociobiology and the related discipline of evolutionary psychology, including work on other aspects of the altruism problem.

Evolutionary Paths and Processes

One of the most prominent debates arising during the 1970s was over the theory of punctuated equilibrium. Niles Eldredge and Stephen Jay Gould proposed that there was a pattern of fossil species that remained largely unchanged for long periods (what they termed *stasis*), interspersed with relatively brief periods of rapid change during speciation.

Improvements in sequencing methods resulted in a large increase of sequenced genomes, allowing the testing and refining of evolutionary theories using this huge amount of genome data. Comparisons between these genomes provide insights into the molecular mechanisms of speciation and adaptation. These genomic analyses have produced fundamental changes in the understanding of the evolutionary history of life, such as the proposal of the three-domain system by Carl Woese. Advances in computational hardware and software allow the testing and extrapolation of increasingly advanced evolutionary models and the development of the field of systems biology. One of the results has been an exchange of ideas between theories of biological evolution and the field of computer science known as evolutionary computation, which attempts to mimic biological evolution for the purpose of developing new computer algorithms. Discoveries in biotechnology now allow the modification of entire genomes, advancing evolutionary studies to the level where future experiments may involve the creation of entirely synthetic organisms.

Microbiology, Horizontal Gene Transfer and Endosymbiosis

Microbiology was largely ignored by early evolutionary theory. This was due to the paucity of morphological traits and the lack of a species concept in microbiology, particularly amongst prokaryotes. These studies are revealing unanticipated levels of diversity amongst microbes.

One particularly important outcome from studies on microbial evolution was the discovery in Japan of horizontal gene transfer in 1959. This transfer of genetic material between different species of bacteria was first recognized because it played a major role in the spread of antibiotic resistance. More recently, as knowledge of genomes has continued to expand, it has been suggested that lateral transfer of genetic material has played an important role in the evolution of all organisms. These high levels of horizontal gene transfer have led to suggestions that the family tree of today's organisms, the so-called 'tree of life', is more similar to an interconnected web or net.

Indeed, as part of the endosymbiotic theory for the origin of organelles, a form of horizontal gene transfer has been a critical step in the evolution of eukaryotes such as fungi, plants, and animals. The endosymbiotic theory holds that organelles within the cells of eukorytes such as mitochondria and chloroplasts, had descended from independent bacteria that came to live symbiotically within other cells. It had been suggested in the late 19th century when similarities between mitochondria and bacteria were noted, but largely dismissed until it was revived and championed by Lynn Margulis in the 1960s and 70s; Margulis was able to make use of new evidence that such organelles had their own DNA that was inherited independently from that in the cell's nucleus.

Evolutionary Developmental Biology

In the 1980s and 1990s the tenets of the modern evolutionary synthesis came under increasing scrutiny. There was a renewal of structuralist themes in evolutionary biology in the work of biologists such as Brian Goodwin and Stuart Kauffman, which incorporated ideas from cybernetics and systems theory, and emphasized the self-organizing processes of development as factors directing the course of evolution. The evolutionary biologist Stephen Jay Gould revived earlier ideas of heterochrony, alterations in the relative rates of developmental processes over the course of evolution, to account for the generation of novel forms, and, with the evolutionary biologist Richard Lewontin, wrote an influential paper in 1979 suggesting that a change in one biological structure, or even a structural novelty, could arise incidentally as an accidental result of selection on another structure, rather than through direct selection for that particular adaptation. They called such incidental structural changes 'spandrels' after an architectural feature. Later, Gould and Vrba discussed the acquisition of new functions by novel structures arising in this fashion, calling them 'exaptations'.

Molecular data regarding the mechanisms underlying development accumulated rapidly during the 1980s and '90s. It became clear that the diversity of animal morphology was not the result of different sets of proteins regulating the development of different animals, but from changes in the deployment of a small set of proteins that were common to all animals. These proteins became known as the 'developmental toolkit'. Such perspectives influenced the disciplines of phylogenetics, paleontology and comparative developmental biology, and spawned the new discipline of evolutionary developmental biology.

More recent work in this field by Mary Jane West-Eberhard has emphasized phenotypic and developmental plasticity. It has been suggested, for example, that the rapid emergence of basic animal body plans in the Cambrian explosion was due in part to changes in the environment acting on inherent material properties of cell aggregates, such as differential cell adhesion and biochemical oscillation. The resulting forms were later stabilized by natural selection. Experimental and theoretical research on these and related ideas have been presented in the multi-authored volume *Origination of Organismal Form*.

Epigenetic Inheritance

Yet another area where developmental biology has led to the questioning of some tenets of the modern evolutionary synthesis is in the field of epigenetics, the study of how environmental factors affect the way genes express themselves during development. By the first decade of the

21st century it had become accepted that in some cases such environmental factors could affect the expression of genes in subsequent generations even though the offspring were not exposed to the same environmental factors, and there had been no genetic changes. This shows that in some cases non-genetic changes to an organism can be inherited and it has been suggested that such inheritance can help with adaptation to local conditions and affect evolution. Some have suggested that in some cases a form of Lamarckian evolution may occur.

4 Genetics

Genetics is the study of genes, and tries to explain what they are and how they work. Genes are how living organisms inherit features from their ancestors; for example, children usually look like their parents because they have inherited their parents' genes. Genetics tries to identify which features are inherited, and explain how these features are passed from generation to generation.

In genetics, a feature of a living thing is called a 'trait'. Some traits are part of an organism's physical appearance; such as a person's eye-colour, height or weight. Other sorts of traits are not easily seen and include blood types or resistance to diseases. Some traits are inherited through our genes, so tall and thin people tend to have tall and thin children. Other traits come from interactions between our genes and the environment, so a child might inherit the tendency to be tall, but if they are poorly nourished, they will still be short. The way our genes and environment interact to produce a trait can be complicated. For example, the chances of somebody dying of cancer or heart disease seems to depend on both their genes and their lifestyle.

Genes are made from a long molecule called DNA, which is copied and inherited across generations. DNA is made of simple units that line up in a particular order within this large molecule. The order of these units carries genetic information, similar to how the order of letters on a page carry information. The language used by DNA is called the genetic code, which lets organisms read the information in the genes. This information is the instructions for constructing and operating a living organism.

The information within a particular gene is not always exactly the same between one organism and another, so different copies of a gene do not always give exactly the same instructions. Each unique form of a single gene is called an allele. As an example, one allele for the gene for hair colour could instruct the body to produce a lot of pigment, producing black hair, while a different allele of the same gene might give garbled instructions that fail to produce any pigment, giving white hair. Mutations are random changes in genes, and can create new alleles. Mutations can also produce new traits, such as when mutations to an allele for black hair produce a new allele for white hair. This appearance of new traits is important in evolution.

Genes are inherited as units, with two parents dividing out copies of their genes to their offspring. You can think of this process like mixing two hands of cards, shuffling them, and then dealing them out again. Humans have two copies of each of their genes (*i.e.,* two alleles) and when people reproduce they make copies of their genes and put them into eggs or sperm, but only put in one copy of each type of gene. When an egg joins with a sperm, this gives a child a complete set of genes. This child will have the same number of genes as its parents, but for any gene one of their two copies will come from their father, and one from their mother.

The effects of this mixing depends on the types (the alleles) of the gene you are interested in. If the father has two alleles for green eyes, and the mother has two alleles for brown eyes, all their children will get two alleles that give different instructions, one for green eyes and one for brown. The eye colour of these children depends on how these alleles work together. If one allele overrides the instructions from another, it is called the *dominant* allele, and the allele that is overridden is called the *recessive* allele. In the case of a daughter with both green and brown alleles, brown is dominant and she ends up with brown eyes.

Although the green colour allele is still there in this brown-eyed girl, it doesn't show. This is a difference between what you see on the surface (the traits of an organism, called its phenotype) and the genes within the organism (its genotype). In this example you can call the brown allele '*B*' and the green allele '*g*'. (It is normal to write dominant alleles with capital letters and recessive ones with lower-case letters.) The brown-eyed daughter has the 'brown eye phenotype' but her genotype is *Bg*, with one copy of the *B* allele, and one of the *g* allele.

Now imagine that this woman grows up and has children with a brown-eyed man who also has a *Bg* genotype. Her eggs will be a mixture of two types, one sort containing the *B* allele, and one sort the *g* allele.

Similarly, her partner will produce a mix of two types of sperm containing one or the other of these two alleles. Now, when the alleles are mixed up in their offspring, these children have a chance of getting either brown or green eyes, since they could get a genotype of *BB* = brown eyes, *Bg* = brown eyes or *gg* = green eyes. In this generation, there is therefore a chance of the recessive allele showing itself in the phenotype of the children — some of them may have green eyes like their grandfather.

Many traits are inherited in a more complicated way than the example above. This can happen when there are several genes involved, each contributing a small part to the end result. Tall people tend to have tall children because their children get a package of many alleles that each contribute a bit to how much they grow. However, there are not clear groups of 'short people' and 'tall people', like there are groups of people with brown or green eyes. This is because of the large number of genes involved; this makes the trait very variable and people are of many different heights. Inheritance can also be complicated when the trait depends on the interaction between genetics and the environment. This is quite common, for example, if a child does not eat enough nutritious food this will not change traits like eye colour, but it could stunt their growth.

Inherited Diseases

Some diseases are hereditary and run in families; others, such as infectious diseases, are caused by the environment. Other diseases come from a combination of genes and the environment. Genetic disorders are diseases that are caused by a single allele of a gene and are inherited in families. These include Huntington's disease, Cystic fibrosis or Duchenne muscular dystrophy. Cystic fibrosis, for example, is caused by mutations in a single gene called *CFTR* and is inherited as a recessive trait.

Other diseases are influenced by genetics, but the genes a person gets from their parents only change their risk of getting a disease. Most of these diseases are inherited in a complex way, with either multiple genes involved, or coming from both genes and the environment. As an example, the risk of breast cancer is 50 times higher in the families most at risk, compared to the families least at risk. This variation is probably due to a large number of alleles, each changing the risk a little bit. Several of the genes have been identified, such as *BRCA1* and *BRCA2*, but not all of them. However, although some of the risk is genetic, the risk of this cancer is also increased by being overweight, drinking a lot of alcohol and not exercising. A woman's risk of breast cancer therefore comes from a large number of alleles interacting with her environment, so it is very hard to predict.

The function of genes is to provide the information needed to make molecules called proteins in cells. Cells are the smallest independent parts of organisms: the human body contains about 100 trillion cells, while very small organisms like bacteria are just one single cell. A cell is like a miniature and very complex factory that can make all the parts needed to produce a copy of itself, which happens when cells divide. There is a simple division of labour in cells–genes give instructions and proteins carry out these instructions, tasks like building a new copy of a cell, or repairing damage. Each type of protein is a specialist that only does one job, so if a cell needs to do something new, it must make a new protein to do this job. Similarly, if a cell needs to do something faster or slower than before, it makes more or less of the protein responsible. Genes tell cells what to do by telling them which proteins to make and in what amounts.

Proteins are made of a chain of 20 different types of amino acid molecules. This chain folds up into a compact shape, rather like an untidy ball of string. The shape of the protein is determined by the sequence of amino acids along its chain and it is this shape that, in turn, determines what the protein will do. For example, some proteins have parts of their surface that perfectly match the shape of another molecule, allowing the protein to bind to this molecule very tightly. Other proteins are enzymes, which are like tiny machines that alter other molecules.

The information in DNA is held in the sequence of the repeating units along the DNA chain. These units are four types of nucleotides (A, T, G and C) and the sequence of nucleotides stores information in an alphabet called the genetic code. When a gene is read by a cell the DNA sequence is copied into a very similar molecule called RNA (this process is called transcription). Transcription is controlled by other DNA sequences (such as promoters), which show a cell where genes are, and control how often they are copied. The RNA copy made from a gene is then fed through a structure called a ribosome, which translates the sequence of nucleotides in the RNA into the correct sequence of amino acids and joins these amino acids together to make a complete protein chain. The new protein then folds up into its active form. The process of moving information from the language of DNA into the language of amino acids is called translation.

If the sequence of the nucleotides in a gene changes, the sequence of the amino acids in the protein it produces may also change — if part of a gene is deleted, the protein produced will be shorter and may not work any more. This is the reason why different alleles of a gene can have different effects in an organism. As an example, hair colour depends on how much of a dark substance called melanin is put into the hair as it grows. If a person has a normal set of the genes involved in making melanin, they make all the proteins needed and they grow dark hair. However, if the alleles for a particular protein have different sequences and produce proteins that can't do their jobs, no melanin will be produced and the hair will be white. This condition is called albinism and the person with this condition is called an albino.

Genes are copied each time a cell divides into two new cells. The process that copies DNA is called DNA replication. It is through a similar process that a child inherits genes from its parents, when a copy from the mother is mixed with a copy from the father.

DNA can be copied very easily and accurately because each piece of DNA can direct the creation of a new copy of its information. This is because DNA is made of two strands that pair together like the two sides of a zipper. The nucleotides are in the centre, like the teeth in the zipper, and pair up to hold the two strands together. Importantly, the four different sorts of nucleotides are different shapes, so in order for the strands to close up properly, an *A* nucleotide must go opposite a *t* nucleotide, and a *G* opposite a *C*. This exact pairing is called base pairing.

When DNA is copied, the two strands of the old DNA are pulled apart by enzymes which move along each of the two single strands pairing up new nucleotide units and then zipping the strands closed. This produces two new pieces of DNA, each containing one strand from the old DNA and one newly made strand. This process isn't perfect and sometimes the proteins will make mistakes and put the wrong nucleotide into the strand they are building. This causes a change in the sequence of that gene. These changes in DNA sequence are called mutations. Mutations produce new alleles of genes. Sometimes these changes stop the gene from working properly, like the melanin genes discussed above. In other cases these mutations can change what the gene does or even let it do its job a little better than before. These mutations and their effects on the traits of organisms are one of the causes of evolution.

Genes and Evolution

A population of organisms evolves when an inherited trait becomes more common or less common over time. For instance, all the mice living on an island would be a single population of mice. If over a few generations, white mice went from being rare, to being a large part of this population, then the coat colour of these mice would be evolving. In terms of genetics, this is called a change in allele frequency—such as an increase in the frequency of the allele for white fur.

Alleles become more or less common either just by chance (in a process called genetic drift), or through natural selection. In natural selection, if an allele makes it more likely that an organism will survive and reproduce, then over time this allele will become more common. But if an allele is harmful, natural selection will make it less common. For example, if the island was getting colder each year and was covered with snow for much of the time, then the allele for white fur would become useful for the mice, since it would make them harder to see against the snow. Fewer of the white mice would be eaten by predators, so over time white mice would out-compete mice with dark fur. White fur alleles would become more common, and dark fur alleles would become more rare.

Mutations create new alleles. These alleles have new DNA sequences and can produce proteins with new properties. So if an island was populated entirely by black mice, mutations could happen creating alleles for white fur. The combination of mutations creating new alleles at random, and natural selection picking out those which are useful, causes adaptation. This is when organisms change in ways that help them to survive and reproduce.

Since traits come from the genes in a cell, putting a new piece of DNA into a cell can produce a new trait. This is how genetic engineering works. For example, crop plants can be given a gene from an Arctic fish, so they produce an antifreeze protein in their leaves. This can help prevent frost damage. Other genes that can be put into crops include a natural insecticide from the bacteria *Bacillus thuringiensis*. The insecticide kills insects that eat the plants, but is harmless to people. In these plants the new genes are put into the plant before it is grown, so the genes will be in every part of the plant, including its seeds. The plant's offspring will then inherit the new genes, something which has led to concern about the spread of new traits into wild plants.

The kind of technology used in genetic engineering is also being developed to treat people with genetic disorders in an experimental medical technique called gene therapy. However, here the new gene is put in after the person has grown up and become ill, so any new gene will not be inherited by their children. Gene therapy works by trying to replace the allele that causes the disease with an allele that will work properly.

The fact that living things inherit traits from their parents has been used since prehistoric times to improve crop plants and animals through selective breeding. However, the modern science of genetics, which seeks to understand the process of inheritance, only began with the work of Gregor Mendel in the mid-19th century. Although he did not know the physical basis for heredity, Mendel observed that organisms inherit traits via discrete units of inheritance, which are now called genes.

Genes correspond to regions within DNA, a molecule composed of a chain of four different types of nucleotides—the sequence of these nucleotides is the genetic information organisms inherit. DNA naturally occurs in a double stranded form, with nucleotides on each strand complementary to each other. Each strand can act as a template for creating a new partner strand—this is the physical method for making copies of genes that can be inherited.

The sequence of nucleotides in a gene is translated by cells to produce a chain of amino acids, creating proteins—the order of amino acids in a protein corresponds to the order of nucleotides in the gene. This relationship between nucleotide sequence and amino acid sequence is known as the genetic code. The amino acids in a protein determine how it folds into a three-dimensional shape; this structure is, in turn, responsible for the protein's function. Proteins carry out almost all the functions needed for cells to live. A change to the DNA in a gene can change a protein's amino acids, changing its shape and function: this can have a dramatic effect in the cell and on the organism as a whole.

Although genetics plays a large role in the appearance and behaviour of organisms, it is the combination of genetics with what an organism experiences that determines the ultimate outcome. For example, while genes play a role in determining an organism's size, the nutrition and other conditions it experiences after inception also have a large effect.

Although the science of genetics began with the applied and theoretical work of Gregor Mendel in the mid-19th century, other theories of inheritance preceded Mendel. A popular theory during Mendel's time was the concept of blending inheritance: the idea that individuals inherit a smooth blend of traits from their parents. Mendel's work disproved this, showing that traits are composed of combinations of distinct genes rather than a continuous blend. Another theory that had some support at that time was the inheritance of acquired characteristics: the belief that individuals inherit traits strengthened by their parents. This theory (commonly associated with Jean-Baptiste Lamarck) is now known to be wrong—the experiences of individuals do not affect the genes they pass to their children. Other theories included the pangenesis of Charles Darwin (which had both acquired and inherited aspects) and Francis Galton's reformulation of pangenesis as both particulate and inherited.

The modern science of genetics traces its roots to Gregor Johann Mendel, a German-Czech Augustinian monk and scientist who studied the nature of inheritance in plants. In his paper 'Versuche über Pflanzenhybriden' ('Experiments on Plant Hybridization'), presented in 1865 to the *Naturforschender Verein* (Society for Research in Nature) in Brünn, Mendel traced the inheritance patterns of certain traits in pea plants and described them mathematically. Although this pattern of inheritance could only be observed for a few traits, Mendel's work suggested that heredity was particulate, not acquired, and that the inheritance patterns of many traits could be explained through simple rules and ratios.

The importance of Mendel's work did not gain wide understanding until the 1890s, after his death, when other scientists working on similar problems re-discovered his research. William Bateson, a proponent of Mendel's work, coined the word *genetics* in 1905. (The adjective *genetic*, derived from the Greek word *genesis*—, 'origin' and that from the word *genno*—, 'to give birth', predates the noun and was first used in a biological sense in 1860.) Bateson popularized the usage of the word *genetics* to describe the study of inheritance in his inaugural address to the Third International Conference on Plant Hybridization in London, England, in 1906.

After the rediscovery of Mendel's work, scientists tried to determine which molecules in the cell were responsible for inheritance. In 1910, Thomas Hunt Morgan argued that genes are on chromosomes, based on observations of a sex-linked white eye mutation in fruit flies. In 1913, his student Alfred Sturtevant used the phenomenon of genetic linkage to show that genes are arranged linearly on the chromosome.

Although genes were known to exist on chromosomes, chromosomes are composed of both protein and DNA—scientists did not know which of these is responsible for inheritance. In 1928, Frederick Griffith discovered the phenomenon of transformation (see Griffith's experiment): dead bacteria could transfer genetic material to 'transform' other still-living bacteria. Sixteen years later, in 1944, Oswald Theodore Avery, Colin McLeod and Maclyn McCarty identified the molecule responsible for transformation as DNA. The Hershey-Chase experiment in 1952 also showed that DNA (rather than protein) is the genetic material of the viruses that infect bacteria, providing further evidence that DNA is the molecule responsible for inheritance.

James D. Watson and Francis Crick determined the structure of DNA in 1953, using the X-ray crystallography work of Rosalind Franklin and Maurice Wilkins that indicated DNA had a helical structure (i.e., shaped like a corkscrew). Their double-helix model had two strands of DNA with the nucleotides pointing inward, each matching a complementary nucleotide on the other strand to form what looks like rungs on a twisted ladder. This structure showed that genetic information exists in the sequence of nucleotides on each strand of DNA. The structure also suggested a simple method for duplication: if the strands are separated, new partner strands can be reconstructed for each based on the sequence of the old strand.

Although the structure of DNA showed how inheritance works, it was still not known how DNA influences the behaviour of cells. In the following years, scientists tried to understand how DNA controls the process of protein production. It was discovered that the cell uses DNA as a template to create matching messenger RNA (a molecule with nucleotides, very similar to DNA). The nucleotide sequence of a messenger RNA is used to create an amino acid sequence in protein; this translation between nucleotide and amino acid sequences is known as the genetic code.

With this molecular understanding of inheritance, an explosion of research became possible. One important development was chain-termination DNA sequencing in 1977 by Frederick Sanger. This technology allows scientists to read the nucleotide sequence of a DNA molecule. In 1983, Kary Banks Mullis developed the polymerase chain reaction, providing a quick way to isolate and amplify a specific section of a DNA from a mixture. Through the pooled efforts of the Human Genome Project and the parallel private effort by Celera Genomics, these and other techniques culminated in the sequencing of the human genome in 2003.

At its most fundamental level, inheritance in organisms occurs by means of discrete traits, called genes. This property was first observed by Gregor Mendel, who studied the segregation of heritable traits in pea plants. In his experiments studying the trait for flower colour, Mendel observed that the flowers of each pea plant were either purple or white—but never an intermediate between the two colours. These different, discrete versions of the same gene are called alleles.

In the case of pea, which is a diploid species, each individual plant has two alleles of each gene, one allele inherited from each parent. Many species, including humans, have this pattern of inheritance. Diploid organisms with two copies of the same allele of a given gene are called homozygous at that gene locus, while organisms with two different alleles of a given gene are called heterozygous.

The set of alleles for a given organism is called its genotype, while the observable traits of the organism are called its phenotype. When organisms are heterozygous at a gene, often one allele is called dominant as its qualities dominate the phenotype of the organism, while the other allele is called recessive as its qualities recede and are not observed. Some alleles do not have complete dominance and instead have incomplete dominance by expressing an intermediate phenotype, or codominance by expressing both alleles at once.

When a pair of organisms reproduce sexually, their offspring randomly inherit one of the two alleles from each parent. These observations of discrete inheritance and the segregation of alleles are collectively known as Mendel's first law or the Law of Segregation.

Organisms have thousands of genes, and in sexually reproducing organisms these genes generally assort independently of each other. This means that the inheritance of an allele for yellow or green pea colour is unrelated to the inheritance of alleles for white or purple flowers. This phenomenon, known as 'Mendel's second law' or the 'Law of independent assortment', means that the alleles of different genes get shuffled between parents to form offspring with many different combinations.

Often different genes can interact in a way that influences the same trait. In the Blue-eyed Mary (*Omphalodes verna*), for example, there exists a gene with alleles that determine the colour of flowers: blue or magenta. Another gene, however, controls whether the flowers have colour at all or are white. When a plant has two copies of this white allele, its flowers are white–regardless of whether the first gene has blue or magenta alleles. This interaction between genes is called epistasis, with the second gene epistatic to the first.

Many traits are not discrete features (e.g. purple or white flowers) but are instead continuous features (e.g. human height and skin colour). These complex traits are products of many genes. The influence of these genes is mediated, to varying degrees, by the environment an organism has experienced. The degree to which an organism's genes contribute to a complex trait is called heritability. Measurement of the heritability of a trait is relative–in a more variable environment, the environment has a bigger influence on the total variation of the trait. For example, human height is a complex trait with a heritability of 89 per cent in the United States. In Nigeria, however, where people experience a more variable access to good nutrition and healthcare, height has a heritability of only 62 per cent.

The molecular basis for genes is deoxyribonucleic acid (DNA). DNA is composed of a chain of nucleotides, of which there are four types: adenine (A), cytosine (C), guanine (G), and thymine (T). Genetic information exists in the sequence of these nucleotides, and genes exist as stretches of sequence along the DNA chain. Viruses are the only exception to this rule—sometimes viruses use the very similar molecule RNA instead of DNA as their genetic material.

DNA normally exists as a double-stranded molecule, coiled into the shape of a double-helix. Each nucleotide in DNA preferentially pairs with its partner nucleotide on the opposite strand: A pairs with T, and C pairs with G. Thus, in its two-stranded form, each strand effectively contains all necessary information, redundant with its partner strand. This structure of DNA is the physical basis for inheritance: DNA replication duplicates the genetic information by splitting the strands and using each strand as a template for synthesis of a new partner strand.

Genes are arranged linearly along long chains of DNA sequence, called chromosomes. In bacteria, each cell usually contains a single circular chromosome, while eukaryotic organisms (including plants and animals) have their DNA arranged in multiple linear chromosomes. These DNA strands are often extremely long; the largest human chromosome, for example, is about 247 million base pairs in length. The DNA of a chromosome is associated with structural proteins that organize, compact, and control access to the DNA, forming a material called chromatin; in eukaryotes, chromatin is usually composed of nucleosomes, segments of DNA wound around cores of histone proteins. The full set of hereditary material in an organism (usually the combined DNA sequences of all chromosomes) is called the genome.

While haploid organisms have only one copy of each chromosome, most animals and many plants are diploid, containing two of each chromosome and thus two copies of every gene. The two alleles for a gene are located on identical loci of sister chromatids, each allele inherited from a different parent.

An exception exists in the sex chromosomes, specialized chromosomes many animals have evolved that play a role in determining the sex of an organism. In humans and other mammals, the Y chromosome has very few genes and triggers the development of male sexual characteristics, while the *X* chromosome is similar to the other chromosomes and contains many genes unrelated to sex determination. Females have two copies of the *X* chromosome, but males have one *Y* and only one *X* chromosome; this difference in *X* chromosome copy numbers leads to the unusual inheritance patterns of sex-linked disorders.

When cells divide, their full genome is copied and each daughter cell inherits one copy. This process, called mitosis, is the simplest form of reproduction and is the basis for asexual reproduction. Asexual reproduction can also occur in multicellular organisms, producing offspring that inherit their genome from a single parent. Offspring that are genetically identical to their parents are called clones.

Eukaryotic organisms often use sexual reproduction to generate offspring that contain a mixture of genetic material inherited from two different parents. The process of sexual reproduction alternates between forms that contain single copies of the genome (haploid) and double copies (diploid). Haploid cells fuse and combine genetic material to create a diploid cell with paired chromosomes. Diploid organisms form haploids by dividing, without replicating their DNA, to create daughter cells that randomly inherit one of each pair of chromosomes. Most animals and many plants are diploid for most of their lifespan, with the haploid form reduced to single cell gametes such as sperm or eggs.

Although they do not use the haploid/diploid method of sexual reproduction, bacteria have many methods of acquiring new genetic information. Some bacteria can undergo conjugation, transferring a small circular piece of DNA to another bacterium. Bacteria can also take up raw DNA fragments found in the environment and integrate them into their genomes, a phenomenon known as transformation. These processes result in horizontal gene transfer, transmitting fragments of genetic information between organisms that would be otherwise unrelated.

The diploid nature of chromosomes allows for genes on different chromosomes to assort independently during sexual reproduction, recombining to form new combinations of genes. Genes on the same chromosome would theoretically never recombine, however, were it not for the process of chromosomal crossover. During crossover, chromosomes exchange stretches of DNA, effectively shuffling the gene alleles between the chromosomes. This process of chromosomal crossover generally occurs during meiosis, a series of cell divisions that creates haploid cells.

The probability of chromosomal crossover occurring between two given points on the chromosome is related to the distance between the points. For an arbitrarily long distance, the probability of crossover is high enough that the inheritance of the genes is effectively uncorrelated. For genes that are closer together, however, the lower probability of crossover means that the genes demonstrate genetic linkage—alleles for the two genes tend to be inherited together. The amounts of linkage between a series of genes can be combined to form a linear linkage map that roughly describes the arrangement of the genes along the chromosome.

Genes generally express their functional effect through the production of proteins, which are complex molecules responsible for most functions in the cell. Proteins are chains of amino acids, and the DNA sequence of a gene (through an RNA intermediate) is used to produce a specific protein sequence. This process begins with the production of an RNA molecule with a sequence matching the gene's DNA sequence, a process called transcription.

This messenger RNA molecule is then used to produce a corresponding amino acid sequence through a process called translation. Each group of three nucleotides in the sequence, called a codon, corresponds to one of the twenty possible amino acids in protein; this correspondence is called the genetic code. The flow of information is unidirectional: information is transferred from nucleotide sequences into the amino acid sequence of proteins, but it never transfers from protein back into the sequence of DNA—a phenomenon Francis Crick called the central dogma of molecular biology.

The specific sequence of amino acids results in a unique three-dimensional structure for that protein, and the three-dimensional structures of proteins are related to their functions. Some are simple structural molecules, like the fibers formed by the protein collagen. Proteins can bind to other proteins and simple molecules, sometimes acting as enzymes by facilitating chemical reactions within the bound molecules (without changing the structure of the protein itself). Protein structure is dynamic; the protein hemoglobin bends into slightly different forms as it facilitates the capture, transport, and release of oxygen molecules within mammalian blood.

Although genes contain all the information an organism uses to function, the environment plays an important role in determining the ultimate phenotype—a phenomenon often referred to as "nature vs. nurture". The phenotype of an organism depends on the interaction of genetics with the environment. One example of this is the case of temperature-sensitive mutations. Often, a single amino acid change within the sequence of a protein does not change its behaviour and interactions with other molecules, but it does destabilize the structure. In a high temperature environment, where molecules are moving more quickly and hitting each other, this results in the protein losing its structure and failing to function. In a low temperature environment, however, the protein's structure is stable and it functions normally. This type of mutation is visible in the coat colouration of Siamese cats, where a mutation in an enzyme responsible for pigment production causes it to destabilize and lose function at high temperatures. The protein remains functional in areas of skin that are colder—legs, ears, tail, and face—and so the cat has dark fur at its extremities.

Environment also plays a dramatic role in effects of the human genetic disease phenylketonuria. The mutation that causes phenylketonuria disrupts the ability of the body to break down the amino acid phenylalanine, causing a toxic build-up of an intermediate molecule that, in turn, causes severe symptoms of progressive mental retardation and seizures. If someone with the phenylketonuria mutation follows a strict diet that avoids this amino acid, however, they remain normal and healthy.

A popular method to determine how much role nature and nurture play is to study identical and fraternal twins or siblings of multiple birth. Because identical siblings come from the same zygote they are genetically the same. Fraternal siblings however are as different genetically from one another as normal siblings. By comparing how often the twin of a set has the same disorder between fraternal and identical twins, scientists can see whether there is more of a nature or nurture effect. One famous example of a multiple birth study includes the Genain quadruplets, who were identical quadruplets all diagnosed with schizophrenia.

The genome of a given organism contains thousands of genes, but not all these genes need to be active at any given moment. A gene is expressed when it is being transcribed into mRNA (and translated into protein), and there exist many cellular methods of controlling the expression of genes such that proteins are produced only when needed by the cell. Transcription factors are regulatory proteins that bind to the start of genes, either promoting or inhibiting the transcription of the gene Within the genome of *Escherichia coli* bacteria, for example, there exists a series of genes necessary for the synthesis of the amino acid tryptophan. However, when tryptophan is already available to the cell, these genes for tryptophan synthesis are no longer needed. The presence of tryptophan directly affects the activity of the genes–tryptophan molecules bind to the tryptophan repressor (a transcription factor), changing the repressor's structure such that the repressor binds to the genes. The tryptophan repressor blocks the transcription and expression of the genes, thereby creating negative feedback regulation of the tryptophan synthesis process.

Differences in gene expression are especially clear within multicellular organisms, where cells all contain the same genome but have very different structures and behaviours due to the expression of different sets of genes. All the cells in a multicellular organism derive from a single cell, differentiating into variant cell types in response to external and intercellular signals and gradually establishing different patterns of gene expression to create different behaviours. As no single gene is responsible for the development of structures within multicellular organisms, these patterns arise from the complex interactions between many cells.

Within eukaryotes there exist structural features of chromatin that influence the transcription of genes, often in the form of modifications to DNA and chromatin that are stably inherited by daughter cells. These features are called 'epigenetic' because they exist 'on top' of the DNA sequence and retain inheritance from one cell generation to the next. Because of epigenetic features, different cell types grown within the same medium can retain very different properties. Although epigenetic features are generally dynamic over the course of development, some, like the phenomenon of paramutation, have multigenerational inheritance and exist as rare exceptions to the general rule of DNA as the basis for inheritance.

Gene duplication allows diversification by providing redundancy: one gene can mutate and lose its original function without harming the organism.

During the process of DNA replication, errors occasionally occur in the polymerization of the second strand. These errors, called mutations, can have an impact on the phenotype of an organism, especially if they occur within the protein coding sequence of a gene. Error rates are usually very low—1 error in every 10-100 million bases—due to the 'proofreading' ability of DNA polymerases. (Without proofreading error rates are a thousandfold higher; because many viruses rely on DNA and RNA polymerases that lack proofreading ability, they experience higher mutation rates.) Processes that increase the rate of changes in DNA are called mutagenic: mutagenic chemicals promote errors in DNA replication, often by interfering with the structure of base-pairing, while UV radiation induces mutations by causing damage to the DNA structure. Chemical damage to DNA occurs naturally as well, and cells use DNA repair mechanisms to repair mismatches and breaks in DNA—nevertheless, the repair sometimes fails to return the DNA to its original sequence.

In organisms that use chromosomal crossover to exchange DNA and recombine genes, errors in alignment during meiosis can also cause mutations. Errors in crossover are especially likely when similar sequences cause partner chromosomes to adopt a mistaken alignment; this makes some regions in genomes more prone to mutating in this way. These errors create large structural changes in DNA sequence—duplications, inversions or deletions of entire regions, or the accidental exchanging of whole parts between different chromosomes (called translocation).

Mutations alter an organisms genotype and occasionally this causes different phenotypes to appear. Most mutations have little effect on an organism's phenotype, health, or reproductive fitness. Mutations that do have an effect are usually deleterious, but occasionally some can be beneficial. Studies in the fly *Drosophila melanogaster* suggest that if a mutation changes a protein produced by a gene, about 70 per cent of these mutations will be harmful with the remainder being either neutral or weakly beneficial.

Population genetics studies the distribution of genetic differences within populations and how these distributions change over time. Changes in the frequency of an allele in a population are mainly influenced by natural selection, where a given allele provides a selective or reproductive advantage to the organism, as well as other factors such as genetic drift, artificial selection and migration.

Over many generations, the genomes of organisms can change significantly, resulting in the phenomenon of evolution. Selection for beneficial mutations can cause a species to evolve into forms better able to survive in their environment, a process called adaptation. New species are formed through the process of speciation, often caused by geographical separations that prevent populations from exchanging genes with each other. The application of genetic principles to the study of population biology and evolution is referred to as the modern synthesis.

By comparing the homology between different species' genomes it is possible to calculate the evolutionary distance between them and when they may have diverged (called a molecular clock). Genetic comparisons are generally considered a more accurate method of characterizing the relatedness between species than the comparison of phenotypic characteristics. The evolutionary distances between species can be used to form evolutionary trees; these trees represent the common descent and divergence of species over time, although they do not show the transfer of genetic material between unrelated species (known as horizontal gene transfer and most common in bacteria).

Although geneticists originally studied inheritance in a wide range of organisms, researchers began to specialize in studying the genetics of a particular subset of organisms. The fact that significant research already existed for a given organism would encourage new researchers to choose it for further study, and so eventually a few model organisms became the basis for most genetics research. Common research topics in model organism genetics include the study of gene regulation and the involvement of genes in development and cancer.

Organisms were chosen, in part, for convenience—short generation times and easy genetic manipulation made some organisms popular genetics research tools. Widely used model organisms include the gut bacterium *Escherichia coli*, the plant *Arabidopsis thaliana*, baker's yeast (*Saccharomyces cerevisiae*), the nematode *Caenorhabditis elegans*, the common fruit fly (*Drosophila melanogaster*), and the common house mouse (*Mus musculus*).

Medical Genetics Research

Medical genetics seeks to understand how genetic variation relates to human health and disease. When searching for an unknown gene that may be involved in a disease, researchers commonly use genetic linkage and genetic pedigree charts to find the location on the genome associated with the disease. At the population level, researchers take advantage of Mendelian randomization to look for locations in the genome that are associated with diseases, a technique especially useful for multigenic traits not clearly defined by a single gene. Once a candidate gene is found, further research is often done on the corresponding gene (called an orthologous gene) in model organisms. In addition to studying genetic diseases, the increased availability of genotyping techniques has led to the field of pharmacogenetics—studying how genotype can affect drug responses.

Individuals differ in their inherited tendency to develop cancer, and cancer is a genetic disease. The process of cancer development in the body is a combination of events. Mutations occasionally occur within cells in the body as they divide. Although these mutations will not be inherited by any offspring, they can affect the behaviour of cells, sometimes causing them to grow and divide more frequently. There are biological mechanisms that attempt to stop this process; signals are given to inappropriately dividing cells that should trigger cell death, but sometimes additional mutations occur that cause cells to ignore these messages. An internal process of natural selection occurs within the body and eventually mutations accumulate within cells to promote their own growth, creating a cancerous tumor that grows and invades various tissues of the body.

Research Techniques

DNA can be manipulated in the laboratory. Restriction enzymes are commonly used enzymes that cut DNA at specific sequences, producing predictable fragments of DNA. DNA fragments can be visualized through use of gel electrophoresis, which separates fragments according to their length.

The use of ligation enzymes allows DNA fragments to be connected, and by ligating fragments of DNA together from different sources, researchers can create recombinant DNA. Often associated with genetically modified organisms, recombinant DNA is commonly used in the context of plasmids—short circular DNA fragments with a few genes on them. By inserting plasmids into bacteria and growing those bacteria on plates of agar (to isolate clones of bacteria cells), researchers can clonally amplify the inserted fragment of DNA (a process known as molecular cloning). (Cloning can also refer to the creation of clonal organisms, through various techniques.)

DNA can also be amplified using a procedure called the polymerase chain reaction (PCR). By using specific short sequences of DNA, PCR can isolate and exponentially amplify a targeted region of DNA. Because it can amplify from extremely small amounts of DNA, PCR is also often used to detect the presence of specific DNA sequences.

DNA Sequencing and Genomics

One of the most fundamental technologies developed to study genetics, DNA sequencing allows researchers to determine the sequence of nucleotides in DNA fragments. Developed in 1977 by Frederick Sanger and co-workers, chain-termination sequencing is now routinely used to sequence DNA fragments. With this technology, researchers have been able to study the molecular sequences associated with many human diseases.

As sequencing has become less expensive, researchers have sequenced the genomes of many organisms, using computational tools to stitch together the sequences of many different fragments (a process called genome assembly). These technologies were used to sequence the human genome, leading to the completion of the Human Genome Project in 2003. New high-throughput sequencing technologies are dramatically lowering the cost of DNA sequencing, with many researchers hoping to bring the cost of resequencing a human genome down to a thousand dollars.

The large amount of sequence data available has created the field of genomics, research that uses computational tools to search for and analyze patterns in the full genomes of organisms. Genomics can also be considered a subfield of bioinformatics, which uses computational approaches to analyze large sets of biological data.

Heredity

Heredity is the passing of traits to offspring (from its parent or ancestors). This is the process by which an offspring cell or organism acquires or becomes predisposed to the characteristics of its parent cell or organism. Through heredity, variations exhibited by individuals can accumulate and cause a species to evolve. The study of heredity in biology is called genetics, which includes the field of epigenetics.

The ancients had a variety of ideas about heredity: Theophrastus proposed that male flowers caused female flowers to ripen; Hippocrates speculated that 'seeds' were produced by various body parts and transmitted to offspring at the time of conception, and Aristotle thought that male and female semen mixed at conception. Aeschylus, in 458 BC, proposed the male as the parent, with the female as a "nurse for the young life sown within her".

Various hereditary mechanisms were envisaged without being properly tested or quantified. These included blending inheritance and the inheritance of acquired traits. Nevertheless, people were able to develop domestic breeds of animals as well as crops through artificial selection. The inheritance of acquired traits also formed a part of early Lamarckian ideas on evolution.

In the 9th century AD, the Afro-Arab writer Al-Jahiz considered the effects of the environment on the likelihood of an animal to survive, and first described the struggle for existence. His ideas on the struggle for existence in the *Book of Animals* have been summarized as follows:

"Animals engage in a struggle for existence; for resources, to avoid being eaten and to breed. Environmental factors influence organisms to develop new characteristics to ensure survival, thus transforming into new species. Animals that survive to breed can pass on their successful characteristics to offspring".

In 1000 AD, the Arab physician, Abu al-Qasim al-Zahrawi (known as Albucasis in the West), wrote the first clear description of haemophilia, a hereditary genetic disorder, in his *Al-Tasrif*. In this work, he wrote of an Andalusian family whose males died of bleeding after minor injuries.

During the 18th century, Dutch microscopist Antonie van Leeuwenhoek (1632-1723) discovered 'animalcules' in the sperm of humans and other animals. Some scientists speculated they saw a 'little man' (homunculus) inside each sperm. These scientists formed a school of thought known as the 'spermists'. They contended the only contributions of the female to the next generation were the womb in which the homunculus grew, and prenatal influences of the womb. An opposing school of thought, the ovists, believed that the future human was in the egg, and that sperm merely stimulated the growth of the egg. Ovists thought women carried eggs containing boy and girl children, and that the gender of the offspring was determined well before conception.

Pangenesis was an idea that males and females formed 'pangenes' in every organ. These pangenes subsequently moved through their blood to the genitals and then to the children. The concept originated with the ancient Greeks, and influenced biology until as recently as a century ago. The terms 'blood relative', 'bloodline', 'full-blooded', and 'royal blood' are relics of pangenesis. Francis Galton, Charles Darwin's cousin, experimentally tested and disproved pangenesis during the 1870s.

When Charles Darwin proposed his theory of evolution in 1859, one of its major problems was the lack of an underlying mechanism for heredity. Darwin believed in a mix of blending inheritance and the inheritance of acquired traits (pangenesis). Blending inheritance would lead to uniformity across populations in only a few generations and thus would remove variation from a population on which natural selection could act. This led to Darwin adopting some Lamarckian ideas in later editions of *On the Origin of Species* and his later biological works. Darwin's primary approach to heredity was to outline how it appeared to work (noticing that traits could be inherited which were not expressed explicitly in the parent at the time of reproduction, that certain traits could be sex-linked, etc.) rather than suggesting mechanisms.

Darwin's initial model of heredity was adopted by, and then heavily modified by, his cousin Francis Galton, who laid the framework for the biometric school of heredity. Galton rejected the aspects of Darwin's pangenesis model which relied on acquired traits.

The inheritance of acquired traits was shown to have little basis in the 1880s when August Weismann cut the tails off many generations of mice and found that their offspring continued to develop tails.

Gregor Mendel: Father of Modern Genetics

The idea of particulate inheritance of genes can be attributed to the Moravian monk Gregor Mendel who published his work on pea plants in 1865. However, his work was not widely known and was rediscovered in 1901. It was initially assumed the Mendelian inheritance only accounted for large (qualitative) differences, such as those seen by Mendel in his pea plants—and the idea of additive effect of (quantitative) genes was not realised until R.A. Fisher's (1918) paper, "The Correlation Between Relatives on the Supposition of Mendelian Inheritance".

Modern Development of Genetics and Heredity

In the 1930s, work by Fisher and others resulted in a combination of Mendelian and biometric schools into the modern evolutionary synthesis. The modern synthesis bridged the gap between experimental geneticists and naturalists; and between both and palaeontologists, stating that:

> All evolutionary phenomena can be explained in a way consistent with known genetic mechanisms and the observational evidence of naturalists.

Evolution is gradual: small genetic changes, recombination ordered by natural selection. Discontinuities amongst species (or other taxa) are explained as originating gradually through geographical separation and extinction (not saltation).

Selection is overwhelmingly the main mechanism of change; even slight advantages are important when continued. The object of selection is the phenotype in its surrounding environment. The role of genetic drift is equivocal; though strongly supported initially by Dobzhansky, it was downgraded later as results from ecological genetics were obtained.

The primacy of population thinking: the genetic diversity carried in natural populations is a key factor in evolution. The strength of natural selection in the wild was greater than expected; the effect of ecological factors such as niche occupation and the significance of barriers to gene flow are all important.

In palaeontology, the ability to explain historical observations by extrapolation from micro to macro-evolution is proposed. Historical contingency means explanations at different levels may exist. Gradualism does not mean constant rate of change.

The idea that speciation occurs after populations are reproductively isolated has been much debated. In plants, polyploidy must be included in any view of speciation. Formulations such as 'evolution consists primarily of changes in the frequencies of alleles between one generation and another' were proposed rather later. The traditional view is that developmental biology ('evo-devo') played little part in the synthesis, but an account of Gavin de Beer's work by Stephen Jay Gould suggests he may be an exception.

Almost all aspects of the synthesis have been challenged at times, with varying degrees of success. There is no doubt, however, that the synthesis was a great landmark in evolutionary biology. It cleared up many confusions, and was directly responsible for stimulating a great deal of research in the post-World War II era.

5 Genetic Diversity

Genetic diversity, the level of biodiversity, refers to the total number of genetic characteristics in the genetic makeup of a species. It is distinguished from genetic variability, which describes the tendency of genetic characteristics to vary.

The academic field of population genetics includes several hypotheses and theories regarding genetic diversity. The neutral theory of evolution proposes that diversity is the result of the accumulation of neutral substitutions. Diversifying selection is the hypothesis that two subpopulations of a species live in different environments that select for different alleles at a particular locus. This may occur, for instance, if a species has a large range relative to the mobility of individuals within it. Frequency-dependent selection is the hypothesis that as alleles become more common, they become more vulnerable. This is often invoked in host-pathogen interactions, where a high frequency of a defensive allele among the host means that it is more likely that a pathogen will spread if it is able to overcome that allele.

There are many different ways to measure genetic diversity. The modern causes for the loss of animal genetic diversity have also been studied and identified. A 2007 study conducted by the National Science Foundation found that genetic diversity and biodiversity are dependent upon each other—that diversity within a species is necessary to maintain diversity among species, and vice versa. According to the lead researcher in the study, Dr. Richard Lankau, "If any one type is removed from the system, the cycle can break down, and the community becomes dominated by a single species".

Survival and Adaptation

Genetic diversity plays a very important role in survival and adaptability of a species because when a species's environment changes, slight gene variations are necessary to produce changes in the organisms' anatomy that enables it to adapt and survive. A species that has a large degree of genetic diversity among its population will have more variations from which to choose the most fit alleles. Increase in genetic diversity is also essential for an organism to evolve. Species that have very little genetic variation are at a great risk. With very little gene variation within the species, healthy reproduction becomes increasingly difficult, and offspring often deal with similar problems to those of inbreeding. The vulnerability of a population to certain types of diseases can also increase with reduction in genetic diversity.

Agricultural Relevance

When humans initially started farming, they used selective breeding to pass on desirable traits of the crops while omitting the undesirable ones. Selective breeding leads to monocultures: entire farms of nearly genetically identical plants. Little to no genetic diversity makes crops extremely susceptible to widespread disease. Bacteria morph and change constantly. When a disease causing bacterium changes to attack a specific genetic variation, it can easily wipe out vast quantities of the species. If the genetic variation that the bacterium is best at attacking happens to be that which humans have selectively bred to use for harvest, the entire crop will be wiped out.

A very similar occurrence is the cause of the infamous Potato Famine in Ireland. Since new potato plants do not come as a result of reproduction but rather from pieces of the parent plant, no genetic diversity is developed, and the entire crop is essentially a clone of one potato, it is especially susceptible to an epidemic. In the 1840s, much of Ireland's population depended on potatoes for food. They planted namely the 'lumper' variety of potato, which was susceptible to a rot-causing plasmodiophorid called *Phytophthora infestans*. This plasmodiophorid destroyed the vast majority of the potato crop, and left one million people to starve to death.

Coping with Poor Genetic Diversity

The natural world has several ways of preserving or increasing genetic diversity. Among oceanic plankton, viruses aid in the genetic shifting process. Ocean viruses, which infect the plankton, carry genes of other organisms in addition to their own. When a virus containing the genes of one cell infects another, the genetic makeup of the latter changes. This constant shift of genetic make-up helps to maintain a healthy population of plankton despite complex and unpredictable environmental changes.

Cheetahs are a threatened species. Extremely low genetic diversity and resulting poor sperm quality has made breeding and survivorship difficult for cheetahs — only about 5 per cent of cheetahs survive to adulthood. About 10,000 years ago, all but the *jubatus* species of cheetahs died out. The species encountered a population bottleneck and close family relatives were forced to mate with each other, or inbreed. However, it has been recently discovered that female cheetahs can mate with more than one male per litter of cubs. They undergo induced ovulation, which means that a new egg is produced every time a female mates. By mating with multiple males, the mother increases the genetic diversity within a single litter of cubs.

Genetic Diversity of a population can be assessed by some simple measures.

- ❖ Gene Diversity is the proportion of polymorphic loci across the genome.
- ❖ Heterozygosity is the mean number of individuals with polymorphic loci.
- ❖ Alleles per locus is also used to demonstrate variability.

Population Genetics

Population genetics is the study of allele frequency distribution and change under the influence of the four main evolutionary processes: natural selection, genetic drift, mutation and gene flow. It also takes into account the factors of population subdivision and population structure. It attempts to explain such phenomena as adaptation and speciation.

Population genetics was a vital ingredient in the emergence of the modern evolutionary synthesis. Its primary founders were Sewall Wright, J.B.S. Haldane and R.A. Fisher, who also laid the foundations for the related discipline of quantitative genetics.

Population genetics concerns the genetic constitution of populations and how this constitution changes with time. A population is a set of organisms in which any pair of members can breed together. This implies that all members belong to the same species and live near each other.

For example, all of the moths of the same species living in an isolated forest are a population. A gene in this population may have several alternate forms, which account for variations between the phenotypes of the organisms. An example might be a gene for coloration in moths that has two alleles: black and white. A gene pool is the complete set of alleles for a gene in a single population; the allele frequency for an allele is the fraction of the genes in the pool that is composed of that allele (for example, what fraction of moth colouration genes are the black allele). Evolution occurs when there are changes in the frequencies of alleles within a population of interbreeding organisms; for example, the allele for black colour in a population of moths becoming more common.

To understand the mechanisms that cause a population to evolve, it is useful to consider what conditions are required for a population not to evolve. The *Hardy-Weinberg principle* states that the frequencies of alleles (variations in a gene) in a sufficiently large population will remain constant if the only forces acting on that population are the random reshuffling of alleles during the formation of the sperm or egg, and the random combination of the alleles in these sex cells during fertilization. Such a population is said to be in *Hardy-Weinberg equilibrium* as it is not evolving.

Natural Selection

Natural selection is the process by which heritable traits that make it more likely for an organism to survive and successfully reproduce become more common in a population over successive generations.

The natural genetic variation within a population of organisms means that some individuals will survive more successfully than others in their current environment. Factors which affect reproductive success are also important, an issue which Charles Darwin developed in his ideas on sexual selection.

Natural selection acts on the phenotype, or the observable characteristics of an organism, but the genetic (heritable) basis of any phenotype which gives a reproductive advantage will become more common in a population. Over time, this process can result in adaptations that specialize organisms for particular ecological niches and may eventually result in the emergence of new species.

Natural selection is one of the cornerstones of modern biology. The term was introduced by Darwin in his groundbreaking 1859 book *On the Origin of Species,* in which natural selection was described by analogy to artificial selection, a process by which animals and plants with traits considered desirable by human breeders are systematically favored for reproduction. The concept of natural selection was originally developed in the absence of a valid theory of heredity; at the time of Darwin's writing, nothing was known of modern genetics. The union of traditional Darwinian evolution with subsequent discoveries in classical and molecular genetics is termed the *modern evolutionary synthesis*. Natural selection remains the primary explanation for adaptive evolution.

Gene Flow

Gene flow is the exchange of genes between populations, which are usually of the same species. Examples of gene flow within a species include the migration and then breeding of organisms, or the exchange of pollen. Gene transfer between species includes the formation of hybrid organisms and horizontal gene transfer.

Migration into or out of a population can change allele frequencies, as well as introducing genetic variation into a population. Immigration may add new genetic material to the established gene pool of a population. Conversely, emigration may remove genetic material. As barriers to reproduction between two diverging populations are required for the populations to become new species, gene flow may slow this process by spreading genetic differences between the populations. Gene flow is hindered by mountain ranges, oceans and deserts or even man-made structures such as the Great Wall of China, which has hindered the flow of plant genes.

Depending on how far two species have diverged since their most recent common ancestor, it may still be possible for them to produce offspring, as with horses and donkeys mating to produce mules. Such hybrids are generally infertile, due to the two different sets of chromosomes being unable to pair up during meiosis. In this case, closely related species may regularly interbreed, but hybrids will be selected against and the species will remain distinct. However, viable hybrids are occasionally formed and these new species can either have properties intermediate between their parent species, or possess a totally new phenotype. The importance of hybridization in creating new species of animals is unclear, although cases have been seen in many types of animals, with the gray tree frog being a particularly well-studied example.

Hybridization is, however, an important means of speciation in plants, since polyploidy (having more than two copies of each chromosome) is tolerated in plants more readily than in animals. Polyploidy is important in hybrids as it allows reproduction, with the two different sets of chromosomes each being able to pair with an identical partner during meiosis. Polyploids also have more genetic diversity, which allows them to avoid inbreeding depression in small populations.

Horizontal gene transfer is the transfer of genetic material from one organism to another organism that is not its offspring; this is most common among bacteria. In medicine, this contributes to the spread of antibiotic resistance, as when one bacteria acquires resistance genes it can rapidly transfer them to other species. Horizontal transfer of genes from bacteria to eukaryotes such as the yeast *Saccharomyces cerevisiae* and the adzuki bean beetle *Callosobruchus chinensis* may also have occurred. An example of larger-scale transfers are the eukaryotic bdelloid rotifers, which appear to have received a range of genes from bacteria, fungi, and plants Viruses can also carry DNA between organisms, allowing transfer of genes even across biological domains. Large-scale gene transfer has also occurred between the ancestors of eukaryotic cells and prokaryotes, during the acquisition of chloroplasts and mitochondria.

Gene flow is the transfer of alleles from one population to another.

Migration into or out of a population may be responsible for a marked change in allele frequencies. Immigration may also result in the addition of new genetic variants to the established gene pool of a particular species or population.

There are a number of factors that affect the rate of gene flow between different populations. One of the most significant factors is mobility, as greater mobility of an individual tends to give it greater migratory potential. Animals tend to be more mobile than plants, although pollen and seeds may be carried great distances by animals or wind.

Maintained gene flow between two populations can also lead to a combination of the two gene pools, reducing the genetic variation between the two groups. It is for this reason that gene flow strongly acts against speciation, by recombining the gene pools of the groups, and thus, repairing the developing differences in genetic variation that would have led to full speciation and creation of daughter species.

For example, if a species of grass grows on both sides of a highway, pollen is likely to be transported from one side to the other and vice versa. If this pollen is able to fertilise the plant where it ends up and produce viable offspring, then the alleles in the pollen have effectively been able to move from the population on one side of the highway to the other.

Population genetics was developed as a reconciliation of the Mendelian and biometrician models. A key step was the work of the British biologist and statistician R.A. Fisher. In a series of papers starting in 1918 and culminating in his 1930 book *The Genetical Theory of Natural Selection*, Fisher showed that the continuous variation measured by the biometricians could be produced by the combined action of many discrete genes, and that natural selection could change gene frequencies in a population, resulting in evolution (though lacking the knowledge of what an actual gene was at this time, it should be said in this sense he understood phenotypic trait frequency, rather than specifically identifiable gene frequency). In a series of papers beginning in 1924, another British geneticist, J.B.S. Haldane, applied statistical analysis to real-world examples of natural selection, such as the evolution of industrial melanism in peppered moths, and showed that natural selection worked at an even faster rate than Fisher assumed.

The American biologist Sewall Wright, who had a background in animal breeding experiments, focussed on combinations of interacting genes, and the effects of inbreeding on small, relatively isolated populations that exhibited genetic drift. In 1932, Wright introduced the concept of an adaptive landscape and argued that genetic drift and inbreeding could drive a small, isolated sub-population away from an adaptive peak, allowing natural selection to drive it towards different adaptive peaks. Fisher and Wright had some fundamental disagreements and a controversy about the relative roles of selection and drift continued for much of the century between the Americans and the British. The Frenchman Gustave Malécot was also important early in the development of the discipline.

The work of Fisher, Haldane and Wright founded the discipline of *population genetics*. This integrated natural selection with Mendelian genetics, which was the critical first step in developing a unified theory of how evolution worked.

John Maynard Smith was Haldane's pupil, whilst W.D. Hamilton was heavily influenced by the writings of Fisher. The American George R. Price worked with both Hamilton and Maynard Smith. American Richard Lewontin and Japanese Motoo Kimura were heavily influenced by Wright.

In the first few decades of the 20th century, most field naturalists continued to believe that Lamarckian and orthogenic mechanisms of evolution provided the best explanation for the complexity they observed in the living world. However, as the field of genetics continued to develop, those views became less tenable. Theodosius Dobzhansky, a postdoctoral worker in T. H. Morgan's lab, had been influenced by the work on genetic diversity by Russian geneticists such as Sergei Chetverikov. He helped to bridge the divide between the foundations of microevolution developed by the population geneticists and the patterns of macroevolution observed by field biologists, with his 1937 book *Genetics and the Origin of Species*.

Dobzhansky examined the genetic diversity of wild populations and showed that, contrary to the assumptions of the population geneticists, these populations had large amounts of genetic diversity, with marked differences between sub-populations. The book also took the highly mathematical work of the population geneticists and put it into a more accessible form. In Great Britain E.B. Ford, the pioneer of ecological genetics, continued throughout the 1930s and 1940s to demonstrate the power of selection due to ecological factors including the ability to maintain genetic diversity through genetic polymorphisms such as human blood types. Ford's work would contribute to a shift in emphasis during the course of the modern synthesis towards natural selection over genetic drift.

6 Mutation

Mutations are changes in a genomic sequence: the DNA sequence of a cell's genome or the DNA or RNA sequence of a virus. Mutations are caused by radiation, viruses, transposons and mutagenic chemicals, as well as errors that occur during meiosis or DNA replication. They can also be induced by the organism itself, by cellular processes such as hypermutation.

Mutation can result in several different types of change in DNA sequences; these can either have no effect, alter the product of a gene, or prevent the gene from functioning properly or completely. Studies in the fly *Drosophila melanogaster* suggest that if a mutation changes a protein produced by a gene, this will probably be harmful, with about 70 per cent of these mutations having damaging effects, and the remainder being either neutral or weakly beneficial. Due to the damaging effects that mutations can have on cells, organisms have evolved mechanisms such as DNA repair to remove mutations. Therefore, the optimal mutation rate for a species is a trade-off between costs of a high mutation rate, such as deleterious mutations, and the metabolic costs of maintaining systems to reduce the mutation rate, such as DNA repair enzymes. Viruses that use RNA as their genetic material have rapid mutation rates, which can be an advantage since these viruses will evolve constantly and rapidly, and thus evade the defensive responses of e.g. the human immune system.

Mutations can involve large sections of DNA becoming duplicated, usually through genetic recombination. These duplications are a major source of raw material for evolving new genes, with tens to hundreds of genes duplicated in animal genomes every million years. Most genes belong to larger families of genes of shared ancestry. Novel genes are produced by several methods, commonly through the duplication and mutation of an ancestral gene, or by recombining parts of different genes to form new combinations with new functions. Here, domains act as modules, each with a particular and independent function, that can be mixed together to produce genes encoding new proteins with novel properties. For example, the human eye uses four genes to make structures that sense light: three for colour vision and one for night vision; all four arose from a single ancestral gene. Another advantage of duplicating a gene (or even an entire genome) is that this increases redundancy; this allows one gene in the pair to acquire a new function while the other copy performs the original function. Other types of mutation occasionally create new genes from previously non-coding DNA.

Changes in chromosome number may involve even larger mutations, where segments of the DNA within chromosomes break and then rearrange. For example, two chromosomes in the *Homo* genus fused to produce human chromosome 2; this fusion did not occur in the lineage of the other apes, and they retain these separate chromosomes. In evolution, the most important role of such chromosomal rearrangements may be to accelerate the divergence of a population into new species by making populations less likely to interbreed, and thereby preserving genetic differences between these populations.

Sequences of DNA that can move about the genome, such as transposons, make up a major fraction of the genetic material of plants and animals, and may have been important in the evolution of genomes. For example, more than a million copies of the Alu sequence are present in the human genome, and these sequences have now been recruited to perform functions such as regulating gene expression. Another effect of these mobile DNA sequences is that when they move within a genome, they can mutate or delete existing genes and thereby produce genetic diversity.

A mutation has caused this garden moss rose to produce flowers of different colours. This is a somatic mutation that may also be passed on in the germ line.

In multicellular organisms with dedicated reproductive cells, mutations can be subdivided into germ line mutations, which can be passed on to descendants through their reproductive cells, and somatic mutations (also called acquired mutations), which involve cells outside the dedicated reproductive group and which are not usually transmitted to descendants. If the organism can reproduce asexually through mechanisms such as cuttings or budding the distinction can become blurred.

For example, plants can sometimes transmit somatic mutations to their descendants asexually or sexually where flower buds develop in somatically mutated parts of plants. A new mutation that was not inherited from either parent is called a *de novo* mutation. The source of the mutation is unrelated to the consequence, although the consequences are related to which cells were mutated.

Non-lethal mutations accumulate within the gene pool and increase the amount of genetic variation. The abundance of some genetic changes within the gene pool can be reduced by natural selection, while other 'more favorable' mutations may accumulate and result in adaptive evolutionary changes.

For example, a butterfly may produce offspring with new mutations. The majority of these mutations will have no effect; but one might change the colour of one of the butterfly's offspring, making it harder (or easier) for predators to see. If this colour change is advantageous, the chance of this butterfly surviving and producing its own offspring are a little better, and over time the number of butterflies with this mutation may form a larger percentage of the population.

Neutral mutations are defined as mutations whose effects do not influence the fitness of an individual. These can accumulate over time due to genetic drift. It is believed that the overwhelming majority of mutations have no significant effect on an organism's fitness. Also, DNA repair mechanisms are able to mend most changes before they become permanent mutations, and many organisms have mechanisms for eliminating otherwise permanently mutated somatic cells.

Mutation is generally accepted by biologists as the mechanism by which natural selection acts, generating advantageous new traits that survive and multiply in offspring as well as disadvantageous traits, in less fit offspring, that tend to die out.

Two classes of mutations are spontaneous mutations (molecular decay) and induced mutations caused by mutagens.

Spontaneous mutations on the molecular level can be caused by:

- ❖ Tautomerism — A base is changed by the repositioning of a hydrogen atom, altering the hydrogen bonding pattern of that base resulting in incorrect base pairing during replication.
- ❖ Depurination — Loss of a purine base (A or G) to form an apurinic site (AP site).
- ❖ Deamination – Hydrolysis changes a normal base to an atypical base containing a keto group in place of the original amine group.

Examples include C ? U and A ? HX (hypoxanthine), which can be corrected by DNA repair mechanisms; and 5MeC (5-methylcytosine) ? T, which is less likely to be detected as a mutation because thymine is a normal DNA base.

- Slipped strand mispairing - Denaturation of the new strand from the template during replication, followed by renaturation in a different spot ('slipping'). This can lead to insertions or deletions.
- Chemicals
- Hydroxylamine NH_2OH
- Base analogs (e.g. BrdU)
- Alkylating agents (e.g. *N*-ethyl-*N*-nitrosourea) These agents can mutate both replicating and non-replicating DNA. In contrast, a base analog can only mutate the DNA when the analog is incorporated in replicating the DNA. Each of these classes of chemical mutagens has certain effects that then lead to transitions, transversions, or deletions.
- Agents that form DNA adducts (e.g. ochratoxin A metabolites)
- DNA intercalating agents (e.g. ethidium bromide)
- DNA crosslinkers
- Oxidative damage
- Radiation – Nitrous acid converts amine groups on A and C to diazo groups, altering their hydrogen bonding patterns which leads to incorrect base pairing during replication.
- Ionizing Radiation – Ultraviolet radiation (nonionizing radiation). Two nucleotide bases in DNA – cytosine and thymine – are most vulnerable to radiation that can change their properties. UV light can induce adjacent pyrimidine bases in a DNA strand to become covalently joined as a pyrimidine dimer. UV radiation, particularly longer-wave UVA, can also cause oxidative damage to DNA.
- Viral Infections – DNA has so-called hotspots, where mutations occur up to 100 times more frequently than the normal mutation rate. A hotspot can be at an unusual base, e.g., 5-methylcytosine.

Mutation rates also vary across species. Evolutionary biologists have theorized that higher mutation rates are beneficial in some situations, because they allow organisms to evolve and therefore adapt more quickly to their environments. For example, repeated exposure of bacteria to antibiotics, and selection of resistant mutants, can result in the selection of bacteria that have a much higher mutation rate than the original population (mutator strains).

The sequence of a gene can be altered in a number of ways. Gene mutations have varying effects on health depending on where they occur and whether they alter the function of essential proteins. Mutations in the structure of genes can be classified as:

❖ Small-scale mutations, such as those affecting a small gene in one or a few nucleotides, including:

- *Point mutations*, often caused by chemicals or malfunction of DNA replication, exchange a single nucleotide for another. These changes are classified as transitions or transversions. Most common is the transition that exchanges a purine for a purine or a pyrimidine for a pyrimidine, A transition can be caused by nitrous acid, base mis-pairing, or mutagenic base analogs such as 5-bromo-2-deoxyuridine (BrdU). Less common is a transversion, which exchanges a purine for a pyrimidine or a pyrimidine for a purine An example of a transversion is adenine being converted into a cytosine . A point mutation can be reversed by another point mutation, in which the nucleotide is changed back to its original state (true reversion) or by second-site reversion (a complementary mutation elsewhere that results in regained gene functionality). Point mutations that occur within the protein coding region of a gene may be classified into three kinds, depending upon what the erroneous codon codes for:
  - *Silent mutations:* which code for the same amino acid.
  - *Missense mutations:* which code for a different amino acid.
  - *Nonsense mutations:* which code for a stop and can truncate the protein.

Insertions add one or more extra nucleotides into the DNA. They are usually caused by transposable elements, or errors during replication of repeating elements . Insertions in the coding region of a gene may alter splicing of the mRNA (splice site mutation), or cause a shift in the reading frame (frameshift), both of which can significantly alter the gene product. Insertions can be reverted by excision of the transposable element.

Deletions remove one or more nucleotides from the DNA. Like insertions, these mutations can alter the reading frame of the gene. They are generally irreversible: though exactly the same sequence might theoretically be restored by an insertion, transposable elements able to revert a very short deletion (say 1–2 bases) in *any* location are either highly unlikely to exist or do not exist at all. Note that a deletion is not the exact opposite of an insertion: the former is quite random while the latter consists of a specific sequence inserting at locations that are not entirely random or even quite narrowly defined.

Large-scale mutations in chromosomal structure, including:

- ❖ Amplifications (or gene duplications) leading to multiple copies of all chromosomal regions, increasing the dosage of the genes located within them.
- ❖ *Deletions* of large chromosomal regions, leading to loss of the genes within those regions.
- ❖ Mutations whose effect is to juxtapose previously separate pieces of DNA, potentially bringing together separate genes to form functionally distinct fusion genes (e.g. bcr-abl). These include:
    - ***Chromosomal translocations:*** interchange of genetic parts from nonhomologous chromosomes.
    - ***Interstitial deletions:*** an intra-chromosomal deletion that removes a segment of DNA from a single chromosome, thereby apposing previously distant genes. For example, cells isolated from a human astrocytoma, a type of brain tumor, were found to have a chromosomal deletion removing sequences between the 'fused in glioblastoma' (*fig*) gene and the receptor tyrosine kinase 'ros', producing a fusion protein (*FIG-ROS*). The abnormal *FIG-ROS* fusion protein has constitutively active kinase activity that causes oncogenic transformation (a transformation from normal cells to cancer cells).
    - ***Chromosomal inversions:*** reversing the orientation of a chromosomal segment.
    - ***Loss of heterozygosity:*** loss of one allele, either by a deletion or recombination event, in an organism that previously had two different alleles.

By Effect on Function

Loss-of-function mutations are the result of gene product having less or no function. When the allele has a complete loss of function (null allele) it is often called an amorphic mutation. Phenotypes associated with such mutations are most often recessive. Exceptions are when the organism is haploid, or when the reduced dosage of a normal gene product is not enough for a normal phenotype (this is called .haploinsufficiency).

Gain-of-function mutations change the gene product such that it gains a new and abnormal function. These mutations usually have dominant phenotypes. Often called a neomorphic mutation.

Dominant negative mutations (also called antimorphic mutations) have an altered gene product that acts antagonistically to the wild-type allele. These mutations usually result in an altered molecular function (often inactive) and are characterised by a dominant or semi-dominant phenotype. In humans, Marfan syndrome is an example of a dominant negative mutation occurring in an autosomal dominant disease. In this condition, the defective glycoprotein product of the fibrillin gene (FBN1) antagonizes the product of the normal allele.

Lethal mutations are mutations that lead to the death of the organisms which carry the mutations.

A back mutation or reversion is a point mutation that restores the original sequence and hence the original phenotype.

By Effect on Fitness

In applied genetics it is usual to speak of mutations as either harmful or beneficial.

A harmful mutation is a mutation that decreases the fitness of the organism.

A beneficial mutation is a mutation that increases fitness of the organism, or which promotes traits that are desirable.

In theoretical population genetics, it is more usual to speak of such mutations as deleterious or advantageous. In the neutral theory of molecular evolution, genetic drift is the basis for most variation at the molecular level.

A neutral mutation has no harmful or beneficial effect on the organism. Such mutations occur at a steady rate, forming the basis for the molecular clock.

A deleterious mutation has a negative effect on the phenotype, and thus decreases the fitness of the organism.

An advantageous mutation has a positive effect on the phenotype, and thus increases the fitness of the organism.

A nearly neutral mutation is a mutation that may be slightly deleterious or advantageous, although most nearly neutral mutations are slightly deleterious.

In reality, viewing the fitness effects of mutations in these discrete categories is an oversimplification. Attempts have been made to infer the distribution of fitness effects using mutagenesis experiments or theoretical models applied to molecular sequence data. However, the current distribution is still uncertain, and some aspects of the distribution likely vary between species.

By Inheritance

- ❖ inheritable generic in pro-generic tissue or cells on path to be changed to gametes.

- ❖ non-inheritable somatic (e.g., carcinogenic mutation)
- ❖ non-inheritable post mortem aDNA mutation in decaying remains.

By pattern of inheritance The human genome contains two copies of each gene — a paternal and a maternal allele.

1. A heterozygous mutation is a mutation of only one allele.
2. A homozygous mutation is an identical mutation of both the paternal and maternal alleles.

Compound heterozygous mutations or a genetic compound comprises two different mutations in the paternal and maternal alleles.

- ❖ A wildtype or homozygous non-mutated organism is one in which neither allele is mutated.

By Impact on Protein Sequence

A frameshift mutation is a mutation caused by insertion or deletion of a number of nucleotides that is not evenly divisible by three from a DNA sequence. Due to the triplet nature of gene expression by codons, the insertion or deletion can disrupt the reading frame, or the grouping of the codons, resulting in a completely different translation from the original. The earlier in the sequence the deletion or insertion occurs, the more altered the protein produced is.

A non-sense mutation is a point mutation in a sequence of DNA that results in a premature stop codon, or a *nonsense codon* in the transcribed mRNA, and possibly a truncated, and often nonfunctional protein product.

Missense mutations or *non-synonymous mutations* are types of point mutations where a single nucleotide is changed to cause substitution of a different amino acid. This in turn can render the resulting protein nonfunctional. Such mutations are responsible for diseases such as Epidermolysis bullosa, sickle-cell disease, and SOD1 mediated ALS.

A *neutral mutation* is a mutation that occurs in an amino acid codon which results in the use of a different, but chemically similar, amino acid. The similarity between the two is enough that little or no change is often rendered in the protein. For example, a change from AAA to AGA will encode lysine, a chemically similar molecule to the intended arginine.

Silent mutations are mutations that do not result in a change to the amino acid sequence of a protein. They may occur in a region that does not code for a protein, or they may occur within a codon in a manner that does not alter the final amino acid sequence. The phrase *silent mutation* is often used interchangeably with the phrase *synonymous mutation*; however, synonymous mutations are a subcategory of the former, occurring only within exons. The name silent could be a misnomer. For example, a silent mutation in the exon/intron border may lead to alternative splicing by changing the splice site, thereby leading to a changed protein.

Special Classes

Conditional mutation is a mutation that has wild-type (or less severe) phenotype under certain 'permissive' environmental conditions and a mutant phenotype under certain 'restrictive' conditions. For example, a temperature-sensitive mutation can cause cell death at high temperature (restrictive condition), but might have no deleterious consequences at a lower temperature (permissive condition).

Nomenclature

Nomenclature of mutations specify the type of mutation and base or amino acid changes.

Nucleotide substitution (e.g. 76A>T) — The number is the position of the nucleotide from the 5' end, the first letter represents the wild type nucleotide, and the second letter represents the nucleotide which replaced the wild type. In the given example, the adenine at the 76th position was replaced by a thymine.

If it becomes necessary to differentiate between mutations in genomic DNA, mitochondrial DNA, and RNA, a simple convention is used. For example, if the 100th base of a nucleotide sequence mutated from G to C, then it would be written as g.100G>C if the mutation occurred in genomic DNA, m.100G>C if the mutation occurred in mitochondrial DNA, or r.100g>c if the mutation occurred in RNA. Note that for mutations in RNA, the nucleotide code is written in lower case.

Amino acid substitution (e.g. D111E) — The first letter is the one letter code of the wild type amino acid, the number is the position of the amino acid from the *N* terminus, and the second letter is the one letter code of the amino acid present in the mutation. Nonsense mutations are represented with an *X* for the second amino acid (e.g. D111X).

Amino acid deletion (e.g. ?F508) — The Greek letter ? (delta) indicates a deletion. The letter refers to the amino acid present in the wild type and the number is the position from the *N* terminus of the amino acid were it to be present as in the wild type.

Harmful Mutations

Changes in DNA caused by mutation can cause errors in protein sequence, creating partially or completely non-functional proteins. To function correctly, each cell depends on thousands of proteins to function in the right places at the right times. When a mutation alters a protein that plays a critical role in the body, a medical condition can result. A condition caused by mutations in one or more genes is called a genetic disorder. Some mutations alter a gene's DNA base sequence but do not change the function of the protein made by the gene. Studies of the fly *Drosophila melanogaster* suggest that if a mutation does change a protein, this will probably be harmful, with about 70 per cent of these mutations having damaging effects, and the remainder being either neutral or weakly beneficial. However, studies in yeast have shown that only 7 per cent of mutations that are not in genes are harmful.

If a mutation is present in a germ cell, it can give rise to offspring that carries the mutation in all of its cells. This is the case in hereditary diseases. On the other hand, a mutation may occur in a somatic cell of an organism. Such mutations will be present in all descendants of this cell within the same organism, and certain mutations can cause the cell to become malignant, and thus cause cancer.

Often, gene mutations that could cause a genetic disorder are repaired by the DNA repair system of the cell. Each cell has a number of pathways through which enzymes recognize and repair mistakes in DNA. Because DNA can be damaged or mutated in many ways, the process of DNA repair is an important way in which the body protects itself from disease.

Beneficial Mutations

Although most mutations that change protein sequences are neutral or harmful, some mutations have a positive effect on an organism. In this case, the mutation may enable the mutant organism to withstand particular environmental stresses better than wild-type organisms, or reproduce more quickly. In these cases a mutation will tend to become more common in a population through natural selection.

For example, a specific 32 base pair deletion in human CCR5 confers HIV resistance to homozygotes and delays AIDS onset in heterozygotes. The CCR5 mutation is more common in those of European descent. One possible explanation of the etiology of the relatively high frequency of CCR5-?32 in the European population is that it conferred resistance to the bubonic plague in mid-14th century Europe. People with this mutation were more likely to survive infection; thus its frequency in the population increased. This theory could explain why this mutation is not found in southern Africa, where the bubonic plague never reached. A newer theory suggests that the selective pressure on the CCR5 Delta 32 mutation was caused by smallpox instead of the bubonic plague.

Another example, is Sickle cell disease which is a blood disorder in which the body produces an abnormal type of the oxygen-carrying substance hemoglobin in the red blood cells. One-third of all indigenous inhabitants of Sub-Saharan Africa carry the gene, because in areas where malaria is common, there is a survival value in carrying only a single sickle-cell gene (sickle cell trait). Those with only one of the two alleles of the sickle-cell disease are more resistant to malaria, since the infestation of the malaria plasmodium is halted by the sickling of the cells which it infests.

Molecular Evolution

Molecular evolution is the process of evolution at the scale of DNA, RNA, and proteins. Molecular evolution emerged as a scientific field in the 1960s as researchers from molecular biology, evolutionary biology and population genetics sought to understand recent discoveries on the structure and function of nucleic acids and protein. Some of the key topics that spurred development of the field have been the evolution of enzyme function, the use of nucleic acid divergence as a 'molecular clock' to study species divergence, and the origin of non-functional or junk DNA. Recent advances in genomics, including whole-genome sequencing, high-throughput protein characterization, and bioinformatics have led to a dramatic increase in studies on the topic. In the 2000s, some of the active topics have been the role of gene duplication in the emergence of novel gene function, the extent of adaptive molecular evolution *versus* neutral drift, and the identification of molecular changes responsible for various human characteristics especially those pertaining to infection, disease, and cognition.

Causes of Change in Allele Frequency

There are three known processes that affect the survival of a characteristic; or, more specifically, the frequency of an allele (variant of a gene):

- Genetic drift describes changes in gene frequency that cannot be ascribed to selective pressures, but are due instead to events that are unrelated to inherited traits. This is especially important in small mating populations, which simply cannot have enough offspring to maintain the same gene distribution as the parental generation.
- *Gene flow or Migration:* or gene admixture is the only one of the agents that makes populations closer genetically while building larger gene pools.
- *Selection,* in particular natural selection produced by differential mortality and fertility. Differential mortality is the survival rate of individuals before their reproductive age. If they survive, they are then selected further by differential fertility — that is, their total

genetic contribution to the next generation. In this way, the alleles that these surviving individuals contribute to the gene pool will increase the frequency of those alleles. Sexual selection, the attraction between mates that results from two genes, one for a feature and the other determining a preference for that feature, is also very important.

Molecular Study of Phylogeny

Molecular systematics is a product of the traditional field of systematics and molecular genetics. It is the process of using data on the molecular constitution of biological organisms' DNA, RNA, or both, in order to resolve questions in systematics, i.e. about their correct scientific classification or taxonomy from the point of view of evolutionary biology.

Molecular systematics has been made possible by the availability of techniques for DNA sequencing, which allow the determination of the exact sequence of nucleotides or *bases* in either DNA or RNA. At present it is still a long and expensive process to sequence the entire genome of an organism, and this has been done for only a few species. However, it is quite feasible to determine the sequence of a defined area of a particular chromosome. Typical molecular systematic analyses require the sequencing of around 1000 base pairs.

The Driving Forces of Evolution

Depending on the relative importance assigned to the various forces of evolution, three perspectives provide evolutionary explanations for molecular evolution.

While recognizing the importance of random drift for silent mutations, selectionists hypotheses argue that balancing and positive selection are the driving forces of molecular evolution. Those hypotheses are often based on the broader view called panselectionism, the idea that selection is the only force strong enough to explain evolution, relaying random drift and mutations to minor roles.

Neutralists hypotheses emphasize the importance of mutation, purifying selection and random genetic drift. The introduction of the neutral theory by Kimura, quickly followed by King and Jukes' own findings, lead to a fierce debate about the relevance of neodarwinism at the molecular level. The Neutral theory of molecular evolution states that most mutations are deleterious and quickly removed by natural selection, but of the remaining ones, the vast majority are neutral with respect to fitness while the amount of advantageous mutations is vanishingly small. The fate of neutral mutations are governed by genetic drift, and contribute to both nucleotide polymorphism and fixed differences between species.

Mutationists hypotheses emphasize random drift and biases in mutation patterns. Sueoka was the first to propose a modern mutationist view. He proposed that the variation in GC content was not the result of positive selection, but a consequence of the GC mutational pressure.

Related Fields

An important area within the study of molecular evolution is the use of molecular data to determine the correct biological classification of organisms. This is called molecular systematics or molecular phylogenetics.

Tools and concepts developed in the study of molecular evolution are now commonly used for comparative genomics and molecular genetics, while the influx of new data from these fields has been spurring advancement in molecular evolution.

7 Genetic Recombination

Genetic recombination is a process by which a molecule of nucleic acid (usually DNA, but can also be RNA) is broken and then joined to a different one. Recombination can occur between similar molecules of DNA, as in homologous recombination, or dissimilar molecules, as in non-homologous end joining. Recombination is a common method of DNA repair in both bacteria and eukaryotes. In eukaryotes, recombination also occurs in meiosis, where it facilitates chromosomal crossover. The crossover process leads to offspring's having different combinations of genes from those of their parents, and can occasionally produce new chimeric alleles. In organisms with an adaptive immune system, a type of genetic recombination called V(D)J recombination helps immune cells rapidly diversify to recognize and adapt to new pathogens. The shuffling of genes brought about by genetic recombination is thought to have many advantages, as it is a major engine of genetic variation and also allows asexually reproducing organisms to avoid Muller's ratchet, in which the genomes of an asexual population accumulate deleterious mutations in an irreversible manner.

In genetic engineering, recombination can also refer to artificial and deliberate recombination of disparate pieces of DNA, often from different organisms, creating what is called recombinant DNA. A prime example of such a use of genetic recombination is gene targeting, which can be used to add, delete or otherwise change an organism's genes. This technique is important to biomedical researchers as it allows them to study the effects of specific genes. Techniques based on genetic recombination are also applied in protein engineering to develop new proteins of biological interest.

Genetic recombination is catalyzed by many different enzymes, called *recombinases*. RecA, the chief recombinase found in *Escherichia coli,* is responsible for the repair of DNA double strand breaks (DSBs). In yeast and other eukaryotic organisms there are two recombinases required for repairing DSBs. The RAD51 protein is required for mitotic and meiotic recombination, whereas the DMC1 protein is specific to meiotic recombination.

Chromosomal Crossover

Chromosomal crossover refers to recombination between the paired chromosomes inherited from each of one's parents, generally occurring during meiosis. During prophase I the four available chromatids are in tight formation with one another. While in this formation, homologous sites on two chromatids can mesh with one another, and may exchange genetic information.

Because recombination can occur with small probability at any location along chromosome, the frequency of recombination between two locations depends on their distance. Therefore, for genes sufficiently distant on the same chromosome the amount of crossover is high enough to destroy the correlation between alleles.

Gene Conversion

In gene conversion, a section of genetic material is copied from one chromosome to another, but leaves the donating chromosome unchanged.

Non-homologous Recombination

Recombination can occur between DNA sequences that contain no sequence homology. This is referred to as *non-homologous recombination* or non-homologous end joining.

In B Cells

B cells of the immune system perform genetic recombination, called immunoglobulin class switching. It is a biological mechanism that changes an antibody from one class to another, for example, from an isotype called *IgM* to an isotype called *IgG*.

Sexual Reproduction

Sexual reproduction is characterized by processes that pass a combination of genetic material to offspring, resulting in increased genetic diversity. The two main processes are: meiosis, involving the halving of the number of chromosomes; and fertilization, involving the fusion of two gametes and the restoration of the original number of chromosomes. During meiosis, the chromosomes of each pair usually cross over to achieve homologous recombination.

The evolution of sexual reproduction is a major puzzle. The first fossilized evidence of sexually reproducing organisms is from eukaryotes of the Stenian period, about 1 to 1.2 billion years ago. Sexual reproduction is the primary method of reproduction for the vast majority of macroscopic organisms, including almost all animals and plants. Bacterial conjugation, the transfer of DNA between two bacteria, is often mistakenly confused with sexual reproduction, because the mechanics are similar.

A major question is why sexual reproduction persists when parthenogenesis appears in some ways to be a superior form of reproduction. Contemporary evolutionary thought proposes some explanations. It may be due to selection pressure on the clade itself–the ability for a population to radiate more rapidly in response to a changing environment through sexual recombination than parthenogenesis allows. Alternatively, sexual reproduction may allow for the 'ratcheting' of evolutionary speed as one clade competes with another for a limited resource.

Animals typically produce male gametes called sperm, and female gametes called eggs and ova, following immediately after meiosis. With the gametes produced directly by meiosis. Plants on the other hand have mitosis occurring in spores, which are produced by meiosis. The spores germinate into the gametophyte phase. The gametophytes of different groups of plants vary in size; angiosperms have as few as three cells in pollen, and mosses and other so called primitive plants may have several million cells. Plants have an alternation of generations where the sporophyte phase is succeeded by the gametophyte phase. The sporophyte phase produces spores within the sporangium by meiosis.

Flowering Plants

Flowering plants are the dominant plant form on land and they reproduce by sexual and asexual means. Often their most distinguishing feature is their reproductive organs, commonly called flowers. The anther produces male gametophytes, the sperm is produced in pollen grains, which attach to the stigma on top of a carpel, in which the female gametophytes (inside ovules) are located. After the pollen tube grows through the carpel's style, the sex cell nuclei from the pollen grain migrate into the ovule to fertilize the egg cell and endosperm nuclei within the female gametophyte in a process termed double fertilization. The resulting zygote develops into an embryo, while the triploid endosperm (one sperm cell plus two female cells) and female tissues of the ovule give rise to the surrounding tissues in the developing seed. The ovary, which produced the female gametophyte(s), then grows into a fruit, which surrounds the seed(s). Plants may either self-pollinate or cross-pollinate. Non-flowering plants like ferns, moss and liverworts use other means of sexual reproduction.

Ferns mostly produce large diploid sporophytes with rhizomes, roots and leaves; and on fertile leaves called sporangium, spores are produced. The spores are released and germinate to produce short, thin gametophytes that are typically heart shaped, small and green in colour. The gametophytes or thallus, produce both motile sperm in the antheridia and egg cells in separate archegonia. After rains or when dew deposits a film of water, the motile sperm are splashed away from the antheridia, which are normally produced on the top side of the thallus, and swim in the film of water to the antheridia where they fertilize the egg. To promote out crossing or cross fertilization the sperm are released before the eggs are receptive of the sperm, making it more likely that the sperm will fertilize the eggs of different thallus. A zygote is formed after fertilization, which grows into a new sporophytic plant. The condition of having separate sporephyte and gametophyte plants is called alternation of generations. Other plants with similar reproductive means include the *Psilotum*, *Lycopodium*, *Selaginella* and *Equisetum*.

Bryophytes

The bryophytes, which include liverworts, hornworts and mosses, reproduce both sexually and vegetatively. They are small plants found growing in moist locations and like ferns, have motile sperm with flagella and need water to facilitate sexual reproduction. These plants start as a haploid spore that grows into the dominate form, which is a multicellular haploid body with leaf-like structures that photosynthesize. Haploid gametes are produced in antherida and archegonia by mitosis. The sperm released from the antherida respond to chemicals released by ripe archegonia and swim to them in a film of water and fertilize the egg cells thus producing a zygote. The zygote divides by mitotic division and grows into a sporophyte that is diploid. The multicellular diploid sporophyte produces structures called spore capsules, which are connected by seta to the archegonia. The spore capsules produce spores by meiosis, when ripe the capsules burst open and the spores are released. Bryophytes show considerable variation in their breeding structures and the above is a basic outline. Also in some species each plant is one sex while other species produce both sexes on the same plant.

Fungi

Fungi are classified by the methods of sexual reproduction they employ. The outcome of sexual reproduction most often is the production of resting spores that are used to survive inclement times and to spread. There are typically three phases in the sexual reproduction of fungi: plasmogamy, karyogamy and meiosis.

Insects

Insect species make up more than two-thirds of all extant animal species, and most insect species use sex for reproduction, though some species are facultatively parthenogenetic. Many species have sexual dimorphism, while in others the sexes look nearly identical. Typically they have two sexes with males producing spermatozoa and females ova. The ova develop into eggs that have a covering called the chorion, which forms before internal fertilization. Insects have very diverse mating and reproductive strategies most often resulting in the male depositing spermatophore within the female, which stores the sperm until she is ready for egg fertilization. After fertilization, and the formation of a zygote, and varying degrees of development; the eggs are deposited outside the female in many species, or in some, they develop further within the female and live born offspring are produced.

Mammals

There are three extant kinds of mammals: Monotremes, Placentals and Marsupials, all with internal fertilisation. In placental mammals, offspring are born as juveniles: complete animals with the sex organs present although not reproductively functional. After several months or years, the sex organs develop further to maturity and the animal becomes sexually mature. Most female mammals are only fertile during certain periods during their estrous cycle, at which point they are ready to mate. Individual male and female mammals meet and carry out copulation. For most mammals, males and females exchange sexual partners throughout their adult lives.

Male

The male reproductive system contains two main divisions: the penis, and the testicles, the latter of which is where sperm are produced. In humans, both of these organs are outside the abdominal cavity, but they can be primarily housed within the abdomen in other animals (for instance, in dogs, the penis is internal except when mating). Having the testicles outside the abdomen best facilitates temperature regulation of the sperm, which require specific temperatures to survive. Sperm are the smaller of the two gametes and are generally very short-lived, requiring males to produce them continuously from the time of sexual maturity until death. Prior to ejaculation the produced sperm are stored in the seminal vesicle, a small gland that is located just behind the bladder. The sperm cells are motile and they swim using tail-like flagellum to propel themselves towards the ovum. The sperm follows temperature gradients (thermotaxis) and chemical gradients (chemotaxis) to locate the ovum.

Female

The female reproductive system likewise contains two main divisions: the vagina and uterus, which act as the receptacle for the sperm, and the ovaries, which produce the female's ova. All of these parts are always internal. The vagina is attached to the uterus through the cervix, while the uterus is attached to the ovaries via the Fallopian tubes. At certain intervals, the ovaries release an ovum, which passes through the fallopian tube into the uterus.

If, in this transit, it meets with sperm, the sperm penetrate and merge with the egg, fertilizing it. The fertilization usually occurs in the oviducts, but can happen in the uterus itself. The zygote then implants itself in the wall of the uterus, where it begins the processes of embryogenesis and morphogenesis. When developed enough to survive outside the womb, the cervix dilates and contractions of the uterus propel the fetus through the birth canal, which is the vagina.

The ova, which are the female sex cells, are much larger than the sperm and are normally formed within the ovaries of the fetus before its birth. They are mostly fixed in location within the ovary until their transit to the uterus, and contain nutrients for the later zygote and embryo. Over a regular interval, in response to hormonal signals, a process of oogenesis matures one ovum which is released and sent down the Fallopian tube. If not fertilized, this egg is flushed out of the system through menstruation in humans and other great apes and reabsorbed in other mammals in the estrus cycle.

Gestation

Gestation, called *pregnancy* in humans, is the period of time during which the fetus develops, dividing via mitosis inside the female. During this time, the fetus receives all of its nutrition and oxygenated blood from the female, filtered through the placenta, which is attached to the fetus' abdomen via an umbilical cord. This drain of nutrients can be quite taxing on the female, who is required to ingest slightly higher levels of calories. In addition, certain vitamins and other nutrients are required in greater quantities than normal, often creating abnormal eating habits. The length of gestation, called the gestation period, varies greatly from species to species; it is 40 weeks in humans, 56-60 in giraffes and 16 days in hamsters.

Birth

Once the fetus is sufficiently developed, chemical signals start the process of birth, which begins with contractions of the uterus and the dilation of the cervix. The fetus then descends to the cervix, where it is pushed out into the vagina, and eventually out of the female. The newborn, which is called an infant in humans, should typically begin respiration on its own shortly after birth. Not long after, the placenta is passed as well. Most mammals eat this, as it is a good source of protein and other vital nutrients needed for caring for the young. The end of the umbilical cord attached to the young's abdomen eventually falls off on its own.

Monotremes

Monotremes, only five species of which exist, all from Australia and New Guinea, lay eggs. They have one opening for excretion and reproduction called the cloaca. They hold the eggs internally for several weeks, providing nutrients, and then lay them and cover them like birds. After less than two weeks the young hatches and crawls into its mother's pouch, much like marsupials, where it nurses for several weeks as it grows.

Marsupials

Marsupials reproductive systems differ markedly from those of placental mammals. Females have two vaginas, both of which open externally through one orifice but lead to different compartments within the uterus. Males generally have a two-pronged penis, which corresponds to the females' two vaginae. The penis is used only for discharging semen into females, and is separate from the urinary tract. Both sexes possess a cloaca, which is connected to a urogenital sac used to store waste before expulsion.

The female develops a kind of yolk sack in her womb which delivers nutrients to the embryo. Embryos of bandicoots, koalas and wombats additionally form placenta-like organs that connect them to the uterine wall, although the placenta-like organs are smaller than in placental mammals and it is not certain that they transfer nutrients from the mother to the embryo.

Pregnancy is very short, typically 4 to 5 weeks. The embryo is born at a very young stage of development, and is usually less than 5 cm (2.0 in) long at birth. It has been suggested that the short pregnancy is necessary to reduce the risk that the mother's immune system will attack the embryo.

The newborn marsupial uses its forelimbs (with relatively strong hands) to climb to a nipple, which is usually in a pouch on the mother's belly. The mother feeds the baby by contracting muscles over her mammary glands, as the baby is too weak to suckle. The newborn marsupial's need to use its forelimbs for climbing to the nipple has prevented the forelimbs from evolving into paddles or wings and has therefore prevented the appearance of aquatic or truly flying marsupials (although there are several marsupial gliders).

Fish

The vast majority of fish species lay eggs that are then fertilized by the male, some species lay their eggs on a substrate like a rock or on plants, while others scatter their eggs and the eggs are fertilized as they drift or sink in the water column. Some fish species use internal fertilization and then disperse the developing eggs or give birth to live offspring. Fish that have live-bearing offspring include the Guppy and Mollies or *Poecilia*. Fishes that give birth to live young can be ovoviviparous, where the eggs are fertilized within the female and the eggs simply hatch within the female body, or in seahorses, the male carries the developing young within a pouch, and gives birth to live young. Fishes can also be viviparous, where the female supplies nourishment to the internally growing offspring. Some fish are hermaphrodites, where a single fish is both male and female and can produce eggs and sperm. In hermaphroditic fish, some are male and female at the same time while in other fish they are serially hermaphroditic; starting as one sex and changing to the other. In at least one hermaphroditic species, self-fertilization occurs when the eggs and sperm are released together. Internal self-fertilization may occur in some other species. One fish species does not reproduce by sexual reproduction but uses sex to produce offspring; *Poecilia formosa* is a unisex species that uses a form of parthenogenesis called gynogenesis, where unfertilized eggs develop into embryos that produce female offspring. *Poecilia formosa* mate with males of other fish species that use internal fertilization, the sperm does not fertilize the eggs but stimulates the growth of the eggs which develops into embryos.

8 Gene Flow

In population genetics, gene flow (also known as gene migration) is the transfer of alleles of genes from one population to another.

Migration into or out of a population may be responsible for a marked change in allele frequencies (the proportion of members carrying a particular variant of a gene). Immigration may also result in the addition of new genetic variants to the established gene pool of a particular species or population.

There are a number of factors that affect the rate of gene flow between different populations. One of the most significant factors is mobility, as greater mobility of an individual tends to give it greater migratory potential. Animals tend to be more mobile than plants, although pollen and seeds may be carried great distances by animals or wind.

Maintained gene flow between two populations can also lead to a combination of the two gene pools, reducing the genetic variation between the two groups. It is for this reason that gene flow strongly acts against speciation, by recombining the gene pools of thus, repairing the developing differences in genetic variation that would have led to full speciation and creation of daughter species.

For example, if a species of grass grows on both sides of a highway, pollen is likely to be transported from one side to the other and vice versa. If this pollen is able to fertilize the plant.

Barriers to Gene Flow

Physical barriers to gene flow are usually, but not always, natural. They may include impassable mountain ranges, oceans, or vast deserts.

In some cases, they can be artificial, man-made barriers, such as the Great Wall of China, which has hindered the gene flow of native plant populations. Samples of the same species which grow on either side have been shown to have developed genetic differences, because there is little to no gene flow to provide recombination of the gene pools.

Barriers to gene flow need not always be physical. Species can live in the same environment, yet show very limited gene flow due to limited hybridization or hybridization yielding unfit hybrids.

Gene Flow in Humans

Gene flow has been observed in humans. For example, in the United States, gene flow was observed between a white European population and a black West African population, which were recently brought together. In West Africa, where malaria is prevalent, the Duffy antigen provides some resistance to the disease, and this allele is thus present in nearly all of the West African population. In contrast, Europeans have either the allele Fy^a or Fy^b, because malaria is almost non-existent. By measuring the frequencies of the West African and European groups, scientists found that the allele frequencies became mixed in each population because of movement of individuals. It was also found that this gene flow between European and West African groups is much greater in the Northern U.S. than in the South.

Gene Flow Between Species

Gene flow can occur between species, either through hybridization or gene transfer from bacteria or virus to new hosts.

Gene transfer, defined as the movement of genetic material across species boundaries, which includes horizontal gene transfer, antigenic shift, and reassortment is sometimes an important source of genetic variation. Viruses can transfer genes between species. Bacteria can incorporate genes from other dead bacteria, exchange genes with living bacteria, and can exchange plasmids across species boundaries. "Sequence comparisons suggest recent horizontal transfer of many genes among diverse species including across the boundaries of phylogenetic 'domains'. Thus determining the phylogenetic history of a species can not be done conclusively by determining evolutionary trees for single genes".

Biologist Gogarten suggests "the original metaphor of a tree no longer fits the data from recent genome research". Biologists [should] instead use the metaphor of a mosaic to describe the different histories combined in individual genomes and use the metaphor of an intertwined net to visualize the rich exchange and cooperative effects of horizontal gene transfer.

"Using single genes as phylogenetic markers, it is difficult to trace organismal phylogeny in the presence of HGT (horizontal gene transfer). Combining the simple coalescence model of cladogenesis with rare HGT events suggest there was no single last common ancestor that contained all of the genes ancestral to those shared among the three domains of life. Each contemporary molecule has its own history and traces back to an individual molecule cenancestor. However, these molecular ancestors were likely to be present in different organisms at different times".

Genetic Pollution

Purebred, naturally-evolved, region-specific, wild species can be threatened with extinction through the process of genetic pollution, potentially causing uncontrolled hybridization, introgression and genetic swamping. These processes can lead to homogenization or replacement of local genotypes as a result of either a numerical and/or fitness advantage of introduced plant or animal . Non-native species can bring about a form of extinction of native plants and animals by hybridization and introgression either through purposeful introduction by humans or through habitat modification, bringing previously isolated species into contact. These phenomena can be especially detrimental for rare species coming into contact with more abundant ones. Interbreeding between the species can cause a 'swamping' of the rarer species' gene pool, creating hybrids that drive the originally purebred native stock to complete extinction. The extent of this facet of gene flow is not always apparent from morphological (outward appearance) observations alone. Some degree of gene flow may be due to normal, evolutionarily constructive processes, and all constellations of genes and genotypes cannot be preserved. That being said, hybridization with or without introgression may threaten a rare species' existence nonetheless.

Where it ends up and produce viable offspring, then the alleles in the pollen have effectively been able to move from the population on one side of the highway to the other.

When cultivating genetically modified (GM) plants or livestock, it becomes necessary to prevent "genetic pollution" i.e. their genetic modification from reaching other conventionally hybridized or wild native plant and animal populations by using gene flow mitigation usually through unintentional cross pollination and crossbreeding. Reasons to limit gene flow may include biosafety or agricultural co-existence, in which GM and non-GM cropping systems work side by side.

Scientists in several large research programmes are investigating methods of limiting gene flow in plants. Among these programmes are Transcontainer, which investigates methods for biocontainment, SIGMEA, which focuses on the biosafety of genetically modified plants, and Co-Extra, which studies the co-existence of GM and non-GM product chains.

Generally, there are three approaches to gene flow mitigation: keeping the genetic modification out of the pollen, preventing the formation of pollen, and keeping the pollen inside the flower.

- The first approach requires transplastomic plants. In transplastomic plants, the modified DNA is not situated in the cell's nucleus but is present in plastids, which are cellular compartments outside the nucleus. An example for plastids are chloroplasts, in which photosynthesis occurs. In some plants, the pollen does not contain plastids and, consequently, any modification located in plastids cannot be transmitted by the pollen.
- The second approach relies on male sterile plants. Male sterile plants are unable to produce functioning flowers and therefore cannot release viable pollen. Cytoplasmic male sterile plants are known to produce higher yields. Therefore, researchers are trying to introduce this trait to genetically modified crops.
- The third approach works by preventing the flowers from opening. This trait is called cleistogamy and occurs naturally in some plants. Cleistogamous plants produce flowers which either open only partly or not at all. However, it remains unclear how reliable cleistogamy is for gene flow mitigation: a Co-Extra research project on rapeseed investigating the matter has published preliminary results which cast doubt on the attainment of a high degree of reliability.

Hybrid

In biology and specifically genetics, hybrid has several meanings, all referring to the offspring of sexual reproduction.

In general usage, hybrid is synonymous with heterozygous: any offspring resulting from the mating of two distinctly homozygous individuals.

- a genetic hybrid carries two different alleles of the same gene.
- a structural hybrid results from the fusion of gametes that have differing structure in at least one chromosome, as a result of structural abnormalities.
- a numerical hybrid results from the fusion of gametes having different haploid numbers of chromosomes.
- a permanent hybrid is a situation where only the heterozygous genotype occurs, because all homozygous combinations are lethal.

From a taxonomic perspective, hybrid refers to offspring resulting from the interbreeding between two animals or plants of different taxa.

Hybrids between different subspecies within a species (such as between the Bengal tiger and Siberian tiger) are known as intra-specific hybrids. Hybrids between different species within the same genus (such as between lions and tigers) are sometimes known as interspecific hybrids or crosses. Hybrids between different genera (such as between sheep and goats) are known as intergeneric hybrids. Extremely rare interfamilial hybrids have been known to occur (such as the guineafowl hybrids). No interordinal (between different orders) animal hybrids are known.

The second type of hybrid consists of crosses between populations, breeds or cultivars within a single species. This meaning is often used in plant and animal breeding, where hybrids are commonly produced and selected because they have desirable characteristics not found or inconsistently present in the parent individuals or populations. This flow of genetic material between populations or races is often called hybridization.

Depending on the parents, there are a number of different types of hybrids:

- Single cross hybrids — result from the cross between two true breeding organisms and produces an F1 generation called an F1 hybrid (F1 is short for Filial 1, meaning 'first offspring'). The cross between two different homozygous lines produces an F1 hybrid that is heterozygous; having two alleles, one contributed by each parent and typically one is dominant and the other recessive. The F1 generation is also phenotypically homogeneous, producing offspring that are all similar to each other.
- Double cross hybrids — result from the cross between two different F1 hybrids.
- Three-way cross hybrids — result from the cross between one parent that is an F1 hybrid and the other is from an inbred line.
- Triple cross hybrids — result from the crossing of two different three-way cross hybrids.
- Population hybrids — result from the crossing of plants or animals in a population with another population. These include crosses between organisms such as interspecific hybrids or crosses between different races.

Interspecific hybrids are bred by mating two species, normally from within the same genus. The offspring display traits and characteristics of both parents. The offspring of an interspecific cross are very often sterile;

thus, hybrid sterility prevents the movement of genes from one species to the other, keeping both species distinct. Sterility is often attributed to the different number of chromosomes the two species have, for example donkeys have 62 chromosomes, while horses have 64 chromosomes, and mules and hinnies have 63 chromosomes. Mules, hinnies, and other normally sterile interspecific hybrids cannot produce viable gametes because the extra chromosome cannot make a homologous pair at meiosis, meiosis is disrupted, and viable sperm and eggs are not formed. However, fertility in female mules has been reported with a donkey as the father.

Most often other processes occurring in plants and animals keep gametic isolation and species distinction. Species often have different mating or courtship patterns or behaviours, the breeding seasons may be distinct and even if mating does occur antigenic reactions to the sperm of other species prevent fertilization or embryo development. The Lonicera fly is the first known animal species that resulted from natural hybridization. Until the discovery of the Lonicera fly, this process was known to occur in nature only among plants.

Hybrids are often named by the portmanteau method, combining the names of the two parent species. For example, a zeedonk is a cross between a zebra and a donkey. Since the traits of hybrid offspring often vary depending on which species was mother and which was father, it is traditional to use the father's species as the first half of the portmanteau. For example, a liger is a cross between a male lion and a female tiger, while a tiglon is a cross between a male tiger and a female lion.

Hybrids between domesticated and wild animals in particular may be problematic. Breeders of domesticated species discourage crossbreeding with wild species, unless a deliberate decision is made to incorporate a trait of a wild ancestor back into a given breed or strain. Wild populations of animals and plants have evolved naturally over millions of years through a process of natural selection in contrast to human controlled selective breeding or artificial selection for desirable traits from the human point of view. Normally, these two methods of reproduction operate independently of one another. However, an intermediate form of selective breeding, wherein animals or plants are bred by humans, but with an eye to adaptation to natural region-specific conditions and an acceptance of natural selection to weed out undesirable traits, created many ancient domesticated breeds or types now known as landraces.

Many times, domesticated species live in or near areas which also still hold naturally evolved, region-specific wild ancestor species and subspecies. In some cases, a domesticated species of plant or animal may become feral, living wild. Other times, a wild species will come into an area inhabited by a domesticated species. Some of these situations lead to the creation of hybridized plants or animals, a cross between the native species and a domesticated one. This type of crossbreeding, termed genetic pollution by those who are concerned about preserving the genetic base of the wild species, has become a major concern. Hybridization is also a concern to the breeders of purebred species as well, particularly if the gene pool is small and if such crossbreeding or hybridization threatens the genetic base of the domesticated purebred population.

The concern with genetic pollution of a wild population is that hybridized animals and plants may not be as genetically strong as naturally evolved region specific wild ancestors wildlife which can survive without human husbandry and have high immunity to natural diseases. The concern of purebred breeders with wildlife hybridizing a domesticated species is that it can coarsen or degrade the specific qualities of a breed developed for a specific purpose, sometimes over many generations. Thus, both purebred breeders and wildlife biologists share a common interest in preventing accidental hybridization.

Hybrid Plants

Plant species hybridize more readily than animal species, and the resulting hybrids are more often fertile hybrids and may reproduce, though there still exist sterile hybrids and selective hybrid elimination where the offspring are less able to survive and are thus eliminated before they can reproduce. A number of plant species are the result of hybridization and polyploidy with many plant species easily cross pollinating and producing viable seeds, the distinction between each species is often maintained by geographical isolation or differences in the flowering period. Since plants hybridize frequently without much work, they are often created by humans in order to produce improved plants. These improvements can include the production of more or improved; seeds, fruits or other plant parts for consumption, or to make a plant more winter or heat hardy or improve its growth and/or appearance for use in horticulture. Much work is now being done with hybrids to produce more disease resistant plants for both agricultural and horticultural crops. In many groups of plants hybridization has been used to produce larger and more showy flowers and new flower colours.

A sterile *Trillium* hybrid between *Trillium cernuum* and *Trillium grandiflorum*.

Many plant genera and species have their origins in polyploidy. Autopolyploidy resulting from the sudden multiplication in the number of chromosomes in typical normal populations caused by unsuccessful separation of the chromosomes during meiosis. Tetraploids or plants with four sets of chromosomes are common in a number of different groups of plants and over time these plants can differentiate into distinct species from the normal diploid line. In *Oenothera lamarchiana* the diploid species has 14 chromosomes, this species has spontaneously given rise to plants with 28 chromosomes that have been given the name *Oenthera gigas*. Tetraploids can develop into a breeding population within the diploid population and when hybrids are formed with the diploid population the resulting offspring tend to be sterile triploids, thus effectively stopping the intermixing of genes between the two groups of plants (unless the diploids, in rare cases, produce unreduced gametes).

Another form of polyploidy called allopolyploidy occurs when two different species mate and produce hybrids. Usually the typical chromosome number is doubled in successful allopolyploid species, with four sets of chromosomes the genotypes can sort out to form a complete diploid set from the parent species, thus they can produce fertile offspring that can mate and reproduce with each other but can not back-cross with the parent species. Allopolyploidy in plants often gives them a condition called hybrid vigour, which results in plants that are larger and stronger growing than either of the two parent species. Allopolyploids are often more aggressive growing and can be invaders of new habitats.

Sterility in a hybrid is often a result of chromosome number; if parents are of differing chromosome pair number, the offspring will have an odd number of chromosomes, leaving them unable to produce chromosomally balanced gametes. While this is a negative in a crop such as wheat, when growing a crop which produces no seeds would be pointless, it is an attractive attribute in some fruits. Bananas and seedless watermelon, for instance, are intentionally bred to be triploid, so that they will produce no seeds. Many hybrids are created by humans, but natural hybrids occur as well.

Heterosis

Hybrids are sometimes stronger than either parent variety, a phenomenon most common with plant hybrids, which when present is known as *hybrid vigour* (heterosis) or heterozygote advantage. Plant breeders make use of a number of techniques to produce hybrids, including line breeding and the formation of complex hybrids. An economically important example is hybrid maize (corn), which provides a considerable seed yield advantage over open pollinated varieties. Hybrid seed dominates the commercial maize seed market in the United States, Canada and many other major maize producing countries.

Examples of Species Hybrids

Some plant hybrids include:

- ❖ Leyland cypress, [x *Cupressocyparis leylandii*] hybrid between Monterey Cypress and Nootka Cypress.
- ❖ Limequat, lime and kumquat hybrid.
- ❖ Loganberry, a hybrid between raspberry and blackberry.
- ❖ London plane, a hybrid between *Plantanus orientalis* Oriental plane and *Plantanus occidentalis* American plane (American sycamore). Thus forming [*Plantanus x acerfolia*]
- ❖ Peppermint, a hybrid between spearmint and water mint.
- ❖ Tangelo, a hybrid of a Mandarin orange and a pomelo which may have been developed in Asia about 3,500 years ago.
- ❖ Triticale, a wheat — rye hybrid.

Wheat; most modern and ancient wheat breeds are themselves hybrids. Bread wheat is a hexaploid hybrid of three wild grasses; durum (pasta) wheat is a tetraploid hybrid of two wild grasses.

1. Triangle of U: cabbage, mustard etc.
2. Grapefruit, hybrid between a pomelo and the Jamaican sweet orange.

Some natural hybrids are:

- ❖ *Iris albicans*, a sterile hybrid which spreads by rhizome division.
- ❖ Evening primrose, a flower which was the subject of famous experiments by Hugo de Vries on polyploidy and diploidy.

Some horticultural hybrids:

- ❖ *Dianthus x allwoodii*, is a hybrid between *Dianthus caryophyllus* × *Dianthus plumarius*. This is an "interspecific hybrid" or hybrid between two species in the same genus.
- ❖ *x Heucherella tiarelloides*, or *Heuchera sanguinea* × *Tiarella cordifolia* is an "intergeneric hybrid" a hybrid between two different genera.
- ❖ *Quercus x warei* [*Quercus robur* × *Quercus bicolour*] Kindred Spirit Hybrid Oak.

Hybrids in Nature

Hybridisation between two closely related species is actually a common occurrence in nature. Many hybrid zones are known where the ranges of two species meet, and hybrids are continually produced in great numbers. These hybrid zones are useful as biological model systems for studying the mechanisms of speciation (Hybrid speciation). Recently DNA analysis of a bear shot by a hunter in the North West Territories confirmed the existence of naturally-occurring and fertile grizzly—polar bear hybrids. There have been reports of similar supposed hybrids, but this is the first to be confirmed by DNA analysis. In 1943, Clara Helgason described a male bear shot by hunters during her childhood. It was large and off-white with hair all over its paws. The presence of hair on the bottom of the feet suggests it was a natural hybrid of Kodiak and Polar bear.

In some species, hybridisation plays an important role in evolutionary biology. While most hybrids are disadvantaged as a result of genetic incompatibility, the fittest survive, regardless of species boundaries. They may have a beneficial combination of traits allowing them to exploit new habitats or to succeed in a marginal habitat where the two parent species are disadvantaged. This has been seen in experiments on sunflower species. Unlike mutation, which affects only one gene, hybridisation creates multiple variations across genes or gene combinations simultaneously. Successful hybrids could evolve into new species within 50-60 generations. This leads some scientists to speculate that life is a genetic continuum rather than a series of self-contained species.

Where there are two closely related species living in the same area, less than 1 in 1000 individuals are likely to be hybrids because animals rarely choose a mate from a different species (otherwise species boundaries would completely break down). In some closely related species there are recognized 'hybrid zones'.

Some species of Heliconius butterflies exhibit dramatic geographical polymorphism of their wing patterns, which act as aposematic signals advertising their unpalatability to potential predators. Where different-looking geographical races abut, inter-racial hybrids are common, healthy and fertile. Heliconius hybrids can breed with other hybrid individuals and with individuals of either parental race. These hybrid backcrosses are disadvantaged by natural selection because they lack the parental form's warning colouration, and are therefore not avoided by predators.

A similar case in mammals is hybrid White-Tail/Mule Deer. The hybrids don't inherit either parent's escape strategy. White-tail Deer dash while Mule Deer bound. The hybrids are easier prey than the parent species.

In birds, healthy Galapagos Finch hybrids are relatively common, but their beaks are intermediate in shape and less efficient feeding tools than the specialised beaks of the parental species so they lose out in the competition for food. Following a major storm in 1983, the local habitat changed so that new types of plants began to flourish, and in this changed habitat, the hybrids had an advantage over the birds with specialised beaks — demonstrating the role of hybridization in exploiting new ecological niches. If the change in environmental conditions is permanent or is radical enough that the parental species cannot survive, the hybrids become the dominant form. Otherwise, the parental species will re-establish themselves when the environmental change is reversed, and hybrids will remain in the minority.

Natural hybrids may occur when a species is introduced into a new habitat. In Britain, there is hybridisation of native European Red Deer and introduced Chinese Sika Deer. Conservationists want to protect the Red Deer, but the environment favours the Sika Deer genes. There is a similar situation with White-headed Ducks and Ruddy Ducks.

Expression of Parental Traits in Hybrids

When two distinct types of organisms breed with each other, the resulting hybrids typically have intermediate traits (e.g., one parent has red flowers, the other has white, and the hybrid, pink flowers). Commonly, hybrids also combine traits seen only separately in one parent or the other (e.g., a bird hybrid might combine the yellow head of one parent with the orange belly of the other). Most characteristics of the typical hybrid are of one of these two types, and so, in a strict sense, are not really new. However, an intermediate trait does differ from those seen in the parents (e.g., the pink flowers of the intermediate hybrid just mentioned are not seen in either of its parents). Likewise, combined traits are new when viewed as a combination.

In a hybrid, any trait that falls outside the range of parental variation is termed heterotic. Heterotic hybrids do have new traits, that is, they are not intermediate. *Positive heterosis* produces more robust hybrids, they might be stronger or bigger; while the term *negative heterosis* refers to weaker or smaller hybrids. Heterosis is common in both animal and plant hybrids. For example, hybrids between a lion and a tigress ('ligers') are much larger than either of the two progenitors, while a tigon (lioness × tiger) is smaller. Also the hybrids between the Common Pheasant (*Phasianus colchicus*) and domestic fowl (*Gallus gallus*) are larger than either of their parents, as are those produced between the Common Pheasant and hen Golden Pheasant (*Chrysolophus pictus*). Spurs are absent in hybrids of the former type, although present in both parents.

When populations hybridize, often the first generation (F_1) hybrids are very uniform. Typically, however, the individual members of subsequent hybrid generations are quite variable. High levels of variability in a natural population, then, are indicative of hybridity. Researchers use this fact to ascertain whether a population is of hybrid origin. Since such variability generally occurs only in later hybrid generations, the existence of variable hybrids is also an indication that the hybrids in question are fertile.

Genetic Mixing and Extinction

Regionally developed ecotypes can be threatened with extinction when new alleles or genes are introduced that alter that ecotype. This is sometimes called genetic mixing. Hybridization and introgression of new genetic material can lead to the replacement of local genotypes if the hybrids are more fit and have breeding advantages over the indigenous ecotype or species. These hybridization events can result from the introduction of non native genotypes by humans or through habitat modification, bringing previously isolated species into contact. Genetic mixing can be especially detrimental for rare species in isolated habitats, ultimately affecting the population to such a degree that none of the originally genetically distinct population remains.

Effect on Biodiversity and Food Security

In agriculture and animal husbandry, the green revolution's use of conventional hybridization increased yields by breeding 'high-yielding varieties'. The replacement of locally indigenous breeds, compounded with unintentional cross-pollination and crossbreeding (genetic mixing), has reduced the gene pools of various wild and indigenous breeds resulting in the loss of genetic diversity. Since the indigenous breeds are often well-adapted to local extremes in climate and have immunity to local pathogens this can be a significant genetic erosion of the gene pool for future breeding. Therefore, commercial plant geneticists strive to breed 'widely adapted' cultivars to counteract this tendency.

Limiting Factors

A number of conditions exist that limit the success of hybridization, the most obvious is great genetic diversity between most species. But in animals and plants that are more closely related hybridization barriers can include morphological differences, differing times of fertility, mating behaviours and cues, physiological rejection of sperm cells or the developing embryo.

In plants, barriers to hybridization include blooming period differences, different pollinator vectors, inhibition of pollen tube growth, somatoplastic sterility, cytoplasmic-genic male sterility and structural differences of the chromosomes .

Horizontal Gene Transfer

Horizontal gene transfer (HGT), also Lateral gene transfer (LGT), is any process in which an organism incorporates genetic material from another organism without being the offspring of that organism. By contrast, *vertical transfer* occurs when an organism receives genetic material from its ancestor, e.g., its parent or a species from which it has evolved.

Most thinking in genetics has focused upon vertical transfer, but there is a growing awareness that horizontal gene transfer is a highly significant phenomenon and amongst single-celled organisms perhaps the dominant form of genetic transfer. Artificial horizontal gene transfer is a form of genetic engineering.

Horizontal gene transfer was first described in Japan in a 1959 publication that demonstrated the transfer of antibiotic resistance between different species of bacteria. In the mid-1980s, Syvanen predicted that lateral gene transfer existed, had biological significance, and was involved in shaping evolutionary history from the beginning of life on Earth.

As Jain, Rivera and Lake (1999) put it: "Increasingly, studies of genes and genomes are indicating that considerable horizontal transfer has occurred between prokaryotes". The phenomenon appears to have had some significance for unicellular eukaryotes as well. As Bapteste et. al. (2005) observe, "additional evidence suggests that gene transfer might also be an important evolutionary mechanism in protist evolution".

There is some evidence that even higher plants and animals have been affected and this has raised concerns for safety. However, Richardson and Palmer (2007) state: "Horizontal gene transfer (HGT) has played a major role in bacterial evolution and is fairly common in certain unicellular eukaryotes. However, the prevalence and importance of HGT in the evolution of multicellular eukaryotes remain unclear".

Due to the increasing amount of evidence suggesting the importance of these phenomena for evolution molecular biologists such as Peter Gogarten have described horizontal gene transfer as "A New Paradigm for Biology".

It should also be noted that the process may be a hidden hazard of genetic engineering as it may allow dangerous transgenic DNA to spread from species to species.

Mechanism

There are several mechanisms for horizontal gene transfer:

- Transformation, the genetic alteration of a cell resulting from the introduction, uptake and expression of foreign genetic material (DNA or RNA). This process is relatively common in bacteria, but less so in eukaryotes. Transformation is often used in laboratories to insert novel genes into bacteria for experiments or for industrial or medical applications. See also molecular biology and biotechnology.
- Transduction, the process in which bacterial DNA is moved from one bacterium to another by a bacterial virus (a bacteriophage, or phage).

- Bacterial conjugation, a process in which a bacterial cell transfers genetic material to another cell by cell-to-cell contact.
- Gene transfer agents, viruslike elements encoded by the host that are found in the alphaproteobacteria order Rhodobacterales.

Viruses

The virus called *Mimivirus* infects amoebae. Another virus, called *Sputnik*, also infects amoebae but it cannot reproduce unless mimivirus has already infected the same cell. "Sputnik's genome reveals further insight into its biology. Although 13 of its genes show little similarity to any other known genes, three are closely related to mimivirus and mamavirus genes, perhaps cannibalized by the tiny virus as it packaged up particles sometime in its history. This suggests that the satellite virus could perform horizontal gene transfer between viruses — paralleling the way that bacteriophages ferry genes between bacteria".

Prokaryotes

Horizontal gene transfer is common among bacteria even amongst very distantly-related ones. This process is thought to be a significant cause of increased drug resistance when one bacterial cell acquires resistance and quickly transfers the resistance genes to many species.

Eukaryotes

Analysis of DNA sequences suggests that horizontal gene transfer has also occurred within eukaryotes from the chloroplast and mitochondrial genomes to the nuclear genome. As stated in the endosymbiotic theory, chloroplasts and mitochondria probably originated as bacterial endosymbionts of a progenitor to the eukaryotic cell.

Horizontal transfer of genes from bacteria to some fungi, especially the yeast *Saccharomyces cerevisiae*, has been well documented.

There is also recent evidence that the azuki bean beetle has somehow acquired genetic material from its (non-beneficial) endosymbiont *Wolbachia*. New examples have recently been reported demonstrating that Wolbachia bacteria represent an important potential source of genetic material in arthropods and filarial nematodes.

There is also evidence for horizontal transfer of mitochondrial genes to parasites of the Rafflesiaceae plant family from their hosts (also plants), from chloroplasts of a not-yet-identified plant to the mitochondria of the bean *Phaseolus*, and from a heterokont alga to its predator, the sea slug *Elysia chlorotica*.

"Sequence comparisons suggest recent horizontal transfer of many genes among diverse species including across the boundaries of phylogenetic 'domains'. Thus determining the phylogenetic history of a species can not be done conclusively by determining evolutionary trees for single genes".

Researchers at the University of Arizona have found that the genome of pea aphids contains genes that were horizontally transferred from fungi. The transferred genes enable carotenoid production in the aphids, which is not known to occur in any other animals.

Striga hermonthica, a eudicot, has undergone a horizontal gene transfer from Sorghum (*Sorghum bicolour*) to its nuclear genome. The gene is of unknown functionality.

Importance in Evolution

Horizontal gene transfer is a potential confounding factor in inferring phylogenetic trees based on the sequence of one gene. For example, given two distantly related bacteria that have exchanged a gene a phylogenetic tree including those species will show them to be closely related because that gene is the same even though most other genes are dissimilar. For this reason it is often ideal to use other information to infer robust phylogenies such as the presence or absence of genes or, more commonly, to include as wide a range of genes for phylogenetic analysis as possible.

For example, the most common gene to be used for constructing phylogenetic relationships in prokaryotes is the 16s rRNA gene since its sequences tend to be conserved among members with close phylogenetic distances, but variable enough that differences can be measured. However, in recent years it has also been argued that 16s rRNA genes can also be horizontally transferred. Although this may be infrequent the validity of 16s rRNA-constructed phylogenetic trees must be re-evaluated.

Biologist Johann Peter Gogarten suggests "the original metaphor of a tree no longer fits the data from recent genome research" therefore "biologists should use the metaphor of a mosaic to describe the different histories combined in individual genomes and use the metaphor of a net to visualize the rich exchange and cooperative effects of HGT among microbes".

Using single genes as phylogenetic markers, it is difficult to trace organismal phylogeny in the presence of horizontal gene transfer. Combining the simple coalescence model of cladogenesis with rare HGT horizontal gene transfer events suggest there was no single most recent common ancestor that contained all of the genes ancestral to those shared among the three domains of life. Each contemporary molecule has its own history and traces back to an individual molecule cenancestor. However, these molecular ancestors were likely to be present in different organisms at different times".

Scientific American Article (2000)

Uprooting the Tree of Life by W. Ford Doolittle contains a discussion of the Last Universal Common Ancestor and the problems that arose with respect to that concept when one considers horizontal gene transfer. The article covers a wide area — the endosymbiont hypothesis for eukaryotes, the use of small subunit ribosomal RNA (SSU rRNA) as a measure of evolutionary distances (this was the field Carl Woese worked in when formulating the first modern 'tree of life', and his research results with SSU rRNA led him to propose the Archaea as a third domain of life) and other relevant topics. Indeed, it was while examining the new three-domain view of life that horizontal gene transfer arose as a complicating issue: *Archaeoglobus fulgidus* is cited in the article as being an anomaly with respect to a phylogenetic tree based upon the encoding for the enzyme HMGCoA reductase - the organism in question is a definite Archaean, with all the cell lipids and transcription machinery that are expected of an Archaean, but whose HMGCoA genes are actually of bacterial origin.

"The weight of evidence still supports the likelihood that mitochondria in eukaryotes derived from alpha-proteobacterial cells and that chloroplasts came from ingested cyanobacteria, but it is no longer safe to assume that those were the only lateral gene transfers that occurred after the first eukaryotes arose. Only in later, multicellular eukaryotes do we know of definite restrictions on horizontal gene exchange, such as the advent of separated (and protected) germ cells".

"If there had never been any lateral gene transfer, all these individual gene trees would have the same topology (the same branching order), and the ancestral genes at the root of each tree would have all been present in the last universal common ancestor, a single ancient cell. But extensive transfer means that neither is the case: gene trees will differ (although many will have regions of similar topology) *and* there would never have been a single cell that could be called the last universal common ancestor.

"As Woese has written, 'the ancestor cannot have been a particular organism, a single organismal lineage. It was communal, a loosely knit, diverse conglomeration of primitive cells that evolved as a unit, and it eventually developed to a stage where it broke into several distinct communities, which in their turn became the three primary lines of descent (bacteria, archaea and eukaryotes)' In other words, early cells, each having relatively few genes, differed in many ways. By swapping genes freely, they shared various of their talents with their contemporaries. Eventually this collection of eclectic and changeable cells coalesced into the three basic domains known today. These domains become recognisable because much (though by no means all) of the gene transfer that occurs these days goes on within domains".

With regard to how horizontal gene transfer affects evolutionary theory (common descent, universal phylogenetic tree) Carl Woese says:

> "What elevated common descent to doctrinal status almost certainly was the much later discovery of the universality of biochemistry, which was seemingly impossible to explain otherwise. But that was before horizontal gene transfer (HGT), which could offer an alternative explanation for the universality of biochemistry, was recognized as a major part of the evolutionary dynamic. In questioning the doctrine of common descent, one necessarily questions the universal phylogenetic tree. That compelling tree image resides deep in our representation of biology. But the tree is no more than a graphical device; it is not some a priori form that nature imposes upon the evolutionary process. It is not a matter of whether your data are consistent with a tree, but whether tree topology is a useful way to represent your data. Ordinarily it is, of course, but the universal tree is no ordinary tree, and its root no ordinary root. Under conditions of extreme HGT, there is no (organismal) 'tree'. Evolution is basically reticulate".

Natural Selection

Natural selection is the process by which traits become more or less common in a population due to consistent effects upon the survival or reproduction of their bearers. It is a key mechanism of evolution.

The natural genetic variation within a population of organisms may cause some individuals to survive and reproduce more successfully than others in their current environment. For example, the peppered moth exists in both light and dark colours in the United Kingdom, but during the industrial revolution many of the trees on which the moths rested became blackened by soot, giving the dark-coloured moths an advantage in hiding from predators. This gave dark-coloured moths a better chance of surviving to produce dark-coloured offspring, and in just a few generations the majority of the moths were dark. Factors which affect reproductive success are also important, an issue which Charles Darwin developed in his ideas on sexual selection.

Natural selection acts on the phenotype, or the observable characteristics of an organism, but the genetic (heritable) basis of any phenotype which gives a reproductive advantage will become more common in a population. Over time, this process can result in adaptations that specialize populations for particular ecological niches and may eventually result in the emergence of new species. In other words, natural selection is an important process (though not the only process) by which evolution takes place within a population of organisms. As opposed to artificial selection, in which humans favour specific traits, in natural selection the environment acts as a sieve through which only certain variations can pass.

Natural selection is one of the cornerstones of modern biology. The term was introduced by Darwin in his influential 1859 book *On the Origin of Species*, in which natural selection was described as analogous to artificial selection, a process by which animals and plants with traits considered desirable by human breeders are systematically favoured for reproduction. The concept of natural selection was originally developed in the absence of a valid theory of heredity; at the time of Darwin's writing, nothing was known of modern genetics. The union of traditional Darwinian evolution with subsequent discoveries in classical and molecular genetics is termed the *modern evolutionary synthesis*. Natural selection remains the primary explanation for adaptive evolution.

Natural variation occurs among the individuals of any population of organisms. Many of these differences do not affect survival (such as differences in eye colour in humans), but some differences may improve the chances of survival of a particular individual. A rabbit that runs faster than others may be more likely to escape from predators, and algae that are more efficient at extracting energy from sunlight will grow faster. Individuals that have better odds for survival also have better odds for reproduction.

If the traits that give these individuals a reproductive advantage are also heritable, that is, passed from parent to child, then there will be a slightly higher proportion of fast rabbits or efficient algae in the next generation. This is known as *differential reproduction*. Even if the reproductive advantage is very slight, over many generations any heritable advantage will become dominant in the population, due to exponential growth. In this way the natural environment of an organism 'selects' for traits that confer a reproductive advantage, causing gradual changes or evolution of life. This effect was first described and named by Charles Darwin.

The concept of natural selection predates the understanding of genetics, which is the study of heredity. In modern times, it is understood that selection acts on an organism's phenotype, or observable characteristics, but it is the organism's genetic make-up or genotype that is inherited. The phenotype is the result of the genotype and the environment in which the organism lives.

This is the link between natural selection and genetics, as described in the modern evolutionary synthesis. Although a complete theory of evolution also requires an account of how genetic variation arises in the first place (such as by mutation and sexual reproduction) and includes other evolutionary mechanisms (such as gene flow), natural selection is still understood as a fundamental mechanism for evolution.

Nomenclature and Usage

The term *natural selection* has slightly different definitions in different contexts. It is most often defined to operate on heritable traits, because these are the traits that directly participate in evolution. However, natural selection is 'blind' in the sense that changes in phenotype (physical and behavioural characteristics) can give a reproductive advantage regardless of whether or not the trait is heritable (non-heritable traits can be the result of environmental factors or the life experience of the organism).

Following Darwin's primary usage the term is often used to refer to both the evolutionary consequence of blind selection and to its mechanisms. It is sometimes helpful to explicitly distinguish between selection's mechanisms and its effects; when this distinction is important, scientists define 'natural selection' specifically as 'those mechanisms that contribute to the selection of individuals that reproduce', without regard to whether the basis of the selection is heritable. This is sometimes referred to as 'phenotypic natural selection'.

Traits that cause greater reproductive success of an organism are said to be selected for, whereas those that reduce success are selected against. Selection for a trait may also result in the selection of other correlated traits that do not themselves directly influence reproductive advantage. This may occur as a result of pleioropy or gene linkage.

Fitness

The concept of fitness is central to natural selection. Broadly, individuals which are more 'fit' have better potential for survival, as in the well-known phrase 'survival of the fittest'. However, as with natural selection above, the precise meaning of the term is much more subtle, and Richard Dawkins manages in his later books to avoid it entirely. (He devotes a chapter of his book, *The Extended Phenotype*, to discussing the various senses in which the term is used). Modern evolutionary theory defines fitness not by how long an organism lives, but by how successful it is at reproducing. If an organism lives half as long as others of its species, but has twice as many offspring surviving to adulthood, its genes will become more common in the adult population of the next generation.

Though natural selection acts on individuals, the effects of chance mean that fitness can only really be defined 'on average' for the individuals within a population. The fitness of a particular genotype corresponds to the average effect on all individuals with that genotype. Very low-fitness genotypes cause their bearers to have few or no offspring on average; examples include many human genetic disorders like cystic fibrosis.

Since fitness is an averaged quantity, it is also possible that a favorable mutation arises in an individual that does not survive to adulthood for unrelated reasons. Fitness also depends crucially upon the environment. Conditions like sickle-cell anemia may have low fitness in the general human population, but because the sickle-cell trait confers immunity from malaria, it has high fitness value in populations which have high malaria infection rates.

Types of Selection

Natural selection can act on any phenotypic trait, and selective pressure can be produced by any aspect of the environment, including sexual selection and competition with members of the same species. However, this does not imply that natural selection is always directional and results in adaptive evolution; natural selection often results in the maintenance of the status quo by eliminating less fit variants.

The unit of selection can be the individual or it can be another level within the hierarchy of biological organisation, such as genes, cells, and kin groups. There is still debate about whether natural selection acts at the level of groups or species to produce adaptations that benefit a larger, non-kin group. Selection at a different level such as the gene can result in an increase in fitness for that gene, while at the same time reducing the fitness of the individuals carrying that gene, in a process called intragenomic conflict. Overall, the combined effect of all selection pressures at various levels determines the overall fitness of an individual, and hence the outcome of natural selection.

Sexual Selection

It is useful to distinguish between 'ecological selection' and 'sexual selection'. Ecological selection covers any mechanism of selection as a result of the environment (including relatives, e.g. kin selection, competition, and infanticide), while 'sexual selection' refers specifically to competition for mates.

Sexual selection can be *intrasexual,* as in cases of competition among individuals of the same sex in a population, or *intersexual,* as in cases where one sex controls reproductive access by choosing among a population of available mates. Most commonly, intrasexual selection involves male-male competition and intersexual selection involves female choice of suitable males, due to the generally greater investment of resources for a female than a male in a single offspring. However, some species exhibit sex-role reversed behaviour in which it is males that are most selective in mate choice; the best-known examples of this pattern occur in some fishes of the family *Syngnathidae,* though likely examples have also been found in amphibian and bird species.

Some features that are confined to one sex only of a particular species can be explained by selection exercised by the other sex in the choice of a mate, for example, the extravagant plumage of some male birds. Similarly, aggression between members of the same sex is sometimes associated with very distinctive features, such as the antlers of stags, which are used in combat with other stags. More generally, intrasexual selection is often associated with sexual dimorphism, including differences in body size between males and females of a species.

Examples of Natural Selection

Resistance to antibiotics is increased though the survival of individuals which are immune to the effects of the antibiotic, whose offspring then inherit the resistance, creating a new population of resistant bacteria.

A well-known example of natural selection in action is the development of antibiotic resistance in microorganisms. Since the discovery of penicillin in 1928 by Alexander Fleming, antibiotics have been used to fight bacterial diseases. Natural populations of bacteria contain, among their vast numbers of individual members, considerable variation in their genetic material, primarily as the result of mutations. When exposed to antibiotics, most bacteria die quickly, but some may have mutations that make them slightly less susceptible. If the exposure to antibiotics is short, these individuals will survive the treatment. This selective elimination of maladapted individuals from a population is natural selection.

These surviving bacteria will then reproduce again, producing the next generation. Due to the elimination of the maladapted individuals in the past generation, this population contains more bacteria that have some resistance against the antibiotic. At the same time, new mutations occur, contributing new genetic variation to the existing genetic variation. Spontaneous mutations are very rare, and advantageous mutations are even rarer. However, populations of bacteria are large enough that a few individuals will have beneficial mutations. If a new mutation reduces their susceptibility to an antibiotic, these individuals are more likely to survive when next confronted with that antibiotic.

Given enough time, and repeated exposure to the antibiotic, a population of antibiotic-resistant bacteria will emerge. This new changed population of antibiotic-resistant bacteria is optimally adapted to the context it evolved in. At the same time, it is not necessarily optimally adapted any more to the old antibiotic free environment. The end result of natural selection is two populations that are both optimally adapted to their specific environment, while both perform substandard in the other environment.

The widespread use and misuse of antibiotics has resulted in increased microbial resistance to antibiotics in clinical use, to the point that the methicillin-resistant *Staphylococcus aureus* (MRSA) has been described as a 'superbug' because of the threat it poses to health and its relative invulnerability to existing drugs. Response strategies typically include the use of different, stronger antibiotics; however, new strains of MRSA have recently emerged that are resistant even to these drugs.

This is an example of what is known as an evolutionary arms race, in which bacteria continue to develop strains that are less susceptible to antibiotics, while medical researchers continue to develop new antibiotics that can kill them. A similar situation occurs with pesticide resistance in plants and insects. Arms races are not necessarily induced by man; a well-documented example involves the spread of a gene in the butterfly Hypolimnas bolina suppressing male-killing activity by Wolbachia bacteria parasites on the island of Samoa, where the spread of the gene is known to have occurred over a period of just five years.

The life cycle of a sexually reproducing organism. Various components of natural selection are indicated for each life stage.

Natural selection occurs at every life stage of an individual. An individual organism must survive until adulthood before it can reproduce, and selection of those that reach this stage is called *viability selection*. In many species, adults must compete with each other for mates via sexual selection, and success in this competition determines who will parent the next generation. When individuals can reproduce more than once, a longer survival in the reproductive phase increases the number of offspring, called *survival selection*.

The fecundity of both females and males (for example, giant sperm in certain species of *Drosophila*) can be limited via 'fecundity selection'. The viability of produced gametes can differ, while intragenomic conflicts such as meiotic drive between the haploid gametes can result in gametic or 'genic selection'. Finally, the union of some combinations of eggs and sperm might be more compatible than others; this is termed *compatibility selection*.

A pre-requisite for natural selection to result in adaptive evolution, novel traits and speciation, is the presence of heritable genetic variation that results in fitness differences. Genetic variation is the result of mutations, recombinations and alterations in the karyotype (the number, shape, size and internal arrangement of the chromosomes). Any of these changes might have an effect that is highly advantageous or highly disadvantageous, but large effects are very rare. In the past, most changes in the genetic material were considered neutral or close to neutral because they occurred in non-coding DNA or resulted in a synonymous substitution.

However, recent research suggests that many mutations in non-coding DNA do have slight deleterious effects. Although both mutation rates and average fitness effects of mutations are dependent on the organism, estimates from data in humans have found that a majority of mutations are slightly deleterious.

The exuberant tail of the peacock is thought to be the result of sexual selection by females. This peacock is an albino; selection against albinos in nature is intense because they are easily spotted by predators or are unsuccessful in competition for mates.

By the definition of fitness, individuals with greater fitness are more likely to contribute offspring to the next generation, while individuals with lesser fitness are more likely to die early or fail to reproduce. As a result, alleles which on average result in greater fitness become more abundant in the next generation, while alleles which generally reduce fitness become rarer. If the selection forces remain the same for many generations, beneficial alleles become more and more abundant, until they dominate the population, while alleles with a lesser fitness disappear. In every generation, new mutations and re-combinations arise spontaneously, producing a new spectrum of phenotypes. Therefore, each new generation will be enriched by the increasing abundance of alleles that contribute to those traits that were favoured by selection, enhancing these traits over successive generations.

Some mutations occur in so-called regulatory genes. Changes in these can have large effects on the phenotype of the individual because they regulate the function of many other genes. Most, but not all, mutations in regulatory genes result in non-viable zygotes. Examples of non-lethal regulatory mutations occur in HOX genes in humans, which can result in a cervical rib or polydactyly, an increase in the number of fingers or toes. When such mutations result in a higher fitness, natural selection will favour these phenotypes and the novel trait will spread in the population.

Established traits are not immutable; traits that have high fitness in one environmental context may be much less fit if environmental conditions change. In the absence of natural selection to preserve such a trait, it will become more variable and deteriorate over time, possibly resulting in a vestigial manifestation of the trait, also called evolutionary baggage. In many circumstances, the apparently vestigial structure may retain a limited functionality, or may be co-opted for other advantageous traits in a phenomenon known as preadaptation. A famous example of a vestigial structure, the eye of the blind mole rat, is believed to retain function in photoperiod perception.

Speciation

Speciation requires selective mating, which result in a reduced gene flow. Selective mating can be the result of:

1. Geographic isolation;
2. Behavioural isolation; or
3. Temporal isolation.

For example, a change in the physical environment (geographic isolation by an extrinsic barrier) would follow number:

1. a change in camouflage for number;
2 or a shift in mating times (i.e., one species of deer shifts location and therefore changes its 'rut') for number; and
3. Over time, these subgroups might diverge radically to become different species, either because of differences in selection pressures on the different subgroups, or because different mutations arise spontaneously in the different populations, or because of founder effects — some potentially beneficial alleles may, by chance, be present in only one or other of two subgroups when they first become separated.

A lesser-known mechanism of speciation occurs via hybridization, well-documented in plants and occasionally observed in species-rich groups of animals such as cichlid fishes. Such mechanisms of rapid speciation can reflect a mechanism of evolutionary change known as punctuated equilibrium, which suggests that evolutionary change and particularly speciation typically happens quickly after interrupting long periods of stasis.

Genetic changes within groups result in increasing incompatibility between the genomes of the two subgroups, thus reducing gene flow between the groups. Gene flow will effectively cease when the distinctive mutations characterizing each subgroup become fixed. As few as two mutations can result in speciation: if each mutation has a neutral or positive effect on fitness when they occur separately, but a negative effect when they occur together, then fixation of these genes in the respective subgroups will lead to two reproductively isolated populations. According to the biological species concept, these will be two different species.

Pre-Darwinian Theories

Several ancient philosophers expressed the idea that nature produces a huge variety of creatures, apparently randomly, and that only those creatures survive that manage to provide for themselves and reproduce successfully; well-known examples include Empedocles and his intellectual successor, Lucretius, while related ideas were later refined by Aristotle.

The struggle for existence was later described by Al-Jahiz, who argued that environmental factors influence animals to develop new characteristics to ensure survival. Abu Rayhan Biruni described the idea of artificial selection and argued that nature works in much the same way. Similar ideas were later expressed by Nasir al-Din Tusi and Ibn Khaldun. Such classical arguments were reintroduced in the 18th century by Pierre Louis Maupertuis and others, including Charles Darwin's grandfather Erasmus Darwin. While these forerunners had an influence on Darwinism, they later had little influence on the trajectory of evolutionary thought after Charles Darwin.

Until the early 19th century, the prevailing view in Western societies was that differences between individuals of a species were uninteresting departures from their Platonic idealism (or typus) of created kinds. However, the theory of uniformitarianism in geology promoted the idea that simple, weak forces could act continuously over long periods of time to produce radical changes in the Earth's landscape. The success of this theory raised awareness of the vast scale of geological time and made plausible the idea that tiny, virtually imperceptible changes in successive generations could produce consequences on the scale of differences between species. Early 19th century evolutionists such as Jean Baptiste Lamarck suggested the inheritance of acquired characteristics as a mechanism for evolutionary change; adaptive traits acquired by an organism during its lifetime could be inherited by that organism's progeny, eventually causing transmutation of species. This theory has come to be known as Lamarckism and was an influence on the anti-genetic ideas of the Stalinist Soviet biologist Trofim Lysenko.

Darwin's Theory

In 1859, Charles Darwin set out his theory of evolution by natural selection as an explanation for adaptation and speciation. He defined natural selection as the "principle by which each slight variation [of a trait], if useful, is preserved". The concept was simple but powerful: individuals best adapted to their environments are more likely to survive and reproduce. As long as there is some variation between them, there will be an inevitable selection of individuals with the most advantageous variations. If the variations are inherited, then differential reproductive success will lead to a progressive evolution of particular populations of a species, and populations that evolve to be sufficiently different eventually become different species.

Darwin's ideas were inspired by the observations that he had made on the *Beagle* voyage, and by the work of a political economist, the Reverend Thomas Malthus, who in *An Essay on the Principle of*

Population, noted that population (if unchecked) increases exponentially whereas the food supply grows only arithmetically; thus inevitable limitations of resources would have demographic implications, leading to a 'struggle for existence'. When Darwin read Malthus in 1838 he was already primed by his work as a naturalist to appreciate the 'struggle for existence' in nature and it struck him that as population outgrew resources, "favourable variations would tend to be preserved, and unfavourable ones to be destroyed. The result of this would be the formation of new species".

Here is Darwin's own summary of the idea, which can be found in the fourth chapter of the Origin:

> If during the long course of ages and under varying conditions of life, organic beings vary at all in the several parts of their organisation, and I think this cannot be disputed; if there be, owing to the high geometrical powers of increase of each species, at some age, season, or year, a severe struggle for life, and this certainly cannot be disputed; then, considering the infinite complexity of the relations of all organic beings to each other and to their conditions of existence, causing an infinite diversity in structure, constitution, and habits, to be advantageous to them, I think it would be a most extraordinary fact if no variation ever had occurred useful to each being's own welfare, in the same way as so many variations have occurred useful to man. But if variations useful to any organic being do occur, assuredly individuals thus characterised will have the best chance of being preserved in the struggle for life; and from the strong principle of inheritance they will tend to produce offspring similarly characterised. This principle of preservation, I have called, for the sake of brevity, Natural Selection.

Once he had his theory 'by which to work', Darwin was meticulous about gathering and refining evidence as his 'prime hobby' before making his idea public. He was in the process of writing his 'big book' to present his researches when the naturalist Alfred Russel Wallace independently conceived of the principle and described it in an essay he sent to Darwin to forward to Charles Lyell. Lyell and Joseph Dalton Hooker decided (without Wallace's knowledge) to present his essay together with unpublished writings which Darwin had sent to fellow naturalists, and *on the Tendency of Species to form Varieties; and on the Perpetuation of Varieties and Species by Natural Means of Selection* was read to the Linnean Society announcing co-discovery of the principle in July 1858. Darwin published a detailed account of his evidence and conclusions in *On the Origin of Species* in 1859. In the 3rd edition of 1861 Darwin acknowledged that others — notably William Charles Wells in 1813, and Patrick Matthew in 1831 — had proposed similar ideas, but had neither developed them nor presented them in notable scientific publications.

Darwin thought of natural selection by analogy to how farmers select crops or livestock for breeding, which he called 'artificial selection'; in his early manuscripts he referred to a 'Nature' which would do the selection. At the time, other mechanisms of evolution such as evolution by genetic drift were not yet explicitly formulated, and Darwin believed that selection was likely only part of the story: "I am convinced that [it] has been the main, but not exclusive means of modification." In a letter to Charles Lyell in September 1860, Darwin regretted the use of the term 'Natural Selection', preferring the term 'Natural Preservation'. For Darwin and his contemporaries, natural selection was essentially synonymous with evolution by natural selection. After the publication of *on the Origin of Species*, educated people generally accepted that evolution had occurred in some form. However, natural selection remained controversial as a mechanism, partly because it was perceived to be too weak to explain the range of observed characteristics of living organisms, and partly because even supporters of evolution balked at its 'unguided' and non-progressive nature, a response that has been characterized as the single most significant impediment to the idea's acceptance. However, some thinkers enthusiastically embraced natural selection; after reading Darwin, Herbert Spencer introduced the term *'survival of the fittest'*, which became a popular summary of the theory. The fifth edition of *On the Origin of Species* published in 1869 included Spencer's phrase as an alternative to natural selection, with credit given: "But the expression often used by Mr. Herbert Spencer, of the Survival of the Fittest, is more accurate, and is sometimes equally convenient". Although the phrase is still often used by non-biologists, modern biologists avoid it because it is tautological if 'fittest' is read to mean 'functionally superior' and is applied to individuals rather than considered as an averaged quantity over populations.

Modern Evolutionary Synthesis

Natural selection relies crucially on the idea of heredity, but it was developed long before the basic concepts of genetics. Although the Austrian monk Gregor Mendel, the father of modern genetics, was a contemporary of Darwin's, his work would lie in obscurity until the early 20th century. Only after the integration of Darwin's theory of evolution with a complex statistical appreciation of Gregor Mendel's 're-discovered' laws of inheritance did natural selection become generally accepted by scientists. The work of Ronald Fisher (who developed the required mathematical language and The Genetical Theory of Natural Selection), J.B.S. Haldane (who introduced the concept of the 'cost' of natural selection), Sewall Wright (who elucidated the nature of selection and adaptation), Theodosius Dobzhansky (who established the idea that mutation, by creating genetic diversity, supplied the raw material for natural selection, William Hamilton (who conceived of kin selection), Ernst Mayr (who recognised the key importance of reproductive isolation for speciation and many others formed the modern evolutionary synthesis. This synthesis cemented natural selection as the foundation of evolutionary theory, where it remains today.

Impact of the Idea

Darwin's ideas, along with those of Adam Smith and Karl Marx, had a profound influence on 19th century thought. Perhaps the most radical claim of the theory of evolution through natural selection is that "elaborately constructed forms, so different from each other, and dependent on each other in so complex a manner" evolved from the simplest forms of life by a few simple principles. This claim inspired some of Darwin's most ardent supporters—and provoked the most profound opposition. The radicalism of natural selection, according to Stephen Jay Gould, lay in its power to "dethrone some of the deepest and most traditional comforts of Western thought". In particular, it challenged long-standing beliefs in such concepts as a special and exalted place for humans in the natural world and a benevolent creator whose intentions were reflected in nature's order and design.

Cell and Molecular Biology

In the 19th century, Wilhelm Roux, a founder of modern embryology, wrote a book entitled '*Der Kampf der Teile im Organismus*' (The struggle of parts in the organism) in which he suggested that the development of an organism results from a Darwinian competition between the parts of the embryo, occurring at all levels, from molecules to organs. In recent years, a modern version of this theory has been proposed by Jean-Jacques Kupiec. According to this cellular Darwinism, stochasticity at the molecular level generates diversity in cell types whereas cell interactions impose a characteristic order on the developing embryo.

Social and Psychological Theory

The social implications of the theory of evolution by natural selection also became the source of continuing controversy. Friedrich Engels, a German political philosopher and co-originator of the ideology of communism, wrote in 1872 that "Darwin did not know what a bitter satire he wrote on mankind when he showed that free competition, the struggle for existence, which the economists celebrate as the highest historical achievement, is the normal state of the animal kingdom". Interpretation of natural selection as necessarily 'progressive', leading to increasing 'advances' in intelligence and civilisation, was used as a justification for colonialism and policies of eugenics, as well as broader socio-political positions now described as Social Darwinism. Konrad Lorenz won the Nobel Prize in Physiology or Medicine in 1973 for his analysis of animal behaviour in terms of the role of natural selection (particularly group selection). However, in Germany in 1940, in writings that he subsequently disowned, he used the theory as a justification for policies of the Nazi state. He wrote ". . . selection for toughness, heroism, and social utility . . . must be accomplished by some human institution, if mankind, in default of selective factors, is not to be ruined by domestication-induced degeneracy. The racial idea as the basis of our state has already accomplished much in this respect." Others have developed ideas that human societies and culture evolve by mechanisms that are analogous to those that apply to evolution of species.

More recently, work among anthropologists and psychologists has led to the development of socio-biology and later evolutionary psychology, a field that attempts to explain features of human psychology in terms of adaptation to the ancestral environment. The most prominent such example, notably advanced in the early work of Noam Chomsky and later by Steven Pinker, is the hypothesis that the human brain is adapted to acquire the grammatical rules of natural language. Other aspects of human behaviour and social structures, from specific cultural norms such as incest avoidance to broader patterns such as gender roles, have been hypothesized to have similar origins as adaptations to the early environment in which modern humans evolved. By analogy to the action of natural selection on genes, the concept of memes — "units of cultural transmission", or culture's equivalents of genes undergoing selection and recombination — has arisen, first described in this form by Richard Dawkins and subsequently expanded upon by philosophers such as Daniel Dennett as explanations for complex cultural activities, including human consciousness. Extensions of the theory of natural selection to such a wide range of cultural phenomena have been distinctly controversial and are not widely accepted.

Information and Systems Theory

In 1922, Alfred Lotka proposed that natural selection might be understood as a physical principle which could be described in terms of the use of energy by a system, a concept that was later developed by Howard Odum as the maximum power principle whereby evolutionary systems with selective advantage maximise the rate of useful energy transformation. Such concepts are sometimes relevant in the study of applied thermodynamics.

The principles of natural selection have inspired a variety of computational techniques, such as 'soft' artificial life, that simulate selective processes and can be highly efficient in 'adapting' entities to an environment defined by a specified fitness function. For example, a class of heuristic optimization algorithms known as genetic algorithms, pioneered by John Holland in the 1970s and expanded upon by David E. Goldberg, identify optimal solutions by simulated reproduction and mutation of a population of solutions defined by an initial probability distribution. Such algorithms are particularly useful when applied to problems whose solution landscape is very rough or has many local minima.

Natural selection acts on an organism's phenotype, or physical characteristics. Phenotype is determined by an organism's genetic make-up (genotype) and the environment in which the organism lives. Often, natural selection acts on specific traits of an individual, and the terms phenotype and genotype are used narrowly to indicate these specific traits.

When different organisms in a population possess different versions of a gene for a certain trait, each of these versions is known as an allele. It is this genetic variation that underlies phenotypic traits. A typical example is that certain combinations of genes for eye colour in humans which, for instance, give rise to the phenotype of blue eyes. (On the other hand, when all the organisms in a population share the same allele for a particular trait, and this state is stable over time, the allele is said to be *fixed* in that population.)

Some traits are governed by only a single gene, but most traits are influenced by the interactions of many genes. A variation in one of the many genes that contributes to a trait may have only a small effect on the phenotype; together, these genes can produce a continuum of possible phenotypic values.

Directionality of Selection

When some component of a trait is heritable, selection will alter the frequencies of the different alleles, or variants of the gene that produces the variants of the trait. Selection can be divided into three classes, on the basis of its effect on allele frequencies.

Directional selection occurs when a certain allele has a greater fitness than others, resulting in an increase of its frequency. This process can continue until the allele is fixed and the entire population shares the fitter phenotype. It is directional selection that is illustrated in the antibiotic resistance example above.

Far more common is stabilizing selection (which is commonly confused with *purifying selection* , which lowers the frequency of alleles that have a deleterious effect on the phenotype — that is, produce organisms of lower fitness. This process can continue until the allele is eliminated from the population. Purifying selection results in functional genetic features, such as protein-coding genes or regulatory sequences, being conserved over time due to selective pressure against deleterious variants.

Finally, a number of forms of balancing selection exist, which do not result in fixation, but maintain an allele at intermediate frequencies in a population. This can occur in diploid species (that is, those that have two pairs of chromosomes) when heterozygote individuals, who have different alleles on each chromosome at a single genetic locus, have a higher fitness than homozygote individuals that have two of the same alleles. This is called heterozygote advantage or overdominance, of which the best-known example is the malarial resistance observed in heterozygous humans who carry only one copy of the gene for sickle cell anaemia. Maintenance of allelic variation can also occur through disruptive or diversifying selection, which favours genotypes that depart from the average in either direction (that is, the opposite of overdominance), and can result in a bimodal distribution of trait values. Finally, balancing selection can occur through frequency-dependent selection, where the fitness of one particular phenotype depends on the distribution of other phenotypes in the population. The principles of game theory have been applied to understand the fitness distributions in these situations, particularly in the study of kin selection and the evolution of reciprocal altruism.

Selection and Genetic Variation

A portion of all genetic variation is functionally neutral in that it produces no phenotypic effect or significant difference in fitness; the hypothesis that this variation accounts for a large fraction of observed genetic diversity is known as the neutral theory of molecular evolution and was originated by Motoo Kimura. When genetic variation does not result in differences in fitness, selection cannot *directly* affect the frequency of such variation. As a result, the genetic variation at those sites will be higher than at sites where variation does influence fitness. However, after a period with no new mutation, the genetic variation at these sites will be eliminated due to genetic drift.

Mutation Selection Balance

Natural selection results in the reduction of genetic variation through the elimination of maladapted individuals and consequently of the mutations that caused the maladaptation. At the same time, new mutations occur, resulting in a mutation-selection balance. The exact outcome of the two processes depends both on the rate at which new mutations occur and on the strength of the natural selection, which is a function of how unfavourable the mutation proves to be. Consequently, changes in the mutation rate or the selection pressure will result in a different mutation-selection balance.

Genetic Linkage

Genetic linkage occurs when the loci of two alleles are *linked*, or in close proximity to each other on the chromosome. During the formation of gametes, recombination of the genetic material results in reshuffling of the alleles. However, the chance that such a reshuffle occurs between two alleles depends on the distance between those alleles; the closer the alleles are to each other, the less likely it is that such a reshuffle will occur. Consequently, when selection targets one allele, this automatically results in selection of the other allele as well; through this mechanism, selection can have a strong influence on patterns of variation in the genome.

Selective sweeps occur when an allele becomes more common in a population as a result of positive selection. As the prevalence of one allele increases, linked alleles can also become more common, whether they are neutral or even slightly deleterious. This is called *genetic hitchhiking*. A strong selective sweep results in a region of the genome where the positively selected haplotype (the allele and its neighbours) are essentially the only ones that exist in the population.

Whether a selective sweep has occurred or not can be investigated by measuring linkage disequilibrium, or whether a given haplotype is over-represented in the population. Normally, genetic recombination results in a reshuffling of the different alleles within a haplotype, and none of the haplotypes will dominate the population. However, during a selective sweep, selection for a specific allele will also result in selection of neighbouring alleles. Therefore, the presence of a block of strong linkage disequilibrium might indicate that there has been a 'recent' selective sweep near the centre of the block, and this can be used to identify sites recently under selection.

Background selection is the opposite of a selective sweep. If a specific site experiences strong and persistent purifying selection, linked variation will tend to be weeded out along with it, producing a region in the genome of low overall variability. Because background selection is a result of deleterious new mutations, which can occur randomly in any haplotype, it does not produce clear blocks of linkage disequilibrium, although with low recombination it can still lead to slightly negative linkage disequilibrium overall.

Gene-centred View of Evolution

The gene-centered view of evolution, gene selection theory or selfish gene theory holds that evolution occurs through the differential survival of competing genes, increasing the frequency of those alleles whose phenotypic effects successfully promote their own propagation. The proponents of this viewpoint argue that, since heritable information is passed from generation to generation almost exclusively by genetic material, natural selection and evolution are best considered from the perspective of genes. This is in contrast to the organism-centred viewpoint adopted historically by biologists. Proponents of the gene-centred viewpoint argue that it permits understanding of diverse phenomena such as altruism and intragenomic conflict that are otherwise difficult to explain from an organism-focussed perspective.

The gene-centred view of evolution is a different way of looking at the basis of evolutionary development. It turns the whole solution of evolution inside-out for the purpose of examination. What this new perspective reveals is a more easily understood model for the evolution of social characteristics such as selfishness and altruism that much of the study of evolution, caught up in the survival of the *individual organisms*, overlooks.

Acquired Characteristics are not Inherited

Discoveries in science such as the formulation of the central dogma of molecular biology made it clear that the inheritance of acquired characters was not an evolutionary factor in a physical sense and identified genes as lasting entities that survive through many generations. Maynard Smith summarized the issue:

> "If the central dogma is true, and if it is also true that nucleic acids are the only means whereby information is transmitted between generations, this has crucial implications for evolution. It would imply that all evolutionary novelty requires changes in nucleic acids, and that these changes — mutations — are essentially accidental and non-adaptive in nature. Changes elsewhere — in the egg cytoplasm, in materials transmitted through the placenta, in the mother's milk — might alter the development of the child, but, unless the changes were in nucleic acids, they would have no long-term evolutionary effects".
>
> —***Maynard Smith***

The rejection of the inheritance of acquired characters combined with the classical mathematical evolutionary biology developed by Ronald Fisher, J. B. S. Haldane and Sewall Wright, they paved the way to the formulation of the selfish gene theory.

Gene as the Unit of Selection

The view of the gene as the unit of selection was developed mainly in the works W.D. Hamilton, Colin Pittendrigh and George C. Williams. It was later popularised by Richard Dawkins in his books *The Selfish Gene* (1976) and *The Extended Phenotype* (1982).

According to Williams' 1966 book *Adaptation and Natural Selection*:

"The essence of the genetical theory of natural selection is a statistical bias in the relative rates of survival of alternatives (genes, individuals, etc.). The effectiveness of such bias in producing adaptation is contingent on the maintenance of certain quantitative relationships among the operative factors. One necessary condition is that the selected entity must have a high degree of permanence and a low rate of endogenous change, relative to the degree of bias (differences in selection coefficients)".

Williams argued that "The natural selection of phenotypes cannot in itself produce cumulative change, because phenotypes are extremely temporary manifestations". Each phenotype is the unique product of the interaction between genome and environment. It does not matter how fit and fertile a phenotype is, it will eventually be destroyed and will never be duplicated.

Since 1954, it has been known that DNA is the main physical substrate to genetic information, and it is capable of high fidelity replication through many generations. So, a particular sequence of DNA can have a high permanence and a low rate of endogenous change.

In normal sexual reproduction, an entire genome is the unique combination of father's and mother's chromosomes produced at the moment of fertilization. It is generally destroyed with its organism, because "meiosis and recombination destroy genotypes as surely as death". Only half of it is transmitted to each descendant due to the independent segregation.

The gene as an informational entity persists for an evolutionary significant span of time through a lineage of many physical copies.

In his book *River out of Eden*, Dawkins coins the phrase *God's utility function* to explain his view on genes as units of selection. He uses this phrase as a synonym of the 'meaning of life' or the 'purpose of life'. By rephrasing the word *purpose* in terms of what economists call a utility function, meaning 'that which is maximized', Dawkins attempts to reverse-engineer the purpose in the mind of the Divine Engineer of Nature, or the *Utility Function of God*. Finally, Dawkins argues that it is a mistake to assume that an ecosystem or a species as a whole exists for a purpose. He writes that it is incorrect to suppose that individual organisms lead a meaningful life either; in nature, only genes have a utility function — to perpetuate their own existence with indifference to great sufferings inflicted upon the organisms they build, exploit and discard.

Organisms as Vehicles

Genes are not naked in the world. They are usually packed together inside a genome, which is itself contained inside an organism. Genes group together into genomes because "genetic replication makes use of energy and substrates that are supplied by the metabolic economy in much greater quantities than would be possible without a genetic division of labour". They build vehicles to promote their mutual interests of jumping into the next generation of vehicles. As Dawkins puts it, organisms are the 'survival machines' of genes.

The phenotypic effect of a particular gene is contingent on its environment, including the fellow genes constituting with it the total genome. A gene never has a fixed effect, so how is it possible to speak of a gene for long legs? It is because of the phenotypic *differences* between alleles. One may say that one allele, all other things being equal or varying within certain limits, causes greater legs than its alternative. This difference enables the scrutiny of natural selection.

"A gene can have multiple phenotypic effects, each of which may be of positive, negative or neutral value. It is the net selective value of a gene's phenotypic effect that determines the fate of the gene". For instance, a gene can cause its bearer to have greater reproductive success at a young age, but also cause a greater likelihood of death at a later age. If the benefit outweighs the harm, averaged out over the individuals and environments in which the gene happens to occur, then phenotypes containing the gene will generally be positively selected and thus the abundance of that gene in the population will increase.

Even so, it becomes necessary to model the genes in combination with their vehicle as well as in combination with the vehicle's environment.

Selfish Gene Theory

The selfish gene theory of natural selection can be restated as follows:

> "Genes do not present themselves naked to the scrutiny of natural selection, instead they present their phenotypic effects. (...) Differences in genes give rise to difference in these phenotypic differences. Natural selection acts on the phenotypic differences and thereby on genes. Thus genes come to be represented in successive generations in proportion to the selective value of their phenotypic effects".

The result is that "the prevalent genes in a sexual population must be those that, as a mean condition, through a large number of genotypes in a large number of situations, have had the most favourable phenotypic effects for their own replication". In other words, we expect selfish genes ('selfish' meaning that it promotes its own survival without necessarily promoting the survival of the organism, group or even species). This theory implies that adaptations are the phenotypic effects of genes to maximize their representation in future generations. An adaptation is maintained by selection if it promotes genetic survival directly, or else some subordinate goal that ultimately contributes to successful reproduction.

Individual Altruism, Genetic Egoism

The gene is a unit of hereditary information that exists in many physical copies in the world, and which particular physical copy will be replicated and originate new copies does not matter from the gene's point of view. A selfish gene could be favoured by selection by producing altruism among organisms containing it. The idea is summarized as follows:

> "If a gene copy confers a benefit B on another vehicle at cost C to its own vehicle, its costly action is strategically beneficial if $pB > C$, where p is the probability that a copy of the gene is present in the vehicle that benefits. Actions with substantial costs therefore require significant values of p. Two kinds of factors ensure high values of p: relatedness (kinship) and recognition (green beards).

A gene in a somatic cell of an individual may forego replication to promote the transmission of its copies in the germ line cells. It ensures the high value of $p = 1$ due to their constant contact and their common origin from the zygote.

The kin selection theory predicts that a gene may promote the recognition of kinship by historical continuity: a mammalian mother learns to identify her own offspring in the act of giving birth; a male preferentially directs resources to the offspring of mothers with whom he has copulated; the other chicks in a nest are siblings; and so on. The expected altruism between kin is calibrated by the value of p, also known as the coefficient of relatedness. For instance, an individual has a $p = 1/2$ in relation to his brother, and $p = 1/8$ to his cousin, so we would expect, *ceteris paribus*, greater altruism among brothers than among cousins. In this vein, geneticist J.B.S. Haldane famously joked, "Would I lay down my life to save my brother? No, but I would to save two brothers or eight cousins". However, examining the human propensity for altruism, kin selection theory seems incapable of explaining cross-familiar, cross-racial and even cross-species acts of kindness.

Green-beard Effect

Green-beard effects gained their name from a thought-experiment of Richard Dawkins, who considered the possibility of a gene that caused its possessors to develop a green beard and to be nice to other green-bearded individuals. Since then, a 'green beard effect' has come to refer to forms of genetic self-recognition in which a gene in one individual might direct benefits to other individuals that possess the gene. Such genes are essentially *especially selfish*, benefiting themselves regardless of the fates of their vehicles.

ALL KINDS OF ALTRUISM

Kindness

On the other hand, a single trait, group reciprocal kindness, is capable of explaining the vast majority of altruism that is generally accepted as 'good' by modern societies. Imagine a green-bearding behavioural trait whose recognition does not depend on the recognition of some external feature such as beard colour, but relies on recognition of the behaviour itself. Imagine now that the behaviour is altruistic. The success of such a trait in sufficiently intelligent and undeceived organisms is implicit. Moreover, the existence of such a trait predicts a tendency for kindness to unrelated organisms that are apparently kind, even if the organisms are of a completely different species. Moreover, the gene need not be exactly the same, so long as the effect is similar. Multiple versions of the gene—or even meme—would have virtually the same effect in a sort of symbiotic green-bearding cycle of altruism.

Deceit

Whenever recognition plays a role in evolution, so does deception. Just like the harmless lizard that has evolved a pattern that mimics its poisonous cousin and therefore tricks predators, the selfish creature may pretend to be kind by 'growing a green beard' (whatever that green beard may be). Thus green-bearding and the selfish gene theory also give rise to an explanation for the evolution of lies and deceit, characteristics that do not benefit the population as a whole.

Intragenomic Conflict

As genes are capable of producing individual altruism, they are capable of producing conflict among genes inside the genome of one individual. This phenomenon was called intragenomic conflict and arises when one gene promotes its own replication in detriment to other genes in the genome. The classic example is segregation distorter genes that cheat during meiosis or gametogenesis and end up in more than half of the functional gametes. These genes persist even resulting in reduced fertility. Egbert Leigh compared the genome to "a parliament of genes: each acts in its own self-interest, but if its acts hurt the others, they will combine together to suppress it" to explain the relative low occurrence of intragenomic conflict.

Challenges to the Gene-centric View

Prominent opponents of this gene-centric view of evolution include evolutionary biologist Ernst Mayr, palaeontologist Stephen Jay Gould, biologist and anthropologist David Sloan Wilson and philosopher Elliot Sober.

Writing in the New York Review of Books, Gould has characterized the gene-centered perspective as confusing book-keeping with causality. Gould views selection as working on many levels, and has called attention to a hierarchical perspective of selection. Gould also called the claims on *Selfish Gene* 'strict adaptationism', 'ultra-Darwinism', and 'Darwinian fundamentalism', describing them as excessively 'reductionist'. He saw the theory as leading to a simplistic 'algorithmic' theory of evolution, or even to the re-introduction of a teleological principle. Mayr went so far as to say "Dawkins' basic theory of the gene being the object of evolution is totally non-Darwinian".

Gould also addressed the issue of selfish genes in his essay 'Caring groups and selfish genes'. Gould acknowledged that Dawkins was not imputing conscious action to genes, but simply using shorthand metaphor commonly found in evolutionary writings. To Gould, the fatal flaw was that "no matter how much power Dawkins wishes to assign to genes, there is one thing that he cannot give them — direct visibility to natural selection". Rather, the unit of selection is the phenotype, not the genotype, because it is phenotypes which interact with the environment at the natural selection interface. So, in Kim Sterelny's summation of Gould's view: "gene differences do not cause evolutionary changes in populations, they register those changes". The problem, however, with this criticism is that if it is a good argument against the gene-centred view of evolution, it is a good argument against the whole of Mendelian genetics. Genes do 'blend', as far as their effects on developing phenotypes are concerned. But, they do not blend as they replicate and recombine down the generations. Richard Dawkins explained in a later book, *The Extended Phenotype*, that Gould confused particulate genetics with particulate embryology.

Since Gould's death in 2002, Niles Eldredge has continued with counter-arguments to gene-centered natural selection. Eldredge notes that in Dawkins' book *A Devil's Chaplain*, which was published just before Eldredge's book, "Richard Dawkins comments on what he sees as the main difference between his position and that of the late Stephen Jay Gould. He concludes that it is his own vision that genes play a causal role in evolution", while Gould (and Eldredge) "sees genes as passive recorders of what worked better than what".

The gene-centred view of evolution is a synthesis of the theory of evolution by natural selection, the particulate inheritance theory and the non-transmission of acquired characters. It states that those genes whose phenotypic effects successfully promote their own propagation will be favourably selected in detriment to their competitors. This process produces adaptations for the benefit of genes that promote the reproductive success of the organism, or of other organisms containing the same gene (kin altruism and green-beard effects), or even only its own propagation in detriment to the other genes of the genome.

10 Genetic Drift

Genetic drift or allelic drift is the change in the frequency of a gene variant (allele) in a population due to random sampling. The alleles in the offspring are a sample of those in the parents, and chance has a role in determining whether a given individúal survives and reproduces. A population's allele frequency is the fraction of the copies of one gene that share a particular form.

Genetic drift is an important evolutionary process, which leads to changes in allele frequencies over time. It may cause gene variants to disappear completely, and thereby reduce genetic variation. In contrast to natural selection, which makes gene variants more common or less common depending on their reproductive success, the changes due to genetic drift are not driven by environmental or adaptive pressures, and may be beneficial, neutral, or detrimental to reproductive success.

The effect of genetic drift is larger in small populations, and smaller in large populations. Vigorous debates wage among scientists over the relative importance of genetic drift compared with natural selection. Ronald Fisher held the view that genetic drift plays at the most a minor role in evolution, and this remained the dominant view for several decades. In 1968 Motoo Kimura rekindled the debate with his neutral theory of molecular evolution which claims that most of the changes in the genetic material (although not necessarily changes in phenotypes) are caused by genetic drift.

The process of genetic drift can be illustrated using 20 marbles in a jar to represent 20 organisms in a population. Half of them are red and half blue, and both colours correspond to two different alleles of one gene in the population. In each new generation the organisms reproduce at random. To represent this reproduction, randomly select a marble from the original jar and deposit a new marble with the same colour as its 'parent' into a new jar. (The selected marble remains in the original jar.) Repeat this process until there are 20 new marbles in the second jar. The second jar will then contain a second generation of 'offspring', consisting of 20 marbles of various colours. Unless the second jar contains exactly 10 red and 10 blue marbles, there will have been a random shift in the allele frequencies.

Repeat this process a number of times, randomly reproducing each generation of marbles to form the next. The numbers of red and blue marbles picked each generation will fluctuate: sometimes more red, sometimes more blue. This fluctuation is genetic drift — a change in the population's allele frequency resulting from a random variation in the distribution of alleles from one generation to the next.

It is even possible that in any one generation no marbles of a particular colour will be chosen, meaning they have no offspring. In this example, if no red marbles are selected the jar representing the new generation will contain only blue offspring. If this happens, the red allele has been lost permanently in the population, while the remaining blue allele has become fixed: all future generations will be entirely blue. In small populations, fixation can occur in just a few generations.

Probability and Allele Frequency

In probability theory, the law of large numbers predicts little change taking place over time when the population is large. When the reproductive population is small, however, the effects of sampling error can alter the allele frequencies significantly. Genetic drift is therefore considered to be a consequential mechanism of evolutionary change primarily within small, isolated populations.

This effect can be illustrated using a simplified example. Consider a very large colony of bacteria which are isolated within a drop of solution. The bacteria are genetically identical except for a single gene for which there are two different alleles. The alleles are labelled *A* and *B*. Half of the bacteria have allele *A* and the other half have allele *B*. Thus both *A* and *B* have allele frequency $^1/_2$.

A and *B* are neutral alleles, meaning they do not affect the bacteria's ability to survive and reproduce. This being the case, all bacteria in this colony are equally likely to survive and reproduce. The drop of solution then shrinks until it has only enough food to sustain four bacteria.

All the others die without reproducing. Among the four who survive, there are sixteen possible combinations for the *A* and *B* alleles:

(A-A-A-A)	(B-A-A-A)	(A-B-A-A)	(B-B-A-A)
(A-A-B-A)	(B-A-B-A)	(A-B-B-A)	(B-B-B-A)
(A-A-A-B)	(B-A-A-B)	(A-B-A-B)	(B-B-A-B)
(A-A-B-B)	(B-A-B-B)	(A-B-B-B)	(B-B-B-B)

Moran Model

The Moran model assumes overlapping generations. At each time step, one individual is chosen to reproduce and one individual is chosen to die. So in each timestep, the number of copies of a given allele can go up by one, go down by one, or can stay the same. This means that the transition matrix is tridiagonal, which means that mathematical solutions are easier for the Moran model than for the Wright-Fisher model. On the other hand, computer simulations are usually easier to perform using the Wright-Fisher model, because fewer time steps need to be calculated. In the Moran model, it takes *N* timesteps to get through one generation, where *N* is the effective population size. In the Wright-Fisher model, it takes just one.

In practice, the Moran model and Wright-Fisher model give qualitatively similar results, but genetic drift runs twice as fast in the Moran model.

Random Effects Other Than Sampling Error

Random changes in allele frequencies can also be caused by other effects than sampling error, for example random changes in selection pressure.

One important alternative source of stochasticity, perhaps more important than genetic drift, is genetic draft. Genetic draft describes the way the fate of a new mutation depends on the luck of which other alleles happen to be nearby at linked loci. Genetic draft has very different mathematical properties; unlike genetic drift, the direction of the random change in allele frequency each generation is strongly autocorrelated instead of independent over time.

Drift and Fixation

The Hardy–Weinberg principle states that within sufficiently large, randomly mating populations the allele frequencies will tend to remain constant from one generation to the next unless the equilibrium is disturbed by migration, genetic mutation, or selection. However, there is no residual influence on this probability from the frequency distribution of alleles in the grandparent, or any earlier, population—only that of the parent population. The predicted distribution of alleles among the offspring is a memory-less probability as described in the Markov property. This means that the mathematical probabilities associated with the distribution of alleles in any generation are only derived from the distribution of alleles in the generation immediately prior. Thus when random fluctuations result in a change of the allele frequency from the parent generation to the offspring generation, that deviation establishes new expected values for the allele distributions in the next generation to follow.

Populations do not gain new alleles from the random sampling of alleles passed to the next generation, but the sampling can cause an existing allele to disappear. Because random sampling can remove but not replace an allele, and because random declines or increases in allele frequency will influence the expected allele distributions for the next following generation, genetic drift drives a population towards genetic uniformity over time. When an allele reaches a frequency of 1 (100%) it is said to be 'fixed' in the population and when an allele reaches a frequency of 0 (0%) it is lost. Once an allele becomes fixed, genetic drift comes to a halt, and the allele frequency cannot change unless a new allele is introduced in the population via mutation or gene flow. Thus even while genetic drift is a random, directionless process, it acts to eliminate genetic variation over time.

Time to Fixation or Loss

Ten simulations of random genetic drift of a single given allele with an initial frequency distribution 0.5 measured over the course of 50 generations, repeated in three reproductively synchronous populations of different sizes. In general, alleles drift to loss or fixation (frequency of 0.0 or 1.0) significantly faster in smaller populations.

Assuming genetic drift is the only evolutionary force acting upon an allele, at any given point in time the probability that an allele will eventually become fixed in the population is simply its frequency in the population at that given point in time. For example, if the frequency p for allele A is 75 per cent and the frequency q for allele B is 25 per cent, then given unlimited time the probability A will ultimately become fixed in the population is 75 per cent and the probability that B becomes fixed is 25 per cent.

The time needed, which is measured by the number of generations, for fixation to occur can be estimated with probability, and is proportional to the population size, such that fixation is predicted to occur much more rapidly in smaller populations. Normally the effective population size, which is smaller than the total population, is used to determine these probabilities. The effective population size (N_e) takes into account factors such as the level of inbreeding, the number of organisms that are too old or young to breed, and the lower probability that two organisms that live far apart will reproduce.

Genetic Drift *Vs.* Natural Selection

Although both processes drive evolution, genetic drift operates randomly while natural selection functions non-randomly. This is because natural selection emblematizes the ecological interaction of a population, whereas drift is regarded as a sampling procedure across successive generations without regard to fitness pressures imposed by the environment. While natural selection is directioned, guiding evolution by impelling heritable adaptations to the environment, genetic drift has no direction and is guided only by the mathematics of chance.

As a result, drift acts upon the genotypic frequencies within a population without regard their relationship to the phenotype. Changes to the genotype caused by genetic drift may or may not result in changes to the phenotype. In drift each allele in a population is randomly and independently affected, yet the fluctuations in their allele frequencies are all driven in a quantitatively similar manner. Drift is blind with respect to any advantage or disadvantage the allele may bring. Alternatively, natural selection acts directly on the phenotype and indirectly on its underlying genotype. Selection responds specifically to the adaptive advantage or disadvantage presented by a phenotypic trait, and thus affects genes differentially. Selection indirectly rewards the alleles that develop adaptively advantageous phenotypes; with an increase in reproductive success for the phenotype comes an increase in allele frequency. By the same token, selection lowers the frequencies for alleles that cause unfavorable traits, and ignores those which are neutral.

In natural populations, genetic drift and natural selection do not act in isolation; both forces are always at play. However, the degree to which alleles are affected by drift or selection varies according to population size. The statistical effect of sampling error during the reproduction of alleles is much greater in small populations than in large ones. When populations are very small, drift will predominate, and may preserve unfavourable alleles and eliminate favourable ones (this means purifying selection has a stronger effect in species with a larger effective population). Weak selective effects may not be seen at all, as the small changes in frequency they would produce are overshadowed by drift.

In a large population, the probability of sampling error is small and little change to the allele frequencies is expected, even over many generations. Even weak selection forces acting upon an allele will push its frequency upwards or downwards (depending on whether the allele's influence is beneficial or harmful). However, in cases where the allele frequency is very small, drift can also overpower selection—even in large populations. For example, while disadvantageous mutations are usually eliminated quickly in large populations, new advantageous mutations are almost as vulnerable to loss through genetic drift as are neutral mutations. It is not until the allele frequency for the advantageous mutation reaches a certain threshold that genetic drift will have little effect.

Most mutations have a clear negative selective effect and cause the gametes that they occur in to disappear after a few generations. It is possible to calculate how many percent of each generation will be removed by such mutations. The size of the remaining population, is said to be a factor f_0, the equilibrium frequency of non-deleterious alleles, times the total population (f_0 is between zero and one). When a neutral mutation spreads by drift in a population, some of the occurrencies will be removed because they are linked to such negative mutations. That is, they are located in chromosomes that are removed because of selection against a mutation in another part of the same chromosome. As a consequence, the effective population size is reduced by the factor f_0. This means that mutation and selection in combination, causes the drift to have more effect. Because strength of genetic linkage varies along the chromosome, effective population size, and thereby genetic drift, also varies. With a higher recombination rate, linkage decreases and with it this local effect on drift. This effect is visible in molecular data as a correlation between local recombination rate and genetic diversity, and negative correlation between gene density and diversity at non-coding sites.

Population Bottleneck

Changes in a population's allele frequency following a population bottleneck: the rapid and radical decline in population size has reduced the population's genetic variation.

A population bottleneck is when a population contracts to a significantly smaller size over a short period of time due to some random environmental event. In a true population bottleneck, the odds for survival of any member of the population are purely random, and are not improved by any particular inherent genetic advantage. The bottleneck can result in radical changes in allele frequencies, completely independent of selection. And its impact can be sustained, even when the bottleneck is caused by a one-time event such as a natural catastrophe. Even when the allele frequency of the original population is carried forward in the surviving population, a radical reduction in population size increases the likelihood of further allele fluctuation from drift in generations to come.

A population's genetic variation can be greatly reduced by a bottleneck, and even beneficial adaptations may be permanently eliminated. The loss of variation leaves the surviving population vulnerable to any new selection pressures such as disease, climate change or shift in the available food source, because adapting in response to environmental changes requires sufficient genetic variation in the population for natural selection to take place.

There have been many known cases of population bottleneck in the recent past. Prior to the arrival of Europeans, North American prairies were habitat for millions of greater prairie chickens. In Illinois alone, their numbers plummeted from about 100 million birds in 1900 to about 50 birds in the 1990s. The declines in population resulted from hunting and habitat destruction, but the random consequence has been a loss of most of the species' genetic diversity. DNA analysis comparing birds from the mid century to birds in the 1990s documents a steep decline in the genetic variation in just in the latter few decades. Currently the greater prairie chicken is experiencing low reproductive success.

The founder effect is a special case of genetic drift, occurring when a small group in a population splinters off from the original population and forms a new one. The random sample of alleles in the just formed new colony is expected to grossly misrepresent the original population in at least some respects. It is even possible that the number of alleles for some genes in the original population is larger than the number of gene copies in the founders, making complete representation impossible. When a newly formed colony is small, its founders can strongly affect the population's genetic make-up far into the future.

A well documented example is found in the Amish migration to Pennsylvania in 1744. Two members of the new colony shared the recessive allele for Ellis-van Creveld syndrome. Members of the colony and their descendants tend to be religious isolates and remain relatively insular. As a result of many generations of inbreeding, Ellis-van Creveld syndrome is now much more prevalent among the Amish than in the general population.

The difference in gene frequencies between the original population and colony may also trigger the two groups to diverge significantly over the course of many generations. As the difference, or genetic distance, increases, the two separated populations may become distinct, both genetically and phenetically, although not only genetic drift but also natural selection, gene flow and mutation will all contribute to this divergence. This potential for relatively rapid changes in the colony's gene frequency led most scientists to consider the founder effect (and by extension, genetic drift) a significant driving force in the evolution of new species. Sewall Wright was the first to attach this significance to random drift and small, newly isolated populations with his shifting balance theory of speciation. Following after Wright, Ernst Mayr created many persuasive models to show that the decline in genetic variation and small population size following the founder effect were critically important for new species to develop. However, there is much less support for this view today since the hypothesis has been tested repeatedly through experimental research and the results have been equivocal at best.

History of the Concept

The concept for genetic drift was first introduced by one of the founders in the field of population genetics, Sewall Wright. His first use of the term 'drift' was in 1929, though at the time he was using it in the sense of a directed process of change, or natural selection. Later that year he used it to refer to a purely random process, or change due to the effects of sampling error. It came to be known as the 'Sewall-Wright effect', though he was never entirely comfortable to see his name given to it. He preferred 'drifting at random', and 'drift' came to be adopted as a technical term in the stochastic sense exclusively.

In the early days of the modern evolutionary synthesis, scientists were just beginning to blend the new science of population genetics with Charles Darwin's theory of natural selection. Working within this new framework, Wright focused on the effects of inbreeding on small relatively isolated populations. He introduced the concept of an adaptive landscape in which phenomena such as cross breeding and genetic drift in small populations could push them away from adaptive peaks, which would in turn allow natural selection to push them towards new adaptive peaks. Wright thought smaller populations were more suited for natural selection because "inbreeding was sufficiently intense to create new interaction systems through random drift but not intense enough to cause random nonadaptive fixation of genes".

Wright's views on the role of genetic drift in the evolutionary scheme were controversial almost from the very beginning. One of the most vociferous and influential critics was colleague Ronald Fisher. Fisher conceded genetic drift played some role in evolution, but an insignificant one. Fisher has been accused of misunderstanding Wright's views because in his criticisms Fisher seemed to argue Wright had rejected selection almost entirely. To Fisher, viewing the process of evolution as a long, steady, adaptive progression was the only way to explain the ever increasing complexity from simpler forms. But the debates have continued between the 'gradualists' and those who lean more toward the Wright model of evolution where selection and drift together play an important role.

Allopatric Speciation

Allopatric speciation (from the ancient Greek allos, 'other' + Greek patra, 'fatherland') or geographic speciation is speciation that occurs when biological populations of the same species become isolated due to geographical changes such as mountain building or social changes such as emigration. The isolated populations then undergo genotypic and/or phenotypic divergence as:

(a) they become subjected to different selective pressures;

(b) they independently undergo genetic drift;

(c) different mutations arise in the populations.

When part of a population becomes geographically isolated from the remainder, it may over time evolve characteristics different from the parent population. If the geographical barriers are later removed, members of the two populations may be unable to successfully mate with each other. At this point, the genetically isolated group may emerge as a new species. Allopatric isolation is a key factor in speciation and a common process by which new species arise. Adaptive radiation, as observed by Charles Darwin in Galapagos finches is a consequence of allopatric speciation among island populations.

Allopatric speciation is thought to be the dominant mode of speciation. Sympatric speciation represents an alternative method of speciation that does not require physical separation; instead speciation occurs within a population sharing the same geographic boundaries. For example, the development of polyploidy in plant species can lead to a new species arising within the geographic range of its parent population.

Allopatric speciation may occur when a species is subdivided into two genetically isolated populations. *Allopatric* and *allopatry* are terms from biogeography, referring to organisms whose ranges are entirely separate such that they do not occur in any one place together. If these organisms are closely related (e.g. sister species), such a distribution is usually the result of *allopatric speciation*. Separation may be attributed to either geological processes or population dispersal.

Geographical Isolation

Geological processes can fragment a population through such events as emergence of mountain ranges, canyon formation, glacial processes, formation/destruction of land bridges, or the subsidence of large bodies of water. On a global scale, plate tectonics is the major geological factor leading to separation of populations and the resulting distribution of species.

Approximately 50,000 years ago, the Death Valley region of the western United States had a rainy climate which produced an interconnecting system of freshwater rivers and lakes. Climatic changes resulted in a drying trend that has continued for the last 10,000 years. As the lakes and rivers shrank, fish populations became geologically isolated. The few remaining isolated springs are home to a variety of fish, many sharing a close common ancestor; yet each uniquely adapted to its own particular pool of water.

The extent to which a geological barrier can effectively isolate a population correlates to the mobility of the organism or its offspring. For example physical barriers such as canyons may effectively block migration and dispersal of small mammals; however, have little impact on flying birds or wind-borne seeds.

Population Dispersal

Population dispersal is used to describe migratory events, either in the form of range expansion (natural movement away from parents) or jump dispersal (crossing of barriers), which may lead to genetic isolation. If the smaller population fragment becomes genetically isolated from the parental group, they may be subjected to their own unique mutations, selection forces, and the effects of genetic drift; thus, follow their own evolutionary pathway. Migrations or accidental relocations (such as birds being blown off course) may lead to population fragments; merely separated by distance. Once gene flow between the two groups is disrupted, speciation becomes a possibility.

Allopatric Speciation in Peripheral Populations

When populations become genetically isolated, gene pools may accumulate differences from those of the parental population. This may lead to both genotypic and phenotypic differences and in time, the possibility exist that may become reproductively isolated.

Peripheral populations (portion of a population that exists along the edges of the parent population's geographic territory) are more likely to experience reproductive isolation for several reasons. *First*, the peripheral isolates are likely to possess genes that are different from the parental population, since such populations tend to represent the extreme genotypic composition. After isolation, the founding population is less likely to represent the gene pool of the parent population. *Second*, because the peripheral isolates are likely to represent a small number of individuals, they are more susceptible to genetic drift (random chance). *Finally*, it is likely that the peripheral population will inhabit an environment different from its ancestral gene pool; thus, it will likely be subjected to different selective pressures as it colonizes a new frontier. The outer periphery of a population's habitat tends to be extreme; hence, the reason range expansion is kept in check. For most peripheral isolates, it is more likely that they die off rather than survive and speciate.

Evolution

Evolution of reproductive isolation is generally thought to be an incidental by-product of genetic divergence of other traits, particularly adaptive changes that evolve through natural selection in response to different environmental conditions in separate geographic areas.

The Biological Species Concept, proposed by Ernst Mayr, in the 1942, emphasizes reproductive isolation as the basis of defining a species. The definition states: "A species is defined as a population or group of populations whose members have the potential to interbreed with one another in nature and to produce viable offspring, but cannot produce viable, fertile offspring with members of other species".

Mayr, a proponent of allopatric speciation, hypothesized that adaptive genetic changes that accumulate between allopatric populations cause negative epistasis in hybrids, resulting in sterility of the offspring. However, if it is of founder effects, or if the population becomes isolated in an environment which makes new demands upon it. Research has shown that this is a major reason why so many different species exist throughout the world.

If there is considerable genetic and phenotypic change without the loss of the capacity for interbreeding, then such hybridization is simply prevented by the geographical separation of populations. In this case the populations are normally regarded as subspecies.

The frequency of other types of speciation, such as sympatric speciation, parapatric speciation, and heteropatric speciation, is debated. Proponents of peripatric speciation contend that small population size in the peripheral isolate (sometimes referred to as a 'splinter population') increases genetic drift, which can be a more powerful force than natural selection in small populations, to deconstruct complex genotypes, allowing the creation of novel gene combinations. Both forms need not be mutually exclusive; in practice, passive isolation or fragmentation as well as active dispersal seem to play a role in many cases of speciation.

The African Elephant has always been regarded as a single species but, because of morphological and DNA differences, some scientists classify them into three subspecies. Researchers at the University of California, San Diego have argued that divergence due to geographical isolation has gone further, and the elephants of West Africa should be regarded as a separate species from both the savanna elephants of Central, Eastern and

Southern Africa, or the forest elephants of Central Africa. A similar situation exists with the Asian Elephant, which has four distinct living sub-species.

Other cases arise where two populations that are quite distinct morphologically, and are native to different continents, have been classified as different species; but when members of one species are introduced into the other's range, they are found to interbreed freely, showing that they were in fact only geographically isolated subspecies. This was found to be the case, for example, when the Mallard was introduced into New Zealand; it interbred freely with the native Grey Duck, which had been classified as a separate species. It is controversial whether its specific status can now be retained.

Founder Effect

In population genetics, the founder effect is the loss of genetic variation that occurs when a new population is established by a very small number of individuals from a larger population. It was first fully outlined by Ernst Mayr in 1952, using existing theoretical work by those such as Sewall Wright. As a result of the loss of genetic variation, the new population may be distinctively different, both genetically and phenotypically, from the parent population from which it is derived. In extreme cases, the founder effect is thought to lead to the speciation and subsequent evolution of new species.

The original population has nearly equal numbers of blue and red individuals. The three smaller founder populations show that one or the other colour may predominate (founder effect), due to random sampling of the original population. A population bottleneck may also cause a founder effect even though it is not strictly a new population.

The founder effect is a special case of genetic drift. In addition to founder effects, the new population is often a very small population and so shows increased sensitivity to genetic drift, an increase in inbreeding, and relatively low genetic variation. This can be observed in the limited gene pool of Iceland, Easter Islanders and those native to Pitcairn Island. Another example is the legendarily high deaf population of Martha's Vineyard, which resulted in the development of Martha's Vineyard Sign Language.

The founder effect is a special case of genetic drift, occurring when a small group in a population splinters off from the original population and forms a new one. The new colony may have less genetic variation than the original population, and through the random sampling of alleles during reproduction of subsequent generations, continue rapidly towards fixation. This consequence of inbreeding makes the colony more vulnerable to extinction.

When a newly formed colony is small, its founders can strongly affect the population's genetic make-up far into the future. In humans, which have a slow reproduction rate, the population will remain small for many generations, effectively amplifying the drift effect generation after generation until the population reaches a certain size. Alleles which were present but relatively rare in the original population can move to one of two extremes. The most common one is that the allele is soon lost altogether, but the other possibility is that the allele survives and within a few generations has become much more dispersed throughout the population. The new colony can experience an increase in the frequency of recessive alleles as well, and as a result, an increased number who are homozygous for certain recessive traits. A well documented example is found in the Amish migration to Pennsylvania in 1744. Two members of the new colony shared the recessive allele for Ellis-van Creveld syndrome. Members of the colony and their descendants tend to be religious isolates and remain relatively insular. As a result of many generations of inbreeding, Ellis-van Creveld syndrome is now much more prevalent among the Amish than in the general population.

The variation in gene frequency between the original population and colony may also trigger the two groups to diverge significantly over the course of many generations. As the variance, or genetic distance, increases, the two separated populations may become distinctively different, both genetically and phenotypically, although not only genetic drift but also natural selection, gene flow and mutation will all contribute to this divergence. This potential for relatively rapid changes in the colony's gene frequency led most scientists to consider the founder effect (and by extension, genetic drift) a significant driving force in the evolution of new species. Sewall Wright was the first to attach this significance to random drift and small, newly isolated populations with his shifting balance theory of speciation. Following behind Wright, Ernst Mayr created many persuasive models to show that the decline in genetic variation and small population size accompanying the founder effect were critically important for new species to develop. However there is much less support for this view today since the hypothesis has been tested repeatedly through experimental research and the results have been equivocal at best.

Serial Founder Effect

Serial founder effect have occurred when populations migrate over long distances. Such long distance migrations typically involve relatively rapid movements followed by periods of settlement. The populations in each migration carry only a subset of the genetic diversity carried from previous migrations. As a result, genetic differentiation tends to increase with geographic distance as described by the 'Isolation by distance' model. The migration of humans out of Africa is characterized by serial founder effects. Africa has the highest genetic diversity which is consistent with an African origin of modern humans. After the initial migration from Africa, the Indian subcontinent was the first major settling point for modern humans. Consequently, India has the second highest genetic diversity in the world. In general, the genetic diversity of the Indian continent is a subset of Africa, and the genetic diversity outside Africa is a subset of India.

Founder Effects in Island Ecology

Founder populations are essential to the study of island biogeography and island ecology. A natural 'blank slate' is not easily found, but a classic series of studies on founder population effects were done following the catastrophic 1883 eruption of Krakatoa, which erased all life on the island remnant. Another continuing study has been following the biocolonization of Surtsey, Iceland, a new volcanic island that erupted offshore between 1963 and 1967. An earlier event, the Toba eruption in Sumatra of about 73,000 YBP, covered some parts of India with 3-6 metres (9.8-20 ft) of ash, and must have coated the Nicobar Islands and Andaman Islands, much nearer in the ash fallout cone, with life-smothering layers, restarting their biodiversity from effectively zero.

Founder Effects in Human Populations

Due to various migrations throughout human history, founder effects are somewhat common among humans in different times and places. The effective founder population of Quebec was only 2,600. After twelve to sixteen generations, with an eightyfold growth but minimal gene dilution from intermarriage, Quebec has what geneticists call optimal linkage disequilibrium (genetic sharing). The result: far fewer genetic variations, including those that have been well studied because they are connected with inheritable diseases.

Founder effects can also occur naturally as competing genetic lines die out. This means that an effective founder population consists only of those whose genetic print is identifiable in subsequent populations. Because in sexual reproduction, genetic recombination ensures that with each generation, only half the genetic material of a parent is represented in the offspring, some genetic lines may die out entirely, even though there are numerous progeny. A recent study concluded that of the people migrating across the Bering land bridge at the close of the ice age, only 70 left their genetic print in modern descendants, a minute effective founder population — which is easily misread as though implying that only 70 people crossed to North America. The misinterpretations of 'Mitochondrial Eve' are a case in point: it may be hard to explain that a 'mitochondrial Eve' was not the only woman of her time.

In humans, founder effects can arise from cultural isolation, and inevitably, endogamy. For example, the Amish populations in the United States, which have grown from a very few founders, have not recruited newcomers, and tend to marry within the community, exhibit founder effects. Though still rare, phenomena such as polydactyly (extra fingers and toes, a symptom of Ellis-van Creveld syndrome) are more common in Amish communities than in the American population at large. Similarly there is a high frequency of fumarase deficiency among the 10,000 members of the Fundamentalist Church of Jesus Christ of Latter Day Saints community which practices both endogamy and polygyny, where it is estimated 75 to 80 per cent of the community are blood relatives of just two men — founders John Y. Barlow and Joseph Smith Jessop.

Another example is the frequency of total colour-blindness among the inhabitants of Pingelap, an island in Micronesia. In approximately 1775, a typhoon reduced the population of the island to only 20. Among survivors, one of them was heterozygous for achromatopsia. After few generations, the prevalence of achromatopsia is 5 per cent of population and 30 per cent as carriers (by comparison, in the United States, only 0.003 per cent of the population has complete achromatopsia.

More severe illnesses exist among certain Jewish groups. Ashkenazi Jews, for example, have a particularly high chance of suffering from Tay-Sachs disease, a fatal condition in young children.

Overpopulation

Overpopulation is a condition where an organism's numbers exceed the carrying capacity of its habitat. In common parlance, the term often refers to the relationship between the human population and its environment, the Earth. Steve Jones, head of the biology department at University College London, has said, "Humans are 10,000 times more common than we should be, according to the rules of the animal kingdom, and we have agriculture to thank for that. Without farming, the world population would probably have reached half a million by now." The world's population has significantly increased in the last 50 years, mainly due to medical advancements and substantial increases in agricultural productivity.

The recent rapid increase in human population over the past two centuries has raised concerns that humans are beginning to overpopulate the Earth, and that the planet may not be able to sustain present or larger numbers of inhabitants. The population has been growing continuously since the end of the Black Death, around the year 1400; at the beginning of the 19th century, it had reached roughly 1,000,000,000 (1 billion). Increases in life expectancy and resource availability during the industrial and green revolutions led to rapid population growth on a worldwide level. By 1960, the world population had reached 3 billion; it doubled to 6 billion over the next four decades. As of 2009, the estimated annual growth rate was 1.10 per cent, down from a peak of 2.2 per cent in 1963, and the world population stood at roughly 6.7 billion. Current projections show a steady decline in the population growth rate, with the population expected to reach between 8 and 10.5 billion between the year 2040 and 2050.

The scientific consensus is that the current population expansion and accompanying increase in usage of resources is linked to threats to the ecosystem. The InterAcademy Panel Statement on Population Growth, which was ratified by 58 member national academies in 1994, called the growth in human numbers "unprecedented", and stated that many environmental problems, such as rising levels of atmospheric carbon dioxide, global warming, and pollution, were aggravated by the population expansion. At the time, the world population stood at 5.5 billion, and optimistic scenarios predicted a peak of 7.8 billion by 2050, a number that current estimates show will be reached around 2030.

Overpopulation does not depend only on the size or density of the population, but on the ratio of population to available sustainable resources. It also depends on the way resources are used and distributed throughout the population. Overpopulation can result from an increase in births, a decline in mortality rates due to medical advances, from an increase in immigration, or from an unsustainable biome and depletion of resources. It is possible for very sparsely populated areas to be overpopulated, as the area in question may have a meager or non-existent capability to sustain human life (e.g. a desert).

The resources to be considered when evaluating whether an ecological niche is overpopulated include clean water, clean air, food, shelter, warmth, and other resources necessary to sustain life. If the quality of human life is addressed, there may be additional resources considered, such as medical care, education, proper sewage treatment and waste disposal. Overpopulation places competitive stress on the basic life sustaining resources, leading to a diminished quality of life.

History of Concern

Concern about overpopulation is relatively recent in origin. Throughout history, populations have grown slowly despite high birth rates, due to the population-reducing effects of war, plagues and high infant mortality. During the 750 years before the Industrial Revolution, the world's population hardly increased, remaining under 250 million.

By the beginning of the 19th century, the world population had grown to a billion individuals, and intellectuals such as Thomas Malthus and physiocratic economists predicted that mankind would outgrow its available resources, since a finite amount of land was incapable of supporting an endlessly increasing population. Mercantillists argued that a large population was a form of wealth, which made it possible to create bigger markets and armies.

History of Population Growth

The human population has gone through a number of periods of growth since the dawn of civilization in the Holocene period, around 10,000 BCE. The beginning of civilization coincides with the final receding of glacial ice following the end of the last glacial period. It is estimated that about 1,000,000 people, subsisting on hunting and foraging, inhabited the Earth in the period before the neolithic revolution, when human activity shifted away from hunter-gathering and towards very primitive farming.

Around 8,000 BCE, at the dawn of agriculture, the population of the world was approximately 5 million. The next several millennia saw minimal changes in the population, with a steady growth beginning in 1,000 BCE, plateauing (or alternatively, peaking) in 1 BCE, at between 200 and 300 million people.

Data from World Population

The Plague of Justinian caused Europe's population to drop by around 50 per cent between 541 and the 8th century. Steady growth resumed in 800 CE. This growth was disrupted by frequent plagues; most notably, the Black Death during the 14th century. the effects of the Black Death are thought to have reduced the world's population, then at an estimated 450 million, to between 350 and 375 million by 1400. The population of Europe stood at over 70 million in 1340; these levels did not return until 200 years later.

On the other side of the globe, China's population at the founding of the Ming dynasty in 1368 stood close to 60 million, approaching 150 million by the end of the dynasty in 1644.

England's population reached an estimated 5.6 million in 1650, up from an estimated 2.6 million in 1500. New crops that had come to Asia and Europe from the Americas via the Spanish colonizers in the 16th century contributed to the population growth.

Since being introduced by Portuguese traders in the 16th century, maize and manioc have replaced traditional African crops as the continent's most important staple food crops.

Alfred W. Crosby speculated that increased production of maize, manioc, and other American crops ". . . enabled the slave traders drew many, perhaps most, of their cargoes from the rain forest areas, *precisely* those areas where American crops enabled heavier settlement than before".

The population of the Americas in 1500 may have been between 50 and 100 million.

Encounters between European explorers and populations in the rest of the world often introduced local epidemics of extraordinary virulence. Archaeological evidence indicates that the death of around 90 per cent of the Native American population of the New World was caused by Old World diseases such as smallpox, measles, and influenza.

Over the centuries, the Europeans had developed high degrees of immunity to these diseases, while the indigenous peoples had no such immunity.

After the effects of the plagues had subsided during the 17th century, shortly before the Industrial Revolution, the world population began to grow once again. In parts of Asia, like China, the population doubled from 60 to 150 million under the Ming dynasty.

After the start of the Industrial Revolution, during the 18th century, the rate of population growth began to increase. By the end of the century, the world's population was estimated at just under 1 billion.

At the turn of the 20th century, the world's population was roughly 1.6 billion By 1940, this figure had increased to 2.3 billion.

Dramatic growth beginning in 1950 (above 1.8% per year) coincided with greatly increased food production as a result of the industrialisation of agriculture brought about by the Green Revolution. The rate of growth peaked in 1964, at about 2.2 per cent per year.

The world population is currently estimated to be 6,876,200,000, with unreported variability.

1900

- Africa — 133 million
- Asia — 946 million
- Europe — 408 million
- Latin America & Caribbean — 74 million
- North America — 82 million

Projections of Population Growth

According to projections, the world population will continue to grow until at least 2050, with the population reaching 9 billion in 2040, and some predictions putting the population in 2050 as high as 11 billion.

According to the United Nations' World Population Prospects report:

- The world population is currently growing by approximately 74 million people per year. Current United Nations predictions estimate that the world population will reach 9.0 billion around 2050, assuming a decrease in average fertility rate from 2.5 down to 2.0.
- Almost all growth will take place in the less developed regions, where today's 5.3 billion population of underdeveloped countries is expected to increase to 7.8 billion in 2050. By contrast, the population of the more developed regions will remain mostly unchanged, at 1.2 billion. An exception is the United States population, which is expected to increase 44 per cent from 305 million in 2008 to 439 million in 2050.
- In 2000-2005, the average world fertility was 2.65 children per woman, about half the level in 1950-1955 (5 children per woman). In the medium variant, global fertility is projected to decline further to 2.05 children per woman.
- During 2005-2050, nine countries are expected to account for half of the world's projected population increase: India, Pakistan, Nigeria, Democratic Republic of the Congo, Bangladesh, Uganda, United States, Ethiopia, and China, listed according to the size of their contribution to population growth. China would be higher still in this list were it not for its.

One Child Policy

Global life expectancy at birth, which is estimated to have risen from 46 years in 1950-1955 to 65 years in 2000-2005, is expected to keep rising to reach 75 years in 2045-2050. In the more developed regions, the projected increase is from 75 years today to 82 years by mid-century. Among the least developed countries, where life expectancy today is just under 50 years, it is expected to be 66 years in 2045-2050.

The population of 51 countries or areas, including Germany, Italy, Japan and most of the successor States of the former Soviet Union, is expected to be lower in 2050 than in 2005.

During 2005-2050, the net number of international migrants to more developed regions is projected to be 98 million. Because deaths are projected to exceed births in the more developed regions by 73 million during 2005-2050, population growth in those regions will largely be due to international migration.

In 2000-2005, net migration in 28 countries either prevented population decline or doubled at least the contribution of natural increase (births minus deaths) to population growth. These countries include Austria, Canada, Croatia, Denmark, Germany, Italy, Portugal, Qatar, Singapore, Spain, Sweden, United Arab Emirates and United Kingdom.

Birth rates are now falling in a small percentage of developing countries, while the actual populations in many developed countries would fall without immigration.

By 2050 (Medium variant), India will have 1.6 billion people, China 1.4 billion, United States 439 million, Pakistan 309 million, Indonesia 280 million, Nigeria 259 million, Bangladesh 258 million, Brazil 245 million, Democratic Republic of the Congo 189 million, Ethiopia 185 million, Philippines 141 million, Mexico 132 million, Egypt 125 million, Vietnam 120 million, Russia 109 million, Japan 103 million, Iran 100 million, Turkey 99 million, Uganda 93 million, Tanzania 85 million, Kenya 85 million and United Kingdom 80 million.

2050

- Africa — 1.9 billion
- Asia — 5.2 billion
- Europe — 674 million
- Latin America & Caribbean — 765 million
- North America — 448 million

Demographic Transition

The theory of demographic transition held that, after the standard of living and life expectancy increase, family sizes and birth rates decline. However, as new data has become available, it has been observed that after a certain level of development the fertility increases again. This means that both the worry the theory generated about aging populations and the complacency it bred regarding the future environmental impact of population growth are misguided.

Factors cited in the old theory included such social factors as later ages of marriage, the growing desire of many women in such settings to seek careers outside child rearing and domestic work, and the decreased need of children in industrialized settings. The latter factor stems from the fact that children perform a great deal of work in small-scale agricultural societies, and work less in industrial ones; it has been cited to explain the decline in birth rates in industrializing regions.

Another version of demographic transition is proposed by anthropologist Virginia Abernethy in her book *Population Politics*, where she claims that the demographic transition occurs primarily in nations where women enjoy a special status. In strongly patriarchal nations, where she claims women enjoy few special rights, a high standard of living tends to result in population growth.

Many countries have high population growth rates but lower total fertility rates because high population growth in the past skewed the age demographic toward a young age, so the population still rises as the more numerous younger generation approaches maturity.

'Demographic entrapment' is a concept developed by Maurice King, Honorary Research Fellow at the University of Leeds, who posits that this phenomenon occurs when a country has a population larger than its carrying capacity, no possibility of migration, and exports too little to be able to import food. This will cause starvation. He claims that for example many sub-Saharan nations are or will become stuck in demographic entrapment, instead of having a demographic transition.

There is wide variability both in the definition and in the proposed size of the Earth's carrying capacity, with estimates ranging from less than 1 to 1000 billion (1 trillion). Around two-thirds of the estimates fall in the range of 4 billion to 16 billion (with unspecified standard errors), with a median of about 10 billion.

In a study titled *Food, Land, Population and the U.S. Economy*, David Pimentel, professor of ecology and agriculture at Cornell University, and Mario Giampietro, senior researcher at the US National Research Institute on Food and Nutrition (INRAN), estimate the maximum U.S. population for a sustainable economy at 200 million. According to this theory, in order to achieve a sustainable economy and avert disaster, the United States would have to reduce its population by at least one-third, and world population would have to be reduced by two-thirds.

Some groups (for example, the World Wide Fund for Nature and Global Footprint Network) have stated that the carrying capacity for the human population has been exceeded as measured using the Ecological Footprint. In 2006, WWF's 'Living Planet Report' stated that in order for all humans to live with the current consumption patterns of Europeans, we would be spending three times more than what the planet can renew. Humanity as a whole was using, by 2006, 40 per cent more than what Earth can regenerate.

But critics question the simplifications and statistical methods used in calculating Ecological Footprints. Therefore Global Footprint Network and its partner organizations have engaged with national governments and international agencies to test the results — reviews have been produced by France, Germany, the European Commission, Switzerland, Luxembourg, Japan and the United Arab Emirates. Some point out that a more refined method of assessing Ecological Footprint is to designate sustainable versus non-sustainable categories of consumption. However, if yield estimates were adjusted for sustainable levels of production, the yield figures would be lower, and hence the overshoot estimated by the Ecological Footprint method even higher.

David Pimentel, Professor Emeritus at Cornell University, has stated that "With the imbalance growing between population numbers and vital life sustaining resources, humans must actively conserve cropland, freshwater, energy, and biological resources. There is a need to develop renewable energy resources. Humans everywhere must understand that rapid population growth damages the Earth's resources and diminishes human well-being".

These reflect the comments also of the United States Geological Survey in their paper The Future of Planet Earth: Scientific Challenges in the Coming Century. "As the global population continues to grow . . . people will place greater and greater demands on the resources of our planet, including mineral and energy resources, open space, water, and plant and animal resources." "Earth's natural wealth: an audit" by *New Scientist* magazine states that many of the minerals that we use for a variety of products are in danger of running out in the near future. A handful of geologists around the world have calculated the costs of new technologies in terms of the materials they use and the implications of their spreading to the developing world. All agree that the planet's booming population and rising standards of living are set to put unprecedented demands on the materials that only Earth itself can provide . Limitations on how much of these materials is available could even mean that some technologies are not worth pursuing long term. . . . "Virgin stocks of several metals appear inadequate to sustain the modern 'developed world' quality of life for all of Earth's people under contemporary technology".

On the other hand, some researchers, such as Julian Simon and Bjorn Lomborg believe that resources exist for further population growth. However, critics warn, this will be at a high cost to the Earth: "the technological optimists are probably correct in claiming that overall world food production can be increased substantially over the next few decades...[however] the environmental cost of what Paul R. and Anne H. Ehrlich describe as 'turning the Earth into a giant human feedlot' could be severe. A large expansion of agriculture to provide growing populations with improved diets is likely to lead to further deforestation, loss of species, soil erosion, and pollution from pesticides and fertilizer runoff as farming intensifies and new land is brought into production". Since we are intimately dependent upon the living systems of the Earth, some scientists have questioned the wisdom of further expansion.

According to the Millennium Ecosystem Assessment, a four-year research effort by 1,360 of the world's leading scientists commissioned to measure the actual value of natural resources to humans and the world, "The structure of the world's ecosystems changed more rapidly in the second half of the twentieth century than at any time in recorded human history, and virtually all of Earth's ecosystems have now been significantly transformed through human actions." "Ecosystem services, particularly food production, timber and fisheries, are important for employment and economic activity. Intensive use of ecosystems often produces the greatest short-term advantage, but excessive and unsustainable use can lead to losses in the long term. A country could cut its forests and deplete its fisheries, and this would show only as a positive gain to GDP, despite the loss of capital assets. If the full economic value of ecosystems were taken into account in decision-making, their degradation could be significantly slowed down or even reversed".

Another study by the United Nations Environment Programme (UNEP) called the Global Environment Outlook which involved 1,400 scientists and took five years to prepare comes to similar conclusions. It "found that human consumption had far outstripped available resources. Each person on Earth now requires a third more land to supply his or her needs than the planet can supply." It faults a failure to "respond to or recognise the magnitude of the challenges facing the people and the environment of the planet . . . 'The systematic destruction of the Earth's natural and nature-based resources has reached a point where the economic viability of economies is being challenged — and where the bill we hand to our children may prove impossible to pay' . . . The report's authors say its objective is 'not to present a dark and gloomy scenario, but an urgent call to action'. It warns that tackling the problems may affect the vested interests of powerful groups, and that the environment must be moved to the core of decision-making.

Although all resources, whether mineral or other, are limited on the planet, there is a degree of self-correction whenever a scarcity or high-demand for a particular kind is experienced. For example in 1990 known reserves of many natural resources were higher, and their prices lower, than in 1970, despite higher demand and higher consumption. Whenever a price spike would occur, the market tended to correct itself whether by substituting an equivalent resource or switching to a new technology.

Fresh Water

Fresh water supplies, on which agriculture depends, are running low worldwide. This water crisis is only expected to worsen as the population increases. Lester R. Brown of the Earth Policy Institute argues that declining water supplies will have future disastrous consequences for agriculture.

Potential problems with dependence on desalination are reviewed below, however, the majority of the world's freshwater supply is contained in the polar icecaps, and underground river systems accessible through springs and wells.

Fresh water can be obtained from salt water by desalination. For example, Malta derives two thirds of its freshwater by desalination. A number of nuclear powered desalination plants exist; these could continuously provide drinking water with few limitations, if the development of breeder reactors results in nuclear fuel becoming a renewable resource. However, the high costs of desalination, especially for poor countries, make impractical the transport of large amounts of desalinated seawater to interiors of large countries. The cost of desalinization varies; Israel is now desalinating water for a cost of 53 cents per cubic metre, Singapore at 49 cents per cubic metre. In the United States, the cost is 81 cents per cubic metre.

According to a 2004 study by Zhoua and Tolb, "one needs to lift the water by 2000 m, or transport it over more than 1600 km to get transport costs equal to the desalination costs. Desalinated water is expensive in places that are both somewhat far from the sea and somewhat high, such as Riyadh and Harare. In other places, the dominant cost is desalination, not transport. This leads to somewhat lower costs in places like Beijing, Bangkok, Zaragoza, Phoenix, and, of course, coastal cities like Tripoli." Thus while the study is generally positive about the technology for affluent areas that are proximate to oceans, it concludes that "Desalinated water may be a solution for some water-stress regions, but not for places that are poor, deep in the interior of a continent, or at high elevation. Unfortunately, that includes some of the places with biggest water problems." Another potential problem with desalination is the byproduction of saline brine, which can be a major cause of marine pollution when dumped back into the oceans at high temperatures".

The world's largest desalination plant is the Jebel Ali Desalination Plant (Phase 2) in the United Arab Emirates, which can produce 300 million cubic metres of water per year, or about 2500 gallons per second. The largest desalination plant in the US is the one at Tampa Bay, Florida, which began desalinizing 25 million gallons (95000 m^3) of water per day in December 2007. A January 17, 2008, article in the *Wall Street Journal* states, "Worldwide, 13,080 desalination plants produce more than 12 billion gallons of water a day, according to the International Desalination Association." After being desalinized at Jubail, Saudi Arabia, water is pumped 200 miles (320 km) inland though a pipeline to the capital city of Riyadh.

Food

Studies agree that there is enough food to support the world population, but critics dispute this, particularly if sustainability is taken into account.

More than 100 countries now import wheat and 40 countries import rice. Egypt and Iran rely on imports for 40 per cent of their grain supply. Algeria, Japan, South Korea and Taiwan import 70 per cent or more. Yemen and Israel import more than 90 per cent. And just 6 countries — Argentina, Australia, Canada, France, Thailand and the USA — supply 90 per cent of grain exports. In recent decades the US alone supplied almost half of world grain exports.

A 2001 United Nations report says population growth is "the main force driving increases in agricultural demand" but "most recent expert assessments are cautiously optimistic about the ability of global food production to keep up with demand for the foreseeable future (that is to say, until approximately 2030 or 2050)", assuming declining population growth rates.

However, the observed figures for 2007 show an actual increase in absolute numbers of undernourished people in the world, 923 million in 2007 versus 832 million in 1995.; the more recent FAO estimates point out to an even more dramatic increase, to 1.02 billion in 2009.

Global Perspective

The amounts of natural resources in this context are not necessarily fixed, and their distribution is not necessarily a zero-sum game. For example, due to the Green Revolution and the fact that more and more land is appropriated each year from wild lands for agricultural purposes, the worldwide production of food had steadily increased up until 1995. World food production per person was considerably higher in 2005 than 1961.

As world population doubled from 3 billion to 6 billion, daily Calorie consumption in poor countries increased from 1,932 to 2,650, and the percentage of people in those countries who were malnourished fell from 45 per cent to 18 per cent. This suggests that Third World poverty and famine are caused by underdevelopment, not overpopulation. However, others question these statistics. From 1950 to 1984, as the Green Revolution transformed agriculture around the world, grain production increased by over 250 per cent. The world population has grown by about four billion since the beginning of the Green Revolution and most believe that, without the Revolution, there would be greater famine and malnutrition than the UN presently documents.

The number of people who are overweight has surpassed the number who are undernourished. In a 2006 news story, MSNBC reported, "There are an estimated 800 million undernourished people and more than a billion considered overweight worldwide." The U.S. has one of the highest rates of obesity in the world.

The Food and Agriculture Organization of the United Nations states in its report *The State of Food Insecurity in the World 2006*, that while the number of undernourished people in the developing countries has declined by about three million, a smaller proportion of the populations of developing countries is undernourished today than in 1990-92: 17 per cent against 20 per cent. Furthermore, FAO's projections suggest that the proportion of hungry people in developing countries could be halved from 1990-92 levels to 10 per cent by 2015. The FAO also states "We have emphasized first and foremost that reducing hunger is no longer a question of means in the hands of the global community. The world is richer today than it was ten years ago. There is more food available and still more could be produced without excessive upward pressure on prices. The knowledge and resources to reduce hunger are there. What is lacking is sufficient political will to mobilize those resources to the benefit of the hungry".

As of 2008, the price of grain has increased due to more farming used in biofuels, world oil prices at over $100 a barrel, global population growth, climate change, loss of agricultural land to residential and industrial development, and growing consumer demand in China and India Food riots have recently taken place in many countries across the world. An epidemic of stem rust on wheat caused by race *Ug*99 is currently spreading across Africa and into Asia and is causing major concern. A virulent wheat disease could destroy most of the world's main wheat crops, leaving millions to starve. The fungus has spread from Africa to Iran, and may already be in Afghanistan and Pakistan.

It is becoming increasingly difficult to maintain food security in a world beset by a confluence of 'peak' phenomena, namely peak oil, peak water, peak phosphorus, peak grain and peak fish. Growing populations, falling energy sources and food shortages will create the 'perfect storm' by 2030, according to the UK government chief scientist. He said food reserves are at a 50-year low but the world requires 50 per cent more energy, food and water by 2030. The world will have to produce 70 per cent more food by 2050 to feed a projected extra 2.3 billion people, the United Nations' Food and Agriculture Organisation (FAO) warned.

The World Resources Institute states that "Agricultural conversion to croplands and managed pastures has affected some 3.3 billion [hectares] — roughly 26 per cent of the land area. All totalled, agriculture has displaced one-third of temperate and tropical forests and one-quarter of natural grasslands". 40 per cent of the land area is under conversion and fragmented; less than one quarter, primarily in the Arctic and the deserts, remains intact. Usable land may become less useful through salinization, deforestation, desertification, erosion, and urban sprawl. Global warming may cause flooding of many of the most productive agricultural areas. The development of energy sources may also require large areas, for example, the building of hydroelectric dams. Thus, available useful land may become a limiting factor. By most estimates, at least half of cultivable land is already being farmed, and there are concerns that the remaining reserves are greatly overestimated.

High crop yield vegetables like potatoes and lettuce use less space on inedible plant parts, like stalks, husks, vines, and inedible leaves. New varieties of selectively bred and hybrid plants have larger edible parts (fruit, vegetable, grain) and smaller inedible parts; however, many of the gains of agricultural technology are now historic, and new advances are more difficult to achieve. With new technologies, it is possible to grow crops on some marginal land under certain conditions. Aquaculture could theoretically increase available area. Hydroponics and food from bacteria and fungi, like quorn, may allow the growing of food without having to consider land quality, climate, or even available sunlight, although such a process may be very energy-intensive. Some argue that not all arable land will remain productive if used for agriculture because some marginal land can only be made to produce food by unsustainable practices like slash-and-burn agriculture. Even with the modern techniques of agriculture, the sustainability of production is in question.

Some countries, such as the United Arab Emirates and particularly the Emirate of Dubai have constructed large artificial islands, or have created large dam and dike systems, like the Netherlands, which reclaim land from the sea to increase their total land area. Some scientists have said that in the future, densely populated cities will use vertical farming to grow food inside skyscrapers. The notion that space is limited has been decried by skeptics, who point out that the Earth's population of roughly 6.8 billion people could comfortably inhabit an area comparable in size to the state of Texas, in the United States (about 269,000 square miles or 696,707 km^2). However, the impact of humanity extends over a far greater area than that required simply for habitation.

11 Adaptation

Adaptation is the evolutionary process whereby a population becomes better suited to its habitat. This process takes place over many generations, and is one of the basic phenomena of biology.

The term *adaptation* may also refer to a feature which is especially important for an organism's survival. For example, the adaptation of horses' teeth to the grinding of grass, or their ability to run fast and escape predators. Such adaptations are produced in a variable population by the better suited forms reproducing more successfully, that is, by natural selection.

Adaptation is, first of all, a *process*, rather than a physical part of a body. The distinction may be seen in an internal parasite (such as a fluke), where the bodily structure is greatly simplified, but nevertheless the organism is highly adapted to its unusual environment. From this we see that adaptation is not just a matter of visible traits: in such parasites critical adaptations take place in the life-cycle, which is often quite complex. However, as a practical term, adaptation is often used for the *product*: those features of a species which result from the process. Many aspects of an animal or plant can be correctly called adaptations, though there are always some features whose function is in doubt. By using the term *adaptation* for the evolutionary *process*, and *adaptive trait* for the bodily part or function (the product), the two senses of the word may be distinguished.

Adaptation is one of the two main processes that explain the diverse species we see in biology, such as the different species of Darwin's finches.

The other is speciation (species-splitting or cladogenesis), caused by geographical isolation or some other mechanism. A favourite example used today to study the interplay of adaptation and speciation is the evolution of cichlid fish in African lakes, where the question of reproductive isolation is much more complex.

Adaptation is not always a simple matter, where the ideal phenotype evolves for a given external environment. An organism must be viable at all stages of its development and at all stages of its evolution. This places *constraints* on the evolution of development, behaviour and structure of organisms. The main constraint, over which there has been much debate, is the requirement that each genetic and phenotypic change during evolution should be relatively small, because developmental systems are so complex and interlinked. However, it is not clear what 'relatively small' should mean, for example polyploidy in plants is a reasonably common large genetic change. The origin of the symbiosis of multiple micro-organisms to form a eukaryota is a more exotic example.

All adaptations help organisms survive in their ecological niches. These adaptive traits may be structural, behavioural or physiological. Structural adaptations are physical features of an organism (shape, body covering, armament; and also the internal organization). Behavioural adaptations are composed of inherited behaviour chains and/or the ability to learn: behaviours may be inherited in detail (instincts), or a tendency for learning may be inherited (see neuropsychology). Examples: searching for food, mating, vocalizations. Physiological adaptations permit the organism to perform special functions (for instance, making venom, secreting slime, phototropism); but also more general functions such as growth and development, temperature regulation, ionic balance and other aspects of homeostasis. Adaptation, then, affects all aspects of the life of an organism.

Definitions

The following definitions are mainly due to Theodosius Dobzhansky:

1. *Adaptation* is the evolutionary process whereby an organism becomes better able to live in its habitat or habitats.
2. *Adaptedness* is the state of being adapted: the degree to which an organism is able to live and reproduce in a given set of habitats.
3. An *adaptive trait* is an aspect of the developmental pattern of the organism which enables or enhances the probability of that organism surviving and reproducing.

Adaptedness and Fitness

From the above definitions, it is clear that there is a relationship between adaptedness and *fitness* (a key population genetics concept).

Differences in fitness between genotypes predict the rate of evolution by natural selection. Natural selection changes the relative frequencies of alternative phenotypes, insofar as they are heritable. Although the two are connected, the one does not imply the other: a phenotype with high adaptedness may not have high fitness. Dobzhansky mentioned the example of the Californian redwood, which is highly adapted, but a relic species in danger of extinction. Elliott Sober commented that adaptation was a retrospective concept since it implied something about the history of a trait, whereas fitness predicts a trait's future.

1. ***Relative fitness:*** The average contribution to the next generation by a phenotype or a class of phenotypes, relative to the contributions of other phenotypes in the population. This is also known as *Darwinian fitness*, *selective coefficient*, and other terms.
2. ***Absolute fitness:*** The absolute contribution to the next generation by a phenotype or a class of phenotypes. Also known as the Malthusian parameter when applied to the population as a whole.
3. ***Adaptedness:*** The extent to which a phenotype fits its local ecological niche. This can sometimes be tested through a reciprocal transplant experiment.

Adaptation as a fact of life has been accepted by all the great thinkers who have tackled the world of living organisms. It is their explanations of how adaptation arises that separates these thinkers. A few of the most significant ideas:

- Empedocles did not believe that adaptation required a final cause (~ purpose), but "came about naturally, since such things survived". Aristotle, however, did believe in final causes.
- In natural theology, adaptation was interpreted as the work of a deity, even as evidence for the existence of God. William Paley believed that organisms were perfectly adapted to the lives they lead, an argument that shadowed Leibniz, who had argued that God had brought about the best of all possible worlds. Voltaire's Dr Pangloss is a parody of this optimistic idea, and Hume also argued against design. The *Bridgewater Treatises* are a product of natural theology, though some of the authors managed to present their work in a fairly neutral manner. The series was lampooned by Robert Knox, who held quasi-evolutionary views, as the *Bilgewater Treatises*. Darwin broke with the tradition by emphasising the flaws and limitations which occurred in the animal and plant worlds.

Lamarck

Lamarck. His is a proto-evolutionary theory of the inheritance of acquired traits, whose main purpose is to explain adaptations by natural means. He proposed a tendency for organisms to become more complex, moving up a ladder of progress, plus "the influence of circumstances", usually expressed as *use and disuse*. His evolutionary ideas, and those of Geoffroy, fail because they cannot be reconciled with heredity. This was known even before Mendel by medical men interested in human races (Wells Lawrence), and especially by Weismann.

Many other students of natural history, such as Buffon, accepted adaptation, and some also accepted evolution, without voicing their opinions as to the mechanism. This illustrates the real merit of Darwin and Wallace, and secondary figures such as Bates, for putting forward a mechanism whose significance had only been glimpsed previously. A century later, experimental field studies and breeding experiments by such as Ford and Dobzhansky produced evidence that natural selection was not only the 'engine' behind adaptation, but was a much stronger force than had previously been thought.

Changes in Habitat

Before Darwin, adaptation was seen as a fixed relationship between an organism and its habitat. It was not appreciated that as the climate changed, so did the habitat; and as the habitat changed, so did the biota. Also, habitats are subject to changes in their biota: for example, invasions of species from other areas. The relative numbers of species in a given habitat are always changing. Change is the rule, though much depends on the speed and degree of the change.

When the habitat changes, three main things may happen to a resident population: habitat tracking, genetic change or extinction. In fact, all three things may occur in sequence. *Of these three effects, only genetic change brings about adaptation*.

Habitat Tracking

When a habitat changes, the most common thing to happen is that the resident population moves to another locale which suits it; this is the typical response of flying insects or oceanic organisms, who have wide (though not unlimited) opportunity for movement. This common response is called *habitat tracking*. It is one explanation put forward for the periods of apparent stasis in the fossil record (the punctuated equilibrium thesis).

Genetic Change

Genetic change is what occurs in a population when natural selection acts on the genetic variability of the population. By this means, the population adapts genetically to its circumstances. Genetic changes may result in visible structures, or may adjust physiological activity in a way that suits the changed habitat.

It is now clear that habitats and biota do frequently change. Therefore, it follows that the process of adaptation is never finally complete. Over time, it may happen that the environment changes little, and the species comes to fit its surroundings better and better. On the other hand, it may happen that changes in the environment occur relatively rapidly, and then the species becomes less and less well adapted. Seen like this, adaptation is a genetic *tracking process*, which goes on all the time to some extent, but especially when the population cannot or does not move to another, less hostile area. Also, to a greater or lesser extent, the process affects every species in a particular ecosystem.

Van Valen thought that even in a stable environment, competing species had to constantly adapt to maintain their relative standing. This became known as the Red Queen hypothesis.

Intimate Relationships: Co-adaptations

In co-evolution, where the existence of one species is tightly bound up with the life of another species, new or 'improved' adaptations which occur in one species are often followed by the appearance and spread of corresponding features in the other species. There are many examples of this; the idea emphasises that the life and death of living things is intimately connected, not just with the physical environment, but with the life of other species. These relationships are intrinsically dynamic, and may continue on a trajectory for millions of years, as has the relationship between flowering plants and insects (pollination).

Henry Walter Bates' work on Amazonian butterflies led him to develop the first scientific account of mimicry, especially the kind of mimicry which bears his name: Batesian mimicry. This is the mimicry by a palatable species of an unpalatable or noxious species. A common example seen in temperate gardens is the hover-fly, many of which — though bearing no sting — mimic the warning colouration of hymenoptera (wasps and bees). Such mimicry does not need to be perfect to improve the survival of the palatable species.

Bates, Wallace and Müller believed that Batesian and Müllerian mimicry provided evidence for the action of natural selection, a view which is now standard amongst biologists. All aspects of this situation can be, and have been, the subject of research. Field and experimental work on these ideas continues to this day; the topic connects strongly to speciation, genetics and development.

The Basic Machinery: Internal Adaptations

There are some important adaptations to do with the overall coordination of the systems in the body. Such adaptations may have significant consequences. Examples, in vertebrates, would be temperature regulation, or improvements in brain function, or an effective immune system. An example in plants would be the development of the reproductive system in flowering plants. Such adaptations may make the clade (monophyletic group) more viable in a wide range of habitats. The acquisition of such major adaptations has often served as the spark for adaptive radiation, and huge success for long periods of time for a whole group of animals or plants.

Compromise and Conflict Between Adaptations

> It is a profound truth that Nature does not know best; that genetical evolution . . . is a story of waste, makeshift, compromise and blunder.
>
> —***Peter Medawar***

All adaptations have a downside: horse legs are great for running on grass, but they can't scratch their backs; mammals' hair helps temperature, but offers a niche for ectoparasites; the only flying penguins do is under water. Adaptations serving different functions may be mutually destructive. Compromise and make-shift occur widely, not perfection. Selection pressures pull in different directions, and the adaptation that results is some kind of compromise.

> Since the phenotype as a whole is the target of selection, it is impossible to improve simultaneously all aspects of the phenotype to the same degree.
>
> —***Ernst Mayr***

Consider the antlers of the Irish elk, (often supposed to be far too large; in deer antler size has an allometric relationship to body size). Obviously antlers serve positively for defence against predators, and to score victories in the annual rut. But they are costly in terms of resource. Their size during the last glacial period presumably depended on the relative gain and loss of reproductive capacity in the population of elks during that time. Another example: camouflage to avoid detection is destroyed when vivid colours are displayed at mating time. Here the risk to life is counterbalanced by the necessity for reproduction.

The peacock's ornamental train (grown anew in time for each mating season) is a famous adaptation. It must reduce his manoeuverability and flight, and is hugely conspicuous; also, its growth costs food resources. Darwin's explanation of its advantage was in terms of sexual selection: "it depends on the advantage which certain individuals have over other individuals of the same sex and species, in exclusive relation to reproduction." The kind of sexual selection represented by the peacock is called 'mate choice', with an implication that the process selects the more fit over the less fit, and so has survival value. The recognition of sexual selection was for a long time in abeyance, but has been rehabilitated. In practice, the blue peafowl *Pavo cristatus* is a pretty successful species, with a big natural range in India, so the overall outcome of their mating system is quite viable.

The conflict between the size of the human foetal brain at birth, (which cannot be larger than about 400ccs, else it will not get through the mother's pelvis) and the size needed for an adult brain (about 1400ccs), means the brain of a newborn child is quite immature. The most vital things in human life (locomotion, speech) just have to wait while the brain grows and matures. That is the result of the birth compromise. Much of the problem comes from our upright bipedal stance, without which our pelvis could be shaped more suitably for birth. Neanderthals had a similar problem.

Pre-adaptations

This occurs when a species or population has characteristics which (by chance) are suited for conditions which have not yet arisen. For example, the polyploid rice-grass *Spartina townsendii* is better adapted than either of its parent species to their own habitat of saline marsh and mud-flats. White Leghorn fowl are markedly more resistant to vitamin B deficiency than other breeds. On a plentiful diet there is no difference, but on a restricted diet this preadaptation could be decisive.

Pre-adaptation may occur because a natural population carries a huge quantity of genetic variability. In diploid eukaryotes, this is a consequence of the system of sexual reproduction, where mutant alleles get partially shielded, for example, by the selective advantage of heterozygotes. Micro-organisms, with their huge populations, also carry a great deal of genetic variability.

The first experimental evidence of the pre-adaptive nature of genetic variants in micro-organisms was provided by Salvador Luria and Max Delbrück who developed fluctuation analysis, a method to show the random fluctuation of pre-existing genetic changes that conferred resistance to phage in the bacterium *Escherichia coli*.

Co-option of Existing Traits: Exaptation

The classic example is the ear ossicles of mammals, which we know from palaeontological and embrological studies originated in the upper and lower jaws and the hyoid of their Synapsid ancestors, and further back still were part of the gill arches of early fish. We owe this esoteric knowledge to the comparative anatomists, who, a century ago, were at the cutting edge of evolutionary studies. The word *exaptation* was coined to cover these shifts in function, which are surprisingly common in evolutionary history. The origin of wings from feathers that were originally used for temperature regulation is a more recent discovery.

Non-adaptive Traits

Some traits do not appear to be adaptive, that is, they appear to have a neutral or even deleterious effect on fitness in the current environment. Because genes have pleiotropic effects, not all traits may be functional (i.e. spandrels). Alternatively, a trait may have been adaptive at some point in an organism's evolutionary history, but a change in habitats caused what used to be an adaptation to become unnecessary or even a hindrance (maladaptations). Such adaptations are termed vestigial.

Vestigial Organs

Many organisms have vestigial organs, which are the remnants of fully functional structures in their ancestors. As a result of changes in lifestyle the organs became redundant, and are either not functional or reduced in functionality. With the loss of function goes the loss of positive selection, and the subsequent accumulation of deleterious mutations. Since any structure represents some kind of cost to the general economy of the body, an advantage may accrue from their elimination once they are not functional. Examples: wisdom teeth in humans; the loss of pigment and functional eyes in cave fauna; the loss of structure in endoparasites.

Fitness Landscapes

Sewall Wright proposed that populations occupy *adaptive peaks* on a fitness landscape. In order to evolve to another, higher peak, a population would first have to pass through a valley of maladaptive intermediate stages. A given population might be "trapped" on a peak that is not optimally adapted.

Extinction

If a population cannot move or change sufficiently to preserve its long-term viability, then obviously, it will become extinct, at least in that locale. The species may or may not survive in other locales. Species extinction occurs when the death rate over the entire species (population, gene pool . . .) exceeds the birth rate for a long enough period for the species to disappear. It was an observation of Van Valen that groups of species tend to have a characteristic and fairly regular rate of extinction.

Co-extinction

Just as we have co-adaptation, there is also co-extinction. Co-extinction refers to the loss of a species due to the extinction of another;

for example, the extinction of parasitic insects following the loss of their hosts. Co-extinction can also occur when a flowering plant loses its pollinator, or through the disruption of a food chain. "Species co-extinction is a manifestation of the interconnectedness of organisms in complex ecosystems ... While co-extinction may not be the most important cause of species extinctions, it is certainly an insidious one".

Flexibility, Acclimatization, Learning

Flexibility deals with the relative capacity of an organism to maintain themselves in different habitats: their degree of specialization. *Acclimatization* is a term used for automatic physiological adjustments during life; *learning* is the term used for improvement in behavioural performance during life. In biology these terms are preferred, not adaptation, for changes during life which improve the performance of individuals. These adjustments are not inherited genetically by the next generation.

Adaptation, on the other hand, occurs over many generations; it is a gradual process caused by natural selection which changes the genetic make-up of a population so the collective performs better in its niche.

Flexibility

Populations differ in their phenotypic plasticity, which is the ability of an organism with a given genotype to change its phenotype in response to changes in its habitat, or to its move to a different habitat.

To a greater or lesser extent, all living things can adjust to circumstances. The degree of flexibility is inherited, and varies to some extent between individuals. A highly specialized animal or plant lives only in a well-defined habitat, eats a specific type of food, and cannot survive if its needs are not met. Many herbivores are like this; extreme examples are koalas which depend on eucalyptus, and pandas which require bamboo. A generalist, on the other hand, eats a range of food, and can survive in many different conditions. Examples are humans, rats, crabs and many carnivores. The *tendency* to behave in a specialized or exploratory manner is inherited — it is an adaptation.

Rather different is *developmental flexibility:* "An animal or plant is developmentally flexible if when it is raised or transferred to new conditions it develops so that it is better fitted to survive in the new circumstances". Once again, there are huge differences between species, and the *capacities* to be flexible are inherited.

Acclimatization

If humans move to a higher altitude, respiration and physical exertion become a problem, but after spending time in high altitude conditions they *acclimatize* to the pressure by increasing production of red blood corpuscles. The *ability* to acclimatize is an adaptation, but not the acclimatization itself. Fecundity goes down, but deaths from some tropical diseases also goes down.

Over a longer period of time, some people will reproduce better at these high altitudes than others. They will contribute more heavily to later generations. Gradually the whole population becomes adapted to the new conditions. This we know takes place, because the performance of long-term communities at higher altitude is significantly better than the performance of new arrivals, even when the new arrivals have had time to make physiological adjustments.

Some kinds of acclimatization happen so rapidly that they are better called reflexes. The rapid colour changes in some flatfish, cephalopods, chameleons are examples.

Learning

Social learning is supreme for humans, and is possible for quite a few mammals and birds: of course, that does not involve genetic transmission except to the extent that the capacities are inherited. Similarly, the *capacity to learn* is an inherited adaptation, but not what is learnt; the capacity for human speech is inherited, but not the details of language.

Function

To say something has a function is to say something about what it does for the organism, obviously. It also says something about its history: how it has come about. A heart pumps blood: that is its function. It also emits sound, which is just an ancillary side-effect. That is not its function. The heart has a history (which may be well or poorly understood), and that history is about how natural selection formed and maintained the heart as a pump. Every aspect of an organism that has a function has a history. Now, an adaptation must have a functional history: therefore we expect it must have undergone selection caused by relative survival in its habitat. It would be quite wrong to use the word adaptation about a trait which arose as a by-product.

It is widely regarded as unprofessional for a biologist to say something like 'A wing is for flying', although that is their normal function. A biologist would be conscious that sometime in the remote past feathers on a small dinosaur had the function of retaining heat, and that later many wings were not used for flying (e.g. penguins, ostriches). So, the biologist would rather say that the wings on a bird or an insect usually had the *function* of aiding flight. That would carry the connotation of being an adaptation with a history of evolution by natural selection.

Teleonomy

'Teleonomy' is a term invented to describe the study of goal-directed functions which are not guided by the conscious forethought of man or any supernatural entity. It is contrasted with Aristotle's teleology, which has connotations of intention, purpose and foresight. Evolution is teleonomic; *adaptation hoards hindsight rather than foresight*. The following is a definition for its use in biology:

- *Teleonomy:* The hypothesis that adaptations arise without the existence of a prior purpose, but by the action of natural selection on genetic variability.

The term may have been suggested by Colin Pittendrigh in 1958; it grew out of cybernetics and self-organising systems. Ernst Mayr, George C. Williams and Jacques Monod picked up the term and used it in evolutionary biology.

Philosophers of science have also commented on the term. Ernest Nagel analysed the concept of goal-directedness in biology; and David Hull commented on the use of teleology and teleonomy by biologists:

> Haldane can be found remarking, "Teleology is like a mistress to a biologist: he cannot live without her but he's unwilling to be seen with her in public". Today the mistress has become a lawfully wedded wife. Biologists no longer feel obligated to apologize for their use of teleological language; they flaunt it. The only concession which they make to its disreputable past is to rename it 'teleonomy'.

Coevolution

In a broad sense, biological coevolution is "the change of a biological object triggered by the change of a related object". Coevolution can occur at multiple levels of biology: it can be as microscopic as correlated mutations between amino acids in a protein, or as macroscopic as covarying traits between different species in an environment. Each party in a coevolutionary relationship exerts selective pressures on the other, thereby affecting each others' evolution. Species-level coevolution includes the evolution of a host species and its parasites (host-parasite co-evolution), and examples of mutualism evolving through time. Evolution in response to abiotic factors, such as climate change, is not co-evolution (since climate is not alive and does not undergo biological evolution). Evolution in a one-on-one interaction, such as that between predator and prey, host-symbiont or host-parasitic pair, is coevolution. But many cases are less clearcut: a species may evolve in response to a number of other species, each of which is also evolving in response to a set of species. This situation has been referred to as 'diffuse coevolution'. And, certainly, for many organisms, the biotic (living) environment is the most prominent selective pressure, resulting in evolutionary change.

The concept of co-evolution was briefly described by Charles Darwin in *On the Origin of Species*, and developed in detail in *Fertilisation of Orchids*. It is likely that viruses and their hosts may have coevolved in a number of cases.

One model of the co-evolution processes was Leigh Van Valen's Red Queen's Hypothesis. Emphasizing the importance of the sexual conflict, Thierry Lodé privileged the role of *antagonist interactions* (notably sexual) in evolution leading to an antagonist co-evolution.

Co-evolution does not imply mutual dependence. The host of a parasite, or prey of a predator, does not depend on its enemy for survival.

The existence of mitochondria within eukaryote cells is an example of co-evolution as the mitochondria has a different DNA sequence than that of the nucleus in the host cell. This concept is described further by the endosymbiotic theory.

Co-evolutionary algorithms are also a class of algorithms used for generating artificial life as well as for optimization, game learning and machine learning. Pioneering results in the use of co-evolutionary methods were by Daniel Hillis (who coevolved sorting networks) and Karl Sims.

Hummingbirds and Ornithophilous Flowers

Hummingbirds and ornithophilous flowers have evolved to form a mutualistic relationship. It is prevalent in the bird's biology as well as in the flower's. Hummingbird flowers have nectar chemistry associated with the bird's diet. Their colour and morphology also coincide with the bird's vision and morphology. The blooming times of these ornithophilous flowers have also been found to coincide with hummingbirds' breeding seasons.

Flowers have converged to take advantage of similar birds. Flowers compete for pollinators and adaptations reduce deleterious effects of this competition. Bird-pollinated flowers usually show higher nectar volumes and sugar production. This reflects high energy requirements of the birds. Energetic criteria are the most important determinants of flower choice by birds. Following their respective breeding seasons, several species of hummingbirds co-occur in North America, and several hummingbird flowers bloom simultaneously in these habitats. These flowers seem to have converged to a common morphology and colour. Different lengths and curvatures of the corolla tubes can affect the efficiency of extraction in hummingbird species in relation to differences in bill morphology. Tubular flowers force a bird to orient its bill in a particular way when probing the flower, especially when the bill and corolla are both curved; this also allows the plant to place pollen on a certain part of the bird's body. This opens the door for a variety of morphological co-adaptations.

An important requisite for attraction is conspicuousness to birds, which reflects the properties of avian vision and habitat features. Birds have their greatest spectral sensitivity and finest hue discrimination at the long wavelength end of the visual spectrum. This is why red is so conspicuous to birds. Hummingbirds may also be able to see ultraviolet 'colours'. The prevalence of ultraviolet patterns and nectar guides in nectar-poor entomophilous flowers allows the bird to avoid these flowers on sight. Two subfamilies in the family Trochilidae are Phaethorninae and Trochlinae. Each of these groups has evolved in conjunction with a particular set of flowers. Most Phaethorninae species are associated with large monocotyledonous herbs, and members of the subfamily Trochilinae are associated with dicotyledonous plant species.

Angracoid Orchids and African Moths

Another example of co-evolution is pollination of Angraecoid orchids by African moths. These species co-evolve because the moths are dependent on the flowers for nectar and the flowers are dependent on the moths to spread pollen so they can reproduce. The evolutionary process has led to deep flowers and moths with long probosci.

Old World Swallowtail and Fringed Rue

An example of *Antagonistic Co-evolution* is the Old World Swallowtail (Papilio machaon) caterpillar which lives on Fringed Rue (Ruta chalepensis) plant. Rue plant produces etheric oils which repel plant-eating insects. The Old World Swallowtail caterpillar developed resistance to these poisonous substances, thus reducing competition of other plant-eating insects.

Garter Snake and Rough-skinned Newt

Co-evolution can occur between predator and prey species as in the case of the Rough-skinned Newt (*Taricha granulosa*) and the common garter snake (*Thamnophis sirtalis*). In this case, the newts produce a potent nerve toxin that concentrates in their skin. Garter snakes have evolved resistance to this toxin through a set of genetic mutations, and prey upon the newts. The relationship between these animals has resulted in an evolutionary arms race that has driven toxin levels in the newt to extreme levels. This is an example of co-evolution because both organisms changed to better increase their chance of survival.

California Buckeye and Pollinators

When bee-hives are kept whose bee species that have not co-evolved with the California Buckeye, toxicity to aesculin, a neurotoxin present in the flower nectar of the *Aesculus californica* tree may be noted; this toxicity is only thought to be present in the case of honeybees and other insecta, which species did not co-evolve with A. californica.

Evolvability

Evolvability is defined as the ability of a population of organisms to generate genetic diversity and evolve through natural selection.

In order for a biological organism to evolve by natural selection, there must be a certain minimum probability that new, heritable variants are beneficial. Random mutations, unless they occur in DNA sequences with no function, are expected to be mostly detrimental. Beneficial mutations are always rare, but if they are too rare, then adaptation cannot occur. Random mutations seem to be beneficial more often than random changes to a typical computer program are. This means that biological genomes are structured in ways that make beneficial changes less unlikely than they would otherwise be. This has been taken as evidence that evolution has created not just fitter organisms, but populations of organisms that are better able to evolve.

Alternative Definitions

Wagner (2005) describes two definitions of evolvability. According to the first definition, a biological system is evolvable:

- if its properties show heritable genetic variation; and
- if natural selection can thus change these properties.

According to the second definition, a biological system is evolvable:

- if it can acquire novel functions through genetic change, functions that help the organism survive and reproduce.

These definitions can be applied on all levels of biological organisation, from macromolecules to mammals. Not all systems that are evolvable in the first sense are evolvable in the second sense.

Pigliucci ecognizes three classes of definition, depending on timescale. The first corresponds to Wagner's first, and represents the very short timescales that are described by quantitative genetics. He divides Wagner's second definition into two categories, one representing the intermediate timescales that can be studied using population genetics, and one representing exceedingly rare long-term innovations of form.

Example

Consider an enzyme with multiple alleles in the population. Each allele catalyzes the same reaction, but with a different level of activity. However, even after millions of years of evolution, exploring many sequences with similar function, no mutation might exist that gives this enzyme the ability to catalyze a different reaction. Thus, although the enzyme's activity is evolvable in the first sense, that does not mean that the enzyme's function is evolvable in the second sense. However, every system evolvable in the second sense must also be evolvable in the first.

Generating More Variation

More heritable phenotypic variation means more evolvability. While mutation is the ultimate source of heritable variation, its permutations and combinations also make a big difference. Sexual reproduction generates more variation (and thereby evolvability) relative to asexual reproduction (see evolution of sexual reproduction). Evolvability is further increased by generating more variation when an organism is stressed, and thus likely to be less well adapted, but less variation when an organism is doing well. The amount of variation generated can be adjusted in many different ways, for example via the mutation rate, via the probability of sexual *vs.* asexual reproduction, via the probability of outcrossing vs. inbreeding, and via dispersal.

Enhancement of Selection

Rather than creating more phenotypic variation, some mechanisms increase the intensity and effectiveness with which selection acts on existing phenotypic variation. For example:

- Mating rituals that allow sexual selection on 'good genes', and so intensify natural selection

Large Population Size

- Recombination decreasing the importance of the Hill-Robertson effect, where different genotypes contain different adaptive mutations. Recombination brings the two alleles together, creating a super-genotype in place of two competing lineages.
- Shorter generation time

Robustness and Evolvability

Robustness will not increase evolvability in the first sense. In organisms with a high level of robustness, mutations will have smaller phenotypic effects than in organisms with a low level of robustness. Thus, robustness reduces the amount of heritable genetic variation on which selection can act. However, robustness may allow exploration of large regions of genotype space, increasing robustness according to the second sense.

For example, one reason many proteins are less robust to mutation is that they have marginal thermodynamic stability, and most mutations reduce this stability further. Proteins that are more thermostable can tolerate a wider range of mutations, and are more evolvable.

Exploration Ahead of Time

When mutational robustness exists, many mutants will persist in a cryptic state. Mutations tend to fall into two categories, having either a very bad effect or very little effect: few mutations fall somewhere in between. Sometimes, these mutations will not be completely invisible, but still have rare effects, with very low penetrance. When this happens, natural selection weeds out the really bad mutations, while leaving the other mutations relatively unaffected. While evolution has no 'foresight' to know which environment will be encountered in the future, some mutations cause major disruption to a basic biological process, and will never be adaptive in any environment. Screening these out in advance leads to preadapted stocks of cryptic genetic variation.

Another way that phenotypes can be explored, prior to strong genetic commitment, is through learning. An organism that learns gets to 'sample' several different phenotypes during its early development, and later sticks to whatever worked best. Later in evolution, the optimal phenotype can be genetically assimilated so it becomes the default behaviour rather than a rare behaviour. This is known as the Baldwin effect, and it can increase evolvability.

Learning biases phenotypes in a beneficial direction. But an exploratory flattening of the fitness landscape can also increase evolvability even when it has no direction, for example when the flattening is a result of random errors in molecular and/or developmental processes. This increase in evolvability can happen when evolution is faced with crossing a 'valley' in an adaptive landscape. This means that two mutations exist that are deleterious by themselves, but beneficial in combination. These combinations can evolve more easily when the landscape is first flattened, and the discovered phenotype is then fixed by genetic assimilation.

Modularity

If every mutation affected every trait, then a mutation that was an improvement for one trait would be a disadvantage for other traits. This means that almost no mutations would be beneficial overall. But if pleiotropy is restricted to within functional modules, then mutations affect only one trait at a time, and adaptation is much easier.

Evolution of Evolvability

While variation yielding high evolvability could be useful in the long term, in the short term most of that variation is likely to be deleterious. For example, naively it would seem that increasing the mutation rate via a mutator allele would increase evolvability. But as an extreme example, if the mutation rate is too high then all individuals will be dead or at least carry a heavy mutation load. Short-term selection for low variation most of the time is usually thought likely to be more powerful than long-term selection for evolvability, making it difficult for natural selection to cause the evolution of evolvability.

When recombination is low, mutator alleles may still sometimes hitchhike on the success of adaptive mutations that they cause. In this case, selection can take place at the level of the lineage. This may explain why mutators are often seen during experimental evolution of microbes. Mutator alleles can also evolve more easily when they only increase mutation rates in nearby DNA sequences, not across the whole genome: this is known as a contingency locus.

The evolution of evolvability is less controversial if it occurs via the evolution of sexual reproduction, or via the tendency of variation-generating mechanisms to become more active when an organism is stressed. The yeast prion [PSI+] may also be an example of the evolution of evolvability through evolutionary capacitance. An evolutionary capacitor is a switch that turns genetic variation on and off. This is very much like bet-hedging the risk that a future environment will be similar or different. Theoretical models also predict the evolution of evolvability via modularity.

Intragenomic Conflict

The selfish gene theory postulates that natural selection will increase the frequency of those genes whose phenotypic effects ensure their successful replication. Generally, a gene achieves this goal by building, in cooperation with other genes, an organism capable of transmitting the gene to descendants. Intragenomic conflict arises when genes inside a genome are not transmitted by the same rules, or when a gene causes its own transmission to the detriment of the rest of the genome (this last kind of gene is usually called selfish genetic element, or ultraselfish gene or parasitic DNA).

Meiotic Drive

All nuclear genes in a given diploid genome cooperate because each allele has an equal probability of being present in a gamete. This fairness is guaranteed by meiosis. However, there is one type of gene, called a segregation distorter, that 'cheats' during meiosis or gametogenesis and thus is present in more than half of the functional gametes. The most studied examples are sd in *Drosophila melanogaster* (fruit fly), *t* haplotype in *Mus musculus* (mouse) and *sk* in *Neurospora sp.* (fungus). Segregation distorters that are present in sexual chromosomes (as the *X* chromosome in several Drosophila species) are denominated sex-ratio distorters, as they induce a sex-ratio bias in the offspring of the carrier individual.

Killer and Target

The most simple model of meiotic drive involves two tightly linked loci: a *Killer* locus and a *Target* locus. The segregation distorter set is composed by the allele *Killer* (in the *Killer* locus) and the allele *Resistant* (in the

Target locus), while its rival set is composed by the alleles *Non-killer* and *Non-resistant*. So, the segregation distorter set produces a toxin to which it is itself resistant, while its rival is not. Thus, it kills those gametes containing the rival set and increases in frequency. The tight linkage between these loci is crucial, so these genes usually lie on low recombination regions of the genome.

True Meiotic Drive

Other systems do not involve gamete destruction, but rather use the asymmetry of meiosis in females: the driving allele ends up in the ovocyte instead of in the polar bodies with a probability greater than one half. This is termed true meiotic drive, as it does not rely on a post-meiotic mechanism. The best-studied examples include the neocentromeres (knobs) of maize, as well as several chromosomal rearrangements in mammals. The general molecular evolution of centromeres is likely to involve such mechanisms.

Lethal Maternal-effects

The Medea gene causes the death of progeny from a heterozygous mother that do not inherit it. It occurs in the flour beetle (*Tribolium castaneum*). Maternal-effect selfish genes have been successfully synthesized in the lab.

Transposons

Transposons are autonomous replicating genes that encode the ability to move to new positions in the genome and therefore accumulate in the genomes. They replicate themselves in spite of being detrimental to the rest of the genome. They are often called 'jumping genes' or parasitic DNA and were discovered by Barbara McClintock in 1944.

Homing Endonuclease Genes

Homing endonuclease genes (HEG) convert their rival allele into a copy of themselves, and are thus inherited by nearly all meiotic daughter cells of a heterozygote cell. They achieve this by encoding an endonuclease which breaks the rival allele. This break is repaired by using the sequence of the HEG as template.

HEGs encode sequence-specific endonucleases. The recognition sequence (RS) is 15-30 *bp* long and usually occurs once in the genome. HEGs are located in the middle of their own recognition sequences. Most HEGs are encoded by self-splicing introns (group I & II) and inteins. Inteins are internal protein fragments produced from protein splicing and usually contain endonuclease and splicing activities. The allele without the HEGs are cleaved by the homing endonuclease and the double-strand break are repaired by homologous recombination (gene conversion) using the allele containing HEGs as template. Both chromosomes will contain the HEGs after repair.

B-chromosome

B-chromosomes are non-essential chromosomes; not homologous with any member of the normal (*A*) chromosome set; morphologically and structurally different from the *A*'s; and they are transmitted at higher-than-expected frequencies, leading to their accumulation in progeny. In some cases, there is strong evidence to support the contention that they are simply *selfish* and that they exist as *parasitic* chromosomes . They are found in all major taxonomic groupings of both plants and animals.

Cytoplasmic Genes

This section deals with conflict between nuclear and cytoplasmic genes. Mitochondria represent one such example of a set of cytoplasmic genes, as do plasmids and bacteria which have integrated themselves into another species' cytoplasm.

Males as Dead-ends to Cytoplasmic Genes

Anisogamy generally produces zygotes that inherit cytoplasmic elements exclusively from the female gamete. Thus, males represent dead-ends to these genes. Because of this fact, cytoplasmic genes have evolved a number of mechanisms to increase the production of female descendants and/or eliminate offspring not containing them.

Feminization

Male organisms are converted into females by cytoplasmic inherited protists (Microsporidia) or bacteria (*Wolbachia*), regardless of nuclear sex-determining factors. This occurs in amphipod and isopod Crustacea and Lepidoptera.

Male-killing

Male embryos (in the case of cytoplasmic inherited bacteria) or male larvae (in the case of Microsporidia) are killed. In the case of embryo death, this diverts investment from males to females who can transmit these cytoplasmic elements (for instance, in ladybird beetles, infected female hosts eat their dead male brothers, which is positive from the viewpoint of the bacterium). In the case of microsporidia-induced larval death, the agent is transmitted out of the male lineage (through which it cannot be transmitted) into the environment, where it may be taken up again infectiously by other individuals. Male-killing occurs in many insects. In the case of male embryo death, a variety of bacteria have been implicated, including *Wolbachia*.

Male-sterility

Anther tissue (male gametophyte) is killed by mitochondria in monoicous angiosperms, increasing energy and material spent in developing female gametophytes.

Parthenogenesis Induction

In certain haplodiploid Hymenoptera and mites, in which males are produced asexually, *Wolbachia* and *Cardinium* can induce duplication of the chromosomes and thus convert the organisms into females. The cytoplasmic bacterium forces haploid cells to go through mitosis to produce diploid cells which therefore will be female. This produces an entirely female population. Interestingly, if antibiotics are administered to populations which have become asexual in this way, they revert back to sexuality instantly, as the cytoplasmic bacteria forcing this behaviour upon them is removed.

Cytoplasmic Incompatibility

In many arthropods, zygotes produced by sperm of infected males and ova of non-infected females can be killed by *Wolbachia* or *Cardinium.*

Plasmids

Plasmids are additional circular chromosomes present in many bacteria. Most plasmids promote conjugation between their host and other bacteria, infecting new cytoplasms while retaining a copy inside the original host. Chromosomal genes are usually not transmitted. Therefore, they bear the costs of replicating the donated plasmid and the costs of increased exposure to viruses, but gain little in return (but the genes on plasmids may direct production of proteins that are beneficial to bacteria such as those that confer antibiotic resistance properties).

12 DNA Replication

DNA replication, the basis for biological inheritance, is a fundamental process occurring in all living organisms to copy their DNA. This process is 'replication' in that each strand of the original double-stranded DNA molecule serves as template for the reproduction of the complementary strand. Therefore, following DNA replication, two identical DNA molecules have been produced from a single double-stranded DNA molecule. Cellular proofreading and error toe-checking mechanisms ensure near perfect fidelity for DNA replication.

In a cell, DNA replication begins at specific locations in the genome, called 'origins'. Unwinding of DNA at the origin, and synthesis of new strands, forms a replication fork. In addition to DNA polymerase, the enzyme that synthesizes the new DNA by adding nucleotides matched to the template strand, a number of other proteins are associated with the fork and assist in the initiation and continuation of DNA synthesis.

DNA replication can also be performed *in vitro* (outside a cell). DNA polymerases, isolated from cells, and artificial DNA primers are used to initiate DNA synthesis at known sequences in a template molecule. The polymerase chain reaction (PCR), a common laboratory technique, employs such artificial synthesis in a cyclic manner to amplify a specific target DNA fragment from a pool of DNA.

DNA usually exists as a double-stranded structure, with both strands coiled together to form the characteristic double-helix. Each single strand of DNA is a chain of four types of nucleotides: adenine, cytosine, guanine, and thymine. A nucleotide is a mono-, di- or triphosphate deoxyribonucleoside; that is, a deoxyribose sugar is attached to one, two or three phosphates. Chemical interaction of these nucleotides forms phosphodiester linkages, creating the phosphate-deoxribose backbone of the DNA double helix with the bases pointing inward. Nucleotides (bases) are matched between strands through hydrogen bonds to form base pairs. Adenine pairs with thymine and cytosine pairs with guanine.

DNA strands have a directionality, and the different ends of a single strand are called the "3' (three-prime) end" and the "5' (five-prime) end." These terms refer to the carbon atom in deoxyribose to which the next phosphate in the chain attaches. In addition to being complementary, the two strands of DNA are antiparallel: they are orientated in opposite directions. This directionality has consequences in DNA synthesis, because DNA polymerase can only synthesize DNA in one direction by adding nucleotides to the 5' (actually 3') end of a DNA strand.

The pairing of bases in DNA through hydrogen bonding means that the information contained within each strand is redundant. The nucleotides on a single strand can be used to reconstruct nucleotides on a newly synthesized partner strand.

DNA Polymerase

DNA polymerases are a family of enzymes that carry out all forms of DNA replication. A DNA polymerase can only extend an existing DNA strand paired with a template strand; it cannot begin the synthesis of a new strand. To begin synthesis of a new strand, a short fragment of DNA or RNA, called a primer, must be created and paired with the template strand before DNA polymerase can synthesize new DNA.

Once a primer pairs with DNA to be replicated, DNA polymerase synthesizes a new strand of DNA by extending the 3' end of an existing nucleotide chain, adding new nucleotides matched to the template strand one at a time via the creation of phosphodiester bonds. The energy for this process of DNA polymerization comes from two of the three total phosphates attached to each unincorporated base. (Free bases with their attached phosphate groups are called nucleoside triphosphates.) When a nucleotide is being added to a growing DNA strand, two of the phosphates are removed and the energy produced creates a phosphodiester (chemical) bond that attaches the remaining phosphate to the growing chain. The energetics of this process also help explain the directionality of synthesis — if DNA were synthesized in the 3' to 5' direction, the energy for the process would come from the 5' end of the growing strand rather than from free nucleotides.

DNA polymerases are generally extremely accurate, making less than one error for every 10^7 nucleotides added. Even so, some DNA polymerases also have proofreading ability; they can remove nucleotides from the end of a strand in order to correct mismatched bases. If the 5' nucleotide needs to be removed during proofreading, the triphosphate end is lost. Hence, the energy source that usually provides energy to add a new nucleotide is also lost.

Origins of Replication

For a cell to divide, it must first replicate its DNA. This process is initiated at particular points within the DNA, known as 'origins', which are targeted by proteins that separate the two strands and initiate DNA synthesis. Origins contain DNA sequences recognized by replication initiator proteins (e.g. dnaA in *E coli'* and the Origin Recognition Complex in yeast). These initiator proteins recruit other proteins to separate the two strands and initiate replication forks.

Initiator proteins recruit other proteins to separate the DNA strands at the origin, forming a bubble. Origins tend to be 'AT-rich' (rich in adenine and thymine bases) to assist this process, because A-T base pairs have two hydrogen bonds (rather than the three formed in a C-G pair)–strands rich in these nucleotides are generally easier to separate due the positive relationship between the number of hydrogen bonds and the difficulty of breaking these bonds. Once strands are separated, RNA primers are created on the template strands. More specifically, the leading strand receives one RNA primer per active origin of replication while the lagging strand receives several; these several fragments of RNA primers found on the lagging strand of DNA are called Okazaki fragments, named after their discoverer. DNA polymerase extends the leading strand in one continuous motion and the lagging strand in a discontinuous motion (due to the Okazaki fragments). RNase removes the RNA fragments used to initiate replication by DNA Polymerase, and another DNA Polymerase enters to fill the gaps. When this is complete, a single nick on the leading strand and several nicks on the lagging strand can be found. Ligase works to fill these nicks in, thus completing the newly replicated DNA molecule.

As DNA synthesis continues, the original DNA strands continue to unwind on each side of the bubble, forming 2 replication forks. In bacteria, which have a single origin of replication on their circular chromosome, this process eventually creates a 'theta structure' (resembling the Greek letter theta:). In contrast, eukaryotes have longer linear chromosomes and initiate replication at multiple origins within these.

The Replication Fork

The replication fork is a structure that forms within the nucleus during DNA replication. It is created by helicases, which break the hydrogen bonds holding the two DNA strands together. The resulting structure has two branching 'prongs', each one made up of a single strand of DNA. These two strands serve as the template for the leading and lagging strands which will be created as DNA polymerase matches complementary nucleotides to the templates; The templates may be properly referred to as the leading strand template and the lagging strand template.

Leading Strand

The leading strand is the template strand of the DNA double helix so that the replication fork moves along it in the 3' to 5' direction. This allows the new strand synthesized complementary to it to be synthesized 5' to 3' in the same direction as the movement of the replication fork.

On the leading strand, a polymerase 'reads' the DNA and adds nucleotides to it continuously. This polymerase is DNA polymerase III (DNA Pol III) in prokaryotes and presumably Pole in eukaryotes.

Lagging Strand

The lagging strand is the strand of the template DNA double helix that is oriented so that the replication fork moves along it in a 5' to 3' manner. Because of its orientation, opposite to the working orientation of DNA polymerase III, which moves on a template in a 3' to 5' manner, replication of the lagging strand is more complicated than that of the leading strand.

On the lagging strand, primase 'reads' the DNA and adds RNA to it in short, separated segments. In eukaryotes, primase is intrinsic to Pol *a*. DNA polymerase III or Pol *d* lengthens the primed segments, forming Okazaki fragments. Primer removal in eukaryotes is also performed by Pol *d*. In prokaryotes, DNA polymerase *I* 'reads' the fragments, removes the RNA using its flap endonuclease domain (RNA primers are removed by 5'-3' exonuclease activity of polymerase I [weaver, 2005], and replaces the RNA nucleotides with DNA nucleotides (this is necessary because RNA and DNA use slightly different kinds of nucleotides). DNA ligase joins the fragments together.

Dynamics at the Replication Fork

As helicase unwinds DNA at the replication fork, the DNA ahead is forced to rotate. This process results in a build-up of twists in the DNA ahead. This build-up would form a resistance that would eventually halt the progress of the replication fork. DNA topoisomerases are enzymes that solve these physical problems in the coiling of DNA. Topoisomerase I cuts a single backbone on the DNA, enabling the strands to swivel around each other to remove the build-up of twists. Topoisomerase II cuts both backbones, enabling one double-stranded DNA to pass through another, thereby removing knots and entanglements that can form within and between DNA molecules.

Bare single-stranded DNA has a tendency to fold back upon itself and form secondary structures; these structures can interfere with the movement of DNA polymerase. To prevent this, single-strand binding proteins bind to the DNA until a second strand is synthesized, preventing secondary structure formation.

Clamp proteins form a sliding clamp around DNA, helping the DNA polymerase maintain contact with its template and thereby assisting with processivity. The inner face of the clamp enables DNA to be threaded through it. Once the polymerase reaches the end of the template or detects double stranded DNA, the sliding clamp undergoes a conformational change which releases the DNA polymerase. Clamp-loading proteins are used to initially load the clamp, recognizing the junction between template and RNA primers.

Eukaryotes

Within eukaryotes, DNA replication is controlled within the context of the cell cycle. As the cell grows and divides, it progresses through stages in the cell cycle; DNA replication occurs during the *S* phase (Synthesis phase). The progress of the eukaryotic cell through the cycle is controlled by cell cycle checkpoints. Progression through checkpoints is controlled through complex interactions between various proteins, including cyclins and cyclin-dependent kinases.

The G1/S checkpoint (or restriction checkpoint) regulates whether eukaryotic cells enter the process of DNA replication and subsequent division. Cells which do not proceed through this checkpoint are quiescent in the 'G0' stage and do not replicate their DNA.

Replication of chloroplast and mitochondrial genomes occurs independent of the cell cycle, through the process of D-loop replication.

Bacteria

Most bacteria do not go through a well-defined cell cycle and instead continuously copy their DNA; during rapid growth this can result in multiple rounds of replication occurring concurrently. Within *E coli*, the most well-characterized bacteria, regulation of DNA replication can be achieved through several mechanisms, including: the hemimethylation and sequestering of the origin sequence, the ratio of ATP to ADP, and the levels of protein DnaA. These all control the process of initiator proteins binding to the origin sequences.

Because *E coli* methylates GATC DNA sequences, DNA synthesis results in hemimethylated sequences. This hemimethylated DNA is recognized by a protein (SeqA) which binds and sequesters the origin sequence; in addition, dnaA (required for initiation of replication) binds less well to hemimethylated DNA. As a result, newly replicated origins are prevented from immediately initiating another round of DNA replication.

ATP builds up when the cell is in a rich medium, triggering DNA replication once the cell has reached a specific size. ATP competes with ADP to bind to DnaA, and the DnaA-ATP complex is able to initiate replication. A certain number of DnaA proteins are also required for DNA replication — each time the origin is copied the number of binding sites for DnaA doubles, requiring the synthesis of more DnaA to enable another initiation of replication.

Termination of Replication

Because bacteria have circular chromosomes, termination of replication occurs when the two replication forks meet each other on the opposite end of the parental chromosome. *E coli* regulate this process through the use of termination sequences which, when bound by the Tus protein, enable only one direction of replication fork to pass through. As a result, the replication forks are constrained to always meet within the termination region of the chromosome.

Eukaryotes initiate DNA replication at multiple points in the chromosome, so replication forks meet and terminate at many points in the chromosome; these are not known to be regulated in any particular manner. Because eukaryotes have linear chromosomes, DNA replication often fails to synthesize to the very end of the chromosomes (telomeres), resulting in telomere shortening. This is a normal process in somatic cells — cells are only able to divide a certain number of times before the DNA loss prevents further division. (This is known as the Hayflick limit.) Within the germ cell line, which passes DNA to the next generation, telomerase extends the repetitive sequences of the telomere region to prevent degradation. Telomerase can become mistakenly active in somatic cells, sometimes leading to cancer formation.

Polymerase Chain Reaction

Researchers commonly replicate DNA *in vitro* using the polymerase chain reaction (PCR). PCR uses a pair of primers to span a target region in template DNA, and then polymerizes partner strands in each direction from these primers using a thermostable DNA polymerase. Repeating this process through multiple cycles produces amplification of the targeted DNA region. At the start of each cycle, the mixture of template and primers is heated, separating the newly synthesized molecule and template. Then, as the mixture cools, both of these become templates for annealing of new primers, and the polymerase extends from these. As a result, the number of copies of the target region doubles each round, increasing exponentially.

Polymerase Chain Reaction

The polymerase chain reaction (PCR) is a scientific technique in molecular biology to amplify a single or a few copies of a piece of DNA across several orders of magnitude, generating thousands to millions of copies of a particular DNA sequence. The method relies on thermal cycling, consisting of cycles of repeated heating and cooling of the reaction for DNA melting and enzymatic replication of the DNA. Primers (short DNA fragments) containing sequences complementary to the target region along with a DNA polymerase (after which the method is named) are key components to enable selective and repeated amplification. As PCR progresses, the DNA generated is itself used as a template for replication, setting in motion a chain reaction in which the DNA template is exponentially amplified. PCR can be extensively modified to perform a wide array of genetic manipulations.

Almost all PCR applications employ a heat-stable DNA polymerase, such as Taq polymerase, an enzyme originally isolated from the bacterium *Thermus aquaticus*. This DNA polymerase enzymatically assembles a new DNA strand from DNA building blocks, the nucleotides, by using single-stranded DNA as a template and DNA oligonucleotides (also called DNA primers), which are required for initiation of DNA synthesis. The vast majority of PCR methods use thermal cycling, i.e., alternately heating and cooling the PCR sample to a defined series of temperature steps. These thermal cycling steps are necessary first to physically separate the two strands in a DNA double helix at a high temperature in a process called DNA melting. At a lower temperature, each strand is then used as the template in DNA synthesis by the DNA polymerase to selectively amplify the target DNA. The selectivity of PCR results from the use of primers that are complementary to the DNA region targeted for amplification under specific thermal cycling conditions.

Developed in 1983 by Kary Mullis, PCR is now a common and often indispensable technique used in medical and biological research labs for a variety of applications. These include DNA cloning for sequencing, DNA-based phylogeny, or functional analysis of genes; the diagnosis of hereditary diseases; the identification of genetic fingerprints (used in forensic sciences and paternity testing); and the detection and diagnosis of infectious diseases. In 1993, Mullis was awarded the Nobel Prize in Chemistry for his work on PCR.

PCR Principles and Procedure

PCR is used to amplify a specific region of a DNA strand (the DNA target). Most PCR methods typically amplify DNA fragments of up to ~10 kilo base pairs (kb), although some techniques allow for amplification of fragments up to 40 kb in size.

A basic PCR set up requires several components and reagents. These components include:

- *DNA template* that contains the DNA region (target) to be amplified.
- Two *primers* that are complementary to the 3' (three prime) ends of each of the sense and anti-sense strand of the DNA target.
- *Taq polymerase* or another DNA polymerase with a temperature optimum at around 70 °C.
- *Deoxynucleoside triphosphates* (dNTPs; also very commonly and erroneously called deoxynucleotide triphosphates), the building blocks from which the DNA polymerases synthesizes a new DNA strand.
- *Buffer solution,* providing a suitable chemical environment for optimum activity and stability of the DNA polymerase.
- *Divalent cations,* magnesium or manganese ions; generally Mg^{2+} is used, but Mn^{2+} can be utilized for PCR-mediated DNA mutagenesis, as higher Mn^{2+} concentration increases the error rate during DNA synthesis.
- *Monovalent cation* potassium ions.

The PCR is commonly carried out in a reaction volume of 10-200 μl in small reaction tubes (0.2-0.5 ml volumes) in a thermal cycler. The thermal cycler heats and cools the reaction tubes to achieve the temperatures required at each step of the reaction. Many modern thermal cyclers make use of the Peltier effect which permits both heating and cooling of the block holding the PCR tubes simply by reversing the electric current. Thin-walled reaction tubes permit favourable thermal conductivity to allow for rapid thermal equilibration. Most thermal cyclers have heated lids to prevent condensation at the top of the reaction tube. Older thermocyclers lacking a heated lid require a layer of oil on top of the reaction mixture or a ball of wax inside the tube.

Typically, PCR consists of a series of 20-40 repeated temperature changes, called cycles, with each cycle commonly consisting of 2-3 discrete temperature steps, usually three. The cycling is often preceded by a single temperature step (called *hold*) at a high temperature (>90 °C), and followed by one hold at the end for final product extension or brief storage. The temperatures used and the length of time they are applied in each cycle depend on a variety of parameters. These include the enzyme used for DNA synthesis, the concentration of divalent ions and dNTPs in the reaction, and the melting temperature (Tm) of the primers.

- *Initialization step*: This step consists of heating the reaction to a temperature of 94-96°C (or 98°C if extremely thermostable polymerases are used), which is held for 1-9 minutes. It is only required for DNA polymerases that require heat activation by hot-start PCR.
- *Denaturation step*: This step is the first regular cycling event and consists of heating the reaction to 94-98 °C for 20-30 seconds. It causes DNA melting of the DNA template by disrupting the hydrogen bonds between complementary bases, yielding single-stranded DNA molecules.
- *Annealing step*: The reaction temperature is lowered to 50-65°C for 20-40 seconds allowing annealing of the primers to the single-stranded DNA template. Typically the annealing temperature is about 3-5 degrees Celsius below the Tm of the primers used. Stable DNA-DNA hydrogen bonds are only formed when the primer sequence very closely matches the template sequence. The polymerase binds to the primer-template hybrid and begins DNA synthesis.
- *Extension/elongation step*: The temperature at this step depends on the DNA polymerase used; Taq polymerase has its optimum activity temperature at 75-80°C, and commonly a temperature of 72°C is used with this enzyme. At this step the DNA polymerase synthesizes a new DNA strand complementary to the DNA template strand by adding dNTPs that are complementary to the template in 5' to 3' direction, condensing the 5'- phosphate group of the dNTPs with the 3'- hydroxyl group at the end of the nascent (extending) DNA strand. The extension time depends both on the DNA polymerase used and on the length of the DNA fragment to be amplified. As a rule-of-thumb, at its optimum temperature, the DNA polymerase will polymerize a thousand bases per minute. Under optimum conditions, i.e., if there are no limitations due to limiting substrates or reagents, at each extension step, the amount of DNA target is doubled, leading to exponential (geometric) amplification of the specific DNA fragment.
- *Final elongation*: This single step is occasionally performed at a temperature of 70-74°C for 5-15 minutes after the last PCR cycle to ensure that any remaining single-stranded DNA is fully extended.
- *Final hold*: This step at 4-15°C for an indefinite time may be employed for short-term storage of the reaction.

To check whether the PCR generated the anticipated DNA fragment (also sometimes referred to as the amplimer or amplicon), agarose gel electrophoresis is employed for size separation of the PCR products. The size(s) of PCR products is determined by comparison with a DNA ladder (a molecular weight marker), which contains DNA fragments of known size, run on the gel alongside the PCR products.

PCR Stages

The PCR process can be divided into three stages:

- *Exponential amplification*: At every cycle, the amount of product is doubled (assuming 100 per cent reaction efficiency). The reaction is very sensitive: only minute quantities of DNA need to be present.
- *Levelling off stage*: The reaction slows as the DNA polymerase loses activity and as consumption of reagents such as dNTPs and primers causes them to become limiting.
- *Plateau*: No more product accumulates due to exhaustion of reagents and enzyme.

PCR Optimization

In practice, PCR can fail for various reasons, in part due to its sensitivity to contamination causing amplification of spurious DNA products. Because of this, a number of techniques and procedures have been developed for optimizing PCR conditions. Contamination with extraneous DNA is addressed with lab protocols and procedures that separate pre-PCR mixtures from potential DNA contaminants. This usually involves spatial separation of PCR-setup areas from areas for analysis or purification of PCR products, use of disposable plasticware, and thoroughly cleaning the work surface between reaction setups. Primer-design techniques are important in improving PCR product yield and in avoiding the formation of spurious products, and the usage of alternate buffer components or polymerase enzymes can help with amplification of long or otherwise problematic regions of DNA.

PCR allows isolation of DNA fragments from genomic DNA by selective amplification of a specific region of DNA. This use of PCR augments many methods, such as generating hybridization probes for Southern or northern hybridization and DNA cloning, which require larger amounts of DNA, representing a specific DNA region. PCR supplies these techniques with high amounts of pure DNA, enabling analysis of DNA samples even from very small amounts of starting material.

Other applications of PCR include DNA sequencing to determine unknown PCR-amplified sequences in which one of the amplification primers may be used in Sanger sequencing, isolation of a DNA sequence to expedite recombinant DNA technologies involving the insertion of a DNA sequence into a plasmid or the genetic material of another organism. Bacterial colonies (E. coli) can be rapidly screened by PCR for correct DNA vector constructs. PCR may also be used for genetic fingerprinting; a forensic technique used to identify a person or organism by comparing experimental DNAs through different PCR-based methods.

Some PCR 'fingerprints' methods have high discriminative power and can be used to identify genetic relationships between individuals, such as parent-child or between siblings, and are used in paternity testing . This technique may also be used to determine evolutionary relationships among organisms.

Amplification and Quantification of DNA

Because PCR amplifies the regions of DNA that it targets, PCR can be used to analyze extremely small amounts of sample. This is often critical for forensic analysis, when only a trace amount of DNA is available as evidence. PCR may also be used in the analysis of ancient DNA that is tens of thousands of years old. These PCR-based techniques have been successfully used on animals, such as a forty-thousand-year-old mammoth, and also on human DNA, in applications ranging from the analysis of Egyptian mummies to the identification of a Russian tsar.

Quantitative PCR methods allow the estimation of the amount of a given sequence present in a sample—a technique often applied to quantitatively determine levels of gene expression. Real-time PCR is an established tool for DNA quantification that measures the accumulation of DNA product after each round of PCR amplification.

PCR in Diagnosis of Diseases

PCR permits early diagnosis of malignant diseases such as leukemia and lymphomas, which is currently the highest developed in cancer research and is already being used routinely. PCR assays can be performed directly on genomic DNA samples to detect translocation-specific malignant cells at a sensitivity which is at least 10,000 fold higher than other methods.

PCR also permits identification of non-cultivatable or slow-growing microorganisms such as mycobacteria, anaerobic bacteria, or viruses from tissue culture assays and animal models. The basis for PCR diagnostic applications in microbiology is the detection of infectious agents and the discrimination of non-pathogenic from pathogenic strains by virtue of specific genes.

Viral DNA can likewise be detected by PCR. The primers used need to be specific to the targeted sequences in the DNA of a virus, and the PCR can be used for diagnostic analyses or DNA sequencing of the viral genome. The high sensitivity of PCR permits virus detection soon after infection and even before the onset of disease. Such early detection may give physicians a significant lead in treatment. The amount of virus ('viral load') in a patient can also be quantified by PCR-based DNA quantitation techniques.

Variations on the Basic PCR Technique

- *Allele-specific PCR*: a diagnostic or cloning technique which is based on single-nucleotide polymorphisms (SNPs) (single-base differences in DNA). It requires prior knowledge of a DNA sequence, including differences between alleles, and uses primers whose 3' ends encompass the SNP. PCR amplification under stringent conditions is much less efficient in the presence of a mismatch between template and primer, so successful amplification with an SNP-specific primer signals presence of the specific SNP in a sequence.
- *Assembly PCR* or *Polymerase Cycling Assembly (PCA)*: artificial synthesis of long DNA sequences by performing PCR on a pool of long oligonucleotides with short overlapping segments. The oligonucleotides alternate between sense and antisense directions, and the overlapping segments determine the order of the PCR fragments, thereby selectively producing the final long DNA product.
- *Asymmetric PCR*: preferentially amplifies one DNA strand in a double-stranded DNA template. It is used in sequencing and hybridization probing where amplification of only one of the two complementary strands is required. PCR is carried out as usual, but with a great excess of the primer for the strand targeted for amplification. Because of the slow (arithmetic) amplification later in the reaction after the limiting primer has been used up, extra cycles of PCR are required. A recent modification on this process, known as *L*inear-*A*fter-*T*he-*E*xponential-PCR (LATE-PCR), uses a limiting primer with a higher melting temperature [Tm) than the excess primer to maintain reaction efficiency as the limiting primer concentration decreases mid-reaction.
- *Helicase-dependent amplification*: similar to traditional PCR, but uses a constant temperature rather than cycling through denaturation and annealing/extension cycles. DNA helicase, an enzyme that unwinds DNA, is used in place of thermal denaturation.
- *Hot-start PCR*: a technique that reduces non-specific amplification during the initial set up stages of the PCR. It may be performed manually by heating the reaction components to the melting

temperature (e.g., 95°C) before adding the polymerase. Specialized enzyme systems have been developed that inhibit the polymerase's activity at ambient temperature, either by the binding of an antibody or by the presence of covalently bound inhibitors that only dissociate after a high-temperature activation step. Hot-start/cold-finish PCR is achieved with new hybrid polymerases that are inactive at ambient temperature and are instantly activated at elongation temperature.

- *Intersequence-specific PCR* (ISSR): a PCR method for DNA fingerprinting that amplifies regions between simple sequence repeats to produce a unique fingerprint of amplified fragment lengths.
- *Inverse PCR*: is commonly used to identify the flanking sequences around genomic inserts. It involves a series of DNA digestions and self ligation, resulting in known sequences at either end of the unknown sequence.
- *Ligation-mediated PCR*: uses small DNA linkers ligated to the DNA of interest and multiple primers annealing to the DNA linkers; it has been used for DNA sequencing, genome walking, and DNA footprinting.
- *Methylation-specific PCR* (MSP): developed by Stephen Baylin and Jim Herman at the Johns Hopkins School of Medicine, and is used to detect methylation of CpG islands in genomic DNA. DNA is first treated with sodium bisulfite, which converts unmethylated cytosine bases to uracil, which is recognized by PCR primers as thymine. Two PCRs are then carried out on the modified DNA, using primer sets identical except at any CpG islands within the primer sequences. At these points, one primer set recognizes DNA with cytosines to amplify methylated DNA, and one set recognizes DNA with uracil or thymine to amplify unmethylated DNA. MSP using qPCR can also be performed to obtain quantitative rather than qualitative information about methylation.
- *Miniprimer PCR*: uses a thermostable polymerase (S-Tbr) that can extend from short primers ('smalligos') as short as 9 or 10 nucleotides. This method permits PCR targeting to smaller primer binding regions, and is used to amplify conserved DNA sequences, such as the 16S (or eukaryotic 18S) rRNA gene.
- *Multiplex Ligation-dependent Probe Amplification* (*MLPA*): permits multiple targets to be amplified with only a single primer pair, thus avoiding the resolution limitations of multiplex PCR.
- *Multiplex-PCR*: consists of multiple primer sets within a single PCR mixture to produce amplicons of varying sizes that are specific to different DNA sequences. By targeting multiple genes at once,

additional information may be gained from a single test run that otherwise would require several times the reagents and more time to perform. Annealing temperatures for each of the primer sets must be optimized to work correctly within a single reaction, and amplicon sizes, i.e., their base pair length, should be different enough to form distinct bands when visualized by gel electrophoresis.

❖ *Nested PCR*: increases the specificity of DNA amplification, by reducing background due to non-specific amplification of DNA. Two sets of primers are used in two successive PCRs. In the first reaction, one pair of primers is used to generate DNA products, which besides the intended target, may still consist of non-specifically amplified DNA fragments. The product(s) are then used in a second PCR with a set of primers whose binding sites are completely or partially different from and located 3' of each of the primers used in the first reaction. Nested PCR is often more successful in specifically amplifying long DNA fragments than conventional PCR, but it requires more detailed knowledge of the target sequences.

❖ *Overlap-extension PCR*: a genetic engineering technique allowing the construction of a DNA sequence with an alteration inserted beyond the limit of the longest practical primer length.

❖ *Quantitative PCR (Q-PCR)*: used to measure the quantity of a PCR product (commonly in real-time). It quantitatively measures starting amounts of DNA, cDNA or RNA. Q-PCR is commonly used to determine whether a DNA sequence is present in a sample and the number of its copies in the sample. *Quantitative real-time PCR* has a very high degree of precision. QRT-PCR methods use fluorescent dyes, such as Sybr Green, EvaGreen or fluorophore-containing DNA probes, such as TaqMan, to measure the amount of amplified product in real time. It is also sometimes abbreviated to RT-PCR (*R*eal *T*ime PCR) or RQ-PCR. QRT-PCR or RTQ-PCR are more appropriate contractions, since RT-PCR commonly refers to reverse transcription PCR, often used in conjunction with Q-PCR.

❖ *R*everse Transcription PCR (RT-PCR): for amplifying DNA from RNA. Reverse transcriptase reverse transcribes RNA into cDNA, which is then amplified by PCR. RT-PCR is widely used in expression profiling, to determine the expression of a gene or to identify the sequence of an RNA transcript, including transcription start and termination sites. If the genomic DNA sequence of a gene is known, RT-PCR can be used to map the location of exons and introns in the gene. The 5' end of a gene (corresponding to the transcription start site) is typically identified by RACE-PCR (*Rapid Amplification of cDNA Ends*).

- *Solid Phase PCR*: encompasses multiple meanings, including Polony Amplification (where PCR colonies are derived in a gel matrix, for example), Bridge PCR (primers are covalently linked to a solid-support surface), conventional Solid Phase PCR (where Asymmetric PCR is applied in the presence of solid support bearing primer with sequence matching one of the aqueous primers) and Enhanced Solid Phase PCR (where conventional Solid Phase PCR can be improved by employing high *Tm* and nested solid support primer with optional application of a thermal 'step' to favour solid support priming).
- *Thermal asymmetric interlaced PCR (TAIL-PCR)*: for isolation of an unknown sequence flanking a known sequence. Within the known sequence, TAIL-PCR uses a nested pair of primers with differing annealing temperatures; a degenerate primer is used to amplify in the other direction from the unknown sequence.
- *Touchdown PCR* (*Step-down PCR*): a variant of PCR that aims to reduce nonspecific background by gradually lowering the annealing temperature as PCR cycling progresses. The annealing temperature at the initial cycles is usually a few degrees (3-5°C) above the T_m of the primers used, while at the later cycles, it is a few degrees (3-5°C) below the primer T_m. The higher temperatures give greater specificity for primer binding, and the lower temperatures permit more efficient amplification from the specific products formed during the initial cycles.
- *PAN-AC*: uses isothermal conditions for amplification, and may be used in living cells.
- *Universal Fast Walking*: for genome walking and genetic fingerprinting using a more specific 'two-sided' PCR than conventional 'one-sided' approaches (using only one gene-specific primer and one general primer — which can lead to artefactual 'noise') by virtue of a mechanism involving lariat structure formation. Streamlined derivatives of UFW are LaNe RAGE (lariat-dependent nested PCR for rapid amplification of genomic DNA ends), 5'RACE LaNe and 3'RACE LaNe.

Convergent Evolution

Convergent evolution describes the acquisition of the same biological trait in unrelated lineages.

The wing is a classic example of convergent evolution in action. Although their last common ancestor did not have wings, birds and bats do, and are capable of powered flight. The wings are similar in construction, due to the physical constraints imposed upon wing shape. Similarity can also be explained by shared ancestry, as evolution can only work with what is already there—thus wings were modified from limbs, as evidenced by their bone structure.

Traits arising through convergent evolution are termed analogous structures, in contrast to homologous structures, which have a common origin. Bat and pterodactyl wings are an example of analogous structures, while the bat wing is homologous to human and other mammal forearms, sharing an ancestral state despite serving different functions. Similarity in species of different ancestry that is the result of convergent evolution is called homoplasy. The opposite of convergent evolution is divergent evolution, whereby related species evolve different traits. On a molecular level, this can happen due to random mutation unrelated to adaptive changes; see long branch attraction. Convergent evolution is similar to, but distinguishable from, the phenomena of evolutionary relay and parallel evolution. Evolutionary relay describes how independent species acquire similar characteristics through their evolution in similar ecosystems at different times—for example the dorsal fins of extinct ichthyosaurs and sharks. Parallel evolution occurs when two independent species evolve together *at the same time in the same ecospace* and acquire similar characteristics—for instance extinct browsing-horses and paleotheres.

Similarity can also result if organisms occupy similar ecological niches—that is, a distinctive way of life. A classic comparison is between the marsupial fauna of Australia and the placental mammals of the Old World. The two lineages are clades—that is, they each share a common ancestor that belongs to their own group, and are more closely related to one another than to any other clade—but very similar forms evolved in each isolated population. Many body plans, for instance sabre-toothed cats and flying squirrels, evolved independently in both populations.

Distinction from Re-evolution

In some cases, it is difficult to tell whether a trait has been lost then re-evolved convergently, or whether a gene has simply been 'switched off' and then re-enabled later. From a mathematical standpoint, an unused gene has a reasonable probability of remaining in the genome in a functional state for around 6 million years, but after 10 million years it is almost certain that the gene will no longer function.

Examples

One of the most famous examples of convergent evolution is the camera eye of cephalopods (e.g., squid), vertebrates (e.g., mammals) and cnidaria (e.g., box jellies). Their last common ancestor had at most a very simple photoreceptive spot, but a range of processes led to the progressive refinement of this structure to the advanced camera eye — with one subtle difference: The cephalopod eye is 'wired' in the opposite direction, with blood and nerve vessels entering from the back of the retina, rather than the front as in vertebrates. The similarity of the structures in other respects, despite the complex nature of the organ, illustrates how there are some biological challenges (vision) that have an optimal solution.

For a particular trait, proceeding in each of two lineages from a specified ancestor to a later descendant, parallel and convergent evolutionary trends can be strictly defined and clearly distinguished from one another. When both descendants are similar in a particular respect, evolution is defined as parallel if the ancestors considered were also similar, and convergent if they were not.

When the ancestral forms are unspecified or unknown, or the range of traits considered is not clearly specified, the distinction between parallel and convergent evolution becomes more subjective. For instance, the striking example of similar placental and marsupial forms is described by Richard Dawkins in *The Blind Watchmaker* as a case of convergent evolution, because mammals on each continent had a long evolutionary history prior to the extinction of the dinosaurs under which to accumulate relevant differences. Stephen Jay Gould describes many of the same examples as parallel evolution starting from the common ancestor of all marsupials and placentals. Many evolved similarities can be described in concept as parallel evolution from a remote ancestor, with the exception of those where quite different structures are co-opted to a similar function. For example, consider *Mixotricha paradoxa*, a microbe that has assembled a system of rows of apparent cilia and basal bodies closely resembling that of ciliates but that are actually smaller symbiont micro-organisms, or the differently oriented tails of fish and whales. On the converse, any case in which lineages do not evolve together at the same time in the same ecospace might be described as convergent evolution at some point in time.

The definition of a trait is crucial in deciding whether a change is seen as divergent, or as parallel or convergent. In the image above, note that, since serine and threonine possess similar structures with an alcohol side-chain, the example marked '*divergent*' would be termed '*parallel*' if the amino acids were grouped by similarity instead of being considered individually. As another example, if genes in two species independently become restricted to the same region of the animals through regulation by a certain transcription factor, this may be described as a case of parallel evolution — but examination of the actual DNA sequence will probably show only divergent changes in individual base-pair positions, since a new transcription factor binding site can be added in a wide range of places within the gene with similar effect.

A similar situation occurs considering the homology of morphological structures. For example, many insects possess two pairs of flying wings. In beetles, the first pair of wings is hardened into wing covers with little role in flight, while in flies the second pair of wings is condensed into small halteres used for balance. If the two pairs of wings are considered as interchangeable, homologous structures, this may be described as a parallel reduction in the number of wings, but otherwise the two changes are each divergent changes in one pair of wings.

Similar to convergent evolution, evolutionary relay describes how independent species acquire similar characteristics through their evolution in similar ecosystems, but not at the same time (dorsal fins of sharks and ichthyosaurs).

Significance

The degree to which convergence affects the products of evolution is the subject of a popular controversy. In his book *Wonderful Life*, Stephen Jay Gould argues that if the tape of life were re-wound and played back, life would have taken a very different course. Simon Conway Morris counters this argument, arguing that convergence is a dominant force in evolution, and that, since the same environmental and physical constraints act on all life, there is an 'optimum' body plan that life will inevitably evolve toward, with evolution bound to stumble upon intelligence — a trait of primates, crows, and dolphins — at some point. Convergence is difficult to quantify, so progress on this issue may require exploitation of engineering specifications (e.g., of wing aerodynamics) and comparably rigorous measures of 'very different course' in terms of phylogenetic (molecular) distances.

Parallel Evolution

Parallel evolution is the development of a similar trait in related, but distinct, species descending from the same ancestor, but from different clades.

Parallel *vs.* Convergent Evolution

For a particular trait, proceeding in each of two lineages from a specified ancestor to a later descendant, parallel and convergent evolutionary trends can be strictly defined and clearly distinguished from one another. When both descendants are similar in a particular respect, evolution is defined as parallel if the ancestors considered were also similar, and convergent if they were not.

When the ancestral forms are unspecified or unknown, or the range of traits considered is not clearly specified, the distinction between parallel and convergent evolution becomes more subjective. For instance, the striking example of similar placental and marsupial forms is described by Richard Dawkins in *The Blind Watchmaker* as a case of convergent evolution, because mammals on each continent had a long evolutionary history prior to the extinction of the dinosaurs under which to accumulate relevant differences. Stephen Jay Gould describes many of the same examples as parallel evolution starting from the common ancestor of all marsupials and placentals. Many evolved similarities can be described in concept as parallel evolution from a remote ancestor, with the exception of those where quite different structures are co-opted to a similar function. For example, consider *Mixotricha paradoxa*, an eukaryotic microbe which has assembled a system of rows of apparent cilia and basal bodies closely resembling that of ciliates but which are actually smaller symbiont microorganisms, or the differently oriented tails of fish and whales. Conversely, any case in which lineages do not evolve together at the same time in the same ecospace might be described as convergent evolution at some point in time.

The definition of a trait is crucial in deciding whether a change is seen as divergent, or as parallel or convergent. In the image above, note that since serine and threonine possess similar structures with an alcohol side chain, the example marked '*divergent*' would be termed '*parallel*' if the amino acids were grouped by similarity instead of being considered individually. As another example, if genes in two species independently become restricted to the same region of the animals through regulation by a certain transcription factor, this may be described as a case of parallel evolution — but examination of the actual DNA sequence will probably show only divergent changes in individual basepair positions, since a new transcription factor binding site can be added in a wide range of places within the gene with similar effect.

A similar situation occurs considering the homology of morphological structures. For example, many insects possess two pairs of flying wings. In beetles, the first pair of wings is hardened into wing covers with little role in flight, while in flies the second pair of wings is condensed into small halteres used for balance. If the two pairs of wings are considered as interchangeable, homologous structures, this may be described as a parallel reduction in the number of wings, but otherwise the two changes are each divergent changes in one pair of wings.

Similar to convergent evolution, evolutionary relay describes how independent species acquire similar characteristics through their evolution in similar ecosystems, but not at the same time (dorsal fins of sharks and ichthyosaurs).

Parallel Speciation

Defined as the repeated independent evolution of the same reproductive isolating mechanism. An example of this may occur when a species colonizes several new areas which are isolated from, but environmentally similar to, each other. Similar selective pressures in these environments result in parallel evolution among the traits that confer reproductive isolation.

Examples

- Colouration that serves as a warning to predators and for mating displays have evolved in many different species.
- In the plant kingdom, the most familiar examples of parallel evolution are the forms of leaves, where very similar patterns have appeared again and again in separate genera and families.
- In butterflies, many close similarities are found in the patterns of wing colouration, both within and between families.
- Old and New world porcupines shared a common ancestor, both evolved strikingly similar quill structures; this is also an example of convergent evolution as similar structures evolved in hedgehogs, echidnas and tenrecs.

- Contemporaneous evolution of the extinct browsing-horses and extinct paleotheres both of which shared the same environmental space.
- Some extinct Archosaurs evolved an upright posture and likely were warm-blooded. These two characteristics are also found in most mammals. Interestingly, modern crocodiles have a four chambered heart and a crurotarsal, the latter being also a characteristic of therian mammals.
- The extinct pterosaurs and the birds both evolved wings as well as a distinct beak, but not from a recent common ancestor.
- Internal fertilization has evolved independently in sharks, some amphibians and amniotes.
- The Patagium is a fleshy membrane that is found in gliding mammals such as: flying lemurs, flying squirrels, sugar gliders and the extinct Volaticotherium. These mammals acquired the patagium independently.
- Pyrotherians have evolved a body plan similar to proboscideans.

Parallel Evolution Between Marsupials and Placentals

One of the most spectacular examples of parallel evolution is provided by the two main branches of the mammals, the placentals and marsupials, which have followed independent evolutionary pathways following the break-up of land-masses such as Gondwanaland roughly 100 million years ago. In South America, marsupials and placentals shared the ecosystem (prior to the Great American Interchange); in Australia, marsupials prevailed; and in the Old World the placentals won out. However, in all these localities mammals were small and filled only limited places in the ecosystem until the mass extinction of dinosaurs sixty-five million years later. At this time, mammals on all three landmasses began to take on a much wider variety of forms and roles. While some forms were unique to each environment, surprisingly similar animals have often emerged in two or three of the separated continents. Examples of these include the litopterns and horses, whose legs are difficult to distinguish; the European sabre-tooth tiger *(Smilodon)* and the South American marsupial sabre-tooth *(Thylacosmilus)*; the Tasmanian wolf and the European wolf; likewise marsupial and placental moles, flying squirrels, and (arguably) mice.

14 Socio-cultural Evolution

Socio-cultural evolution(ism) is an umbrella term for theories of cultural evolution and social evolution, describing how cultures and societies have changed over time. Note that 'socio-cultural evolution' is not an equivalent of 'socio-cultural development' (unified processes of differentiation and integration involving increases in socio-cultural complexity), as socio-cultural evolution also encompasses socio-cultural transformations accompanied by decreases of complexity (degeneration) as well as ones not accompanied by any significant changes of socio-cultural complexity (cladogenesis). Thus, socio-cultural evolution can be defined as "the process by which structural reorganization is affected through time, eventually producing a form or structure which is qualitatively different from the ancestral form. . . . Evolutionism then becomes the scientific activity of finding nomothetic explanations for the occurrence of such structural changes". Although such theories typically provide models for understanding the relationship between technologies, social structure, the values of a society, and how and why they change with time, they vary as to the extent to which they describe specific mechanisms of variation and social change.

Socio-cultural modelling is an umbrella term for theories of cultural and social evolution, which aims to describe how cultures and societies have developed over time. Such theories typically provide models for understanding the relationship between technologies, social structure, the beliefs, values and goals of a society, and how and why they change with time. Such models are of particular interest to the military in helping unstable regions transition to more stable sustainable states. Most 19th century and some 20th century approaches aimed to provide models for the evolution of humankind as a whole, arguing that different societies are at different stages of social development. At present this thread is continued to some extent within the World System approach. Many of the more recent 20th-century approaches focus on changes specific to individual societies and reject the idea of directional change, or social progress. Most archaeologists and cultural anthropologists work within the framework of modern theories of socio-cultural evolution. Modern approaches to socio-cultural evolution include neoevolutionism, socio-biology, theory of modernization and theory of postindustrial society.

Anthropologists and sociologists often assume that human beings have natural social tendencies and that particular human social behaviours have non-genetic causes and dynamics (i.e. they are learned in a social environment and through social interaction). Societies exist in complex social environments (i.e. with natural resources and constraints), and adapt themselves to these environments. It is thus inevitable that all societies change.

Specific theories of social or cultural evolution are usually meant to explain differences between coeval societies, by positing that different societies are at different stages of development. Although such theories typically provide models for understanding the relationship between technologies, social structure, or values of a society, they vary as to the extent to which they describe specific mechanisms of variation and change.

Early socio-cultural evolution theories—the theories of Auguste Comte, Herbert Spencer and Lewis Henry Morgan—developed simultaneously but independently of Charles Darwin's works and were popular from the late 19th century to the end of World War I. These 19th-century unilineal evolution theories claimed that societies start out in a *primitive* state and gradually become more *civilized* over time, and equated the culture and technology of Western civilization with progress. Some forms of early socio-cultural evolution theories (mainly unilineal ones) have led to much criticised theories like social Darwinism, and scientific racism, used in the past to justify existing policies of colonialism and slavery, and to justify new policies such as eugenics.

Most 19th-century and some 20th-century approaches aimed to provide models for the evolution of humankind as a single entity. However, most 20th-century approaches, such as multilineal evolution, focussed on changes specific to individual societies. Moreover, they rejected directional change (i.e. orthogenetic, teleological or progressive change). Most archaeologists work within the framework of multilineal evolution. Other contemporary approaches to social change include neoevolutionism, sociobiology, dual inheritance theory, theory of modernisation and theory of post-industrial society.

Richard Dawkins wrote in *The Selfish Gene* in 1976 that "there are some examples of cultural evolution in birds and monkeys, but . . . it is our own species that really shows what cultural evolution can do".

The 14th century Islamic scholar Ibn Khaldun concluded that societies are living organisms that experience cyclic birth, growth, maturity, decline, and ultimately death due to universal causes several centuries before the Western civilisation developed the science of sociology. Nonetheless, theories of social and cultural evolution were common in modern European thought. Prior to the 18th century, Europeans predominantly believed that societies on Earth were in a state of decline. European society held up the world of antiquity as a standard to aspire to, and Ancient Greece and Ancient Rome produced levels of technical accomplishment which Europeans of the Middle Ages sought to emulate. At the same time, Christianity taught that people lived in a debased world fundamentally inferior to the Garden of Eden and Heaven. During The Age of Enlightenment, however, European self-confidence grew and the notion of progress became increasingly popular. It was during this period that what would later become known as 'sociological and cultural evolution' would have its roots.

Stadial Theory

The Enlightenment thinkers often speculated that societies progressed through stages of increasing development and looked for the logic, order and the set of scientific truths that determined the course of human history. Georg Wilhelm Friedrich Hegel, for example, argued that social development was an inevitable and determined process, similar to an acorn which has no choice but to become an oak tree. Likewise, it was assumed that societies start out primitive, perhaps in a Hobbesian state of nature, and naturally progress toward something resembling industrial Europe.

While earlier authors such as Michel de Montaigne discussed how societies change through time, it was truly the Scottish Enlightenment which proved key in the development of socio-cultural evolution. After Scotland's union with England in 1707, several Scottish thinkers pondered what the relationship between progress and the 'decadence' brought about by increased trade with England and the affluence it produced. The result was a series of 'conjectural histories'. Authors such as Adam Ferguson, John Millar, and Adam Smith argued that all societies pass through a series of four stages: hunting and gathering, pastoralism and nomadism, agricultural, and finally a stage of commerce. These thinkers thus understood the changes Scotland was undergoing as a transition from an agricultural to a mercantile society.

Philosophical concepts of progress (such as those expounded by the German philosopher G.W.F. Hegel) developed as well during this period. In France authors such as Claude Adrien Helvétius and other philosophes were influenced by this Scottish tradition. Later thinkers such as Comte de Saint-Simon developed these ideas. Auguste Comte in particular presented a coherent view of social progress and a new discipline to study it—sociology.

These developments took place in a wider context. The first process was colonialism. Although imperial powers settled most differences of opinion with their colonial subjects with force, increased awareness of non-Western peoples raised new questions for European scholars about the nature of society and culture. Similarly, effective administration required some degree of understanding of other cultures. Emerging theories of socio-cultural evolution allowed Europeans to organise their new knowledge in a way that reflected and justified their increasing political and economic domination of others: colonised people were less evolved, colonising people were more evolved. When the 17th-century English philosopher Thomas Hobbes described indigenous people as having 'no arts, no letters, no society' and their life as 'solitary, poor, nasty, brutish, and short', he was defining the stereotype of a 'savage', one that would last for many years. Modern civilization, understood as the Western civilization, was the result of steady progress from such a state, and such a notion was common to many thinkers of the Enlightenment, including Voltaire.

The second process was the Industrial Revolution and the rise of capitalism which allowed and promoted continual revolutions in the means of production. Emerging theories of socio-cultural evolution reflected a belief that the changes in Europe wrought by the Industrial Revolution and capitalism were improvements. Industrialisation, combined with the intense political change brought about by the French Revolution and the U.S. Constitution, which were paving the way for the dominance of democracy, forced European thinkers to reconsider some of their assumptions about how society was organised.

Eventually, in the 19th century three great classical theories of social and historical change were created: socio-cultural evolutionism, the social cycle theory, and Marxist historical materialism. Those theories had one common factor: they all agreed that the history of humanity is pursuing a certain fixed path, most likely that of social progress. Thus, each past event is not only chronologically, but causally tied to the present and future events. Those theories postulated that by recreating the sequence of those events, sociology could discover the laws of history.

Socio-cultural Evolutionism and the Idea of Progress

While socio-cultural evolutionists agree that an evolution-like process leads to social progress, classical social evolutionists have developed many different theories, known as theories of unilineal evolution. Socio-cultural evolutionism was the prevailing theory of early socio-cultural anthropology and social commentary, and is associated with scholars like Auguste Comte, Edward Burnett Tylor, Lewis Henry Morgan, Benjamin Kidd, L.T. Hobhouse and Herbert Spencer. Socio-cultural evolutionism attempted to formalise social thinking along scientific lines, with the added influence from the biological theory of evolution. If organisms could develop over time according to discernible, deterministic laws, then it seemed reasonable that societies could as well. Human society was compared to a biological organism, and social science equivalents of concepts like variation, natural selection, and inheritance were introduced as factors resulting in the progress of societies. Idea of progress led to that of a fixed 'stages' through which human societies progress, usually numbering three—savagery, barbarism, and civilization—but sometimes many more. As early as the late 18th century Marquis de Condorcet listed 10 stages, or 'epochs', each advancing the rights of man and perfecting the human race. At that time, anthropology was rising as a new scientific discipline, separating from the traditional views of 'primitive' cultures that was usually based on religious views.

Classical social evolutionism is most closely associated with the 19th-century writings of Auguste Comte, Herbert Spencer (coiner of the phrase 'survival of the fittest'). In many ways Spencer's theory of 'cosmic evolution' has much more in common with the works of Jean-Baptiste Lamarck and Auguste Comte than with contemporary works of Charles Darwin. Spencer also developed and published his theories several years earlier than Darwin. In regard to social institutions, however, there is a good case that Spencer's writings might be classified as 'Social Evolutionism'. Although he wrote that societies over time progressed, and that progress was accomplished through competition, he stressed that the individual (rather than the collectivity) is the unit of analysis that evolves, that evolution takes place through natural selection and that it affects social as well as biological phenomenon. Nonetheless, the publication of Darwin's works proved a boon to the proponents of socio-cultural evolution. The ideas of biological evolution was seen as an attractive explanation for many questions about the development of society.

Both Spencer and Comte view the society as a kind of organism subject to the process of growth—from simplicity to complexity, from chaos to order, from generalisation to specialisation, from flexibility to organisation. They agreed that the process of societies growth can be divided into certain stages, have their beginning and eventual end, and that this growth is in fact social progress—each newer, more evolved society is better. Thus progressivism became one of the basic ideas underlying the theory of socio-cultural evolutionism.

Auguste Comte, known as father of sociology, formulated the law of three stages: human development progresses from the theological stage, in which nature was mythically conceived and man sought the explanation of natural phenomena from supernatural beings, through metaphysical stage in which nature was conceived of as a result of obscure forces and man sought the explanation of natural phenomena from them until the final positive stage in which all abstract and obscure forces are discarded, and natural phenomena are explained by their constant relationship. This progress is forced through the development of human mind, and increasing application of thought, reasoning and logic to the understanding of the world. For Comte, it was the science-valuing society that was the highest, most developed type of human organization.

Herbert Spencer, who argued against government intervention, believing that society evolution should be toward increasing individual freedom, differentiated between two phases of development, focussing on the type of internal regulation within societies. Thus he differentiated between military and industrial societies. The earlier, more primitive military society has a goal of conquest and defence, is centralised, economically self-sufficient, collectivistic, puts the good of a group over the good of an individual, uses compulsion, force and repression, rewards loyalty, obedience and discipline. The industrial society has a goal of production and trade, is decentralised, interconnected with other societies via economic relations, achieves its goals through voluntary cooperation and individual self-restraint, treats the good of individual as the highest value, regulates the social life via voluntary relations, values initiative, independence and innovation. The transition process from the military to industrial society is the outcome of steady evolutionary processes within the society.

Regardless of how scholars of Spencer interpret his relation to Darwin, Spencer proved to be an incredibly popular figure in the 1870s, particularly in the United States. Authors such as Edward L. Youmans, William Graham Sumner, John Fiske, John W. Burgess, Lester Frank Ward, Lewis H. Morgan and other thinkers of the gilded age all developed similar theories of social evolutionism as a result of their exposure to Spencer as well as Darwin.

Lewis H. Morgan, an anthropologist whose ideas have had much impact on sociology, in his 1877 classic *Ancient Societies* differentiated between three eras: savagery, barbarism and civilization, which are divided by technological inventions, like fire, bow, pottery in the savage era, domestication of animals, agriculture, metalworking in the barbarian era and alphabet and writing in the civilization era. Thus Morgan introduced a link between social progress and technological progress. Morgan viewed technological progress as a force behind social progress, and any social change—in social institutions, organisations or ideologies—has its beginnings in technological change. Morgan's theories were popularised by Friedrich Engels, who based his famous work *The Origin of the Family, Private Property and the State* on it. For Engels and other Marxists, this theory was important as it supported their conviction that materialistic factors—economic and technological—are decisive in shaping the fate of humanity.

Émile Durkheim, another of the 'fathers' of sociology, developed a similar, dichotomal view of social progress. His key concept was social solidarity, as he defined social evolution in terms of progressing from mechanical solidarity to organic solidarity. In mechanical solidarity, people are self-sufficient, there is little integration and thus there is the need for use of force and repression to keep society together. In organic solidarity, people are much more integrated and interdependent and specialisation and cooperation is extensive. Progress from mechanical to organic solidarity is based first on population growth and increasing population density, second on increasing 'morality density' (development of more complex social interactions) and thirdly, on the increasing specialisation in workplace. To Durkheim, the most important factor in the social progress is the division of labour.

Anthropologists Sir E.B. Tylor in England and Lewis Henry Morgan in the United States worked with data from indigenous people, who they claimed represented earlier stages of cultural evolution that gave insight into the process and progression of evolution of culture. Morgan would later have a significant influence on Karl Marx and Friedrich Engels, who developed a theory of socio-cultural evolution in which the internal contradictions in society created a series of escalating stages that ended in a socialist society . Tylor and Morgan elaborated the theory of unilinear evolution, specifying criteria for categorising cultures according to their standing within a fixed system of growth of humanity as a whole and examining the modes and mechanisms of this growth. Theirs was often a concern with culture in general, not with individual cultures.

Their analysis of cross-cultural data was based on three assumptions:

1. Contemporary societies may be classified and ranked as more 'primitive' or more 'civilized'.
2. There are a determinate number of stages between 'primitive' and 'civilized' (e.g. band, tribe, chiefdom, and state).
3. All societies progress through these stages in the same sequence, but at different rates.

Theorists usually measured progression (that is, the difference between one stage and the next) in terms of increasing social complexity (including class differentiation and a complex division of labour), or an increase in intellectual, theological, and aesthetic sophistication. These 19th-century ethnologists used these principles primarily to explain differences in religious beliefs and kinship terminologies among various societies.

Lester Frank Ward developed Spencer's theory but unlike Spencer, who considered evolution to be general process applicable to the entire world, physical and sociological, Ward differentiated sociological evolution from biological evolution. He stressed that humans create goals for themselves and strive to realise them, whereas there is no such intelligence and awareness guiding the non-human world, which develops more or less at random. He created a hierarchy of evolution processes. First, there is cosmogenesis, creation and evolution of the world. Then, when life arises, there is biogenesis. Development of humanity leads to anthropogenesis, which is influenced by the human mind. Finally, when society develops, so does sociogenesis, which is the science of shaping the society to fit with various political, cultural and ideological goals.

Edward Burnett Tylor, pioneer of anthropology, focussed on the evolution of culture worldwide, noting that culture is an important part of every society and that it is also subject to the process of evolution. He believed that societies were at different stages of cultural development and that the purpose of anthropology was to reconstruct the evolution of culture, from primitive beginnings to the modern state.

Ferdinand Tönnies describes evolution as the development from informal society, where people have many liberties and there are few laws and obligations, to modern, formal rational society, dominated by traditions and laws and people are restricted from acting as they wish. He also notes that there is a tendency of standardisation and unification, when all smaller societies are absorbed into a single, large, modern society. Thus Tönnies can be said to describe part of the process known today as globalization. Tönnies was also one of the first sociologists to claim that the evolution of society is not necessarily going in the right direction, that social progress is not perfect, and it can even be called a regression as the newer, more evolved societies are obtained only after paying a high cost, resulting in decreasing satisfaction of individuals making up that society. Tönnies' work became the foundation of neoevolutionism.

Although not usually counted as a socio-cultural evolutionist, Max Weber's theory of tripartite classification of authority can be viewed as an evolutionary theory as well. Weber distinguishes three ideal types of political leadership, domination and authority: charismatic domination (familial and religious), traditional domination (patriarchs, patrimonalism, feudalism) and legal (rational) domination (modern law and state, bureaucracy). He also notes that legal domination is the most advanced, and that societies evolve from having mostly traditional and charismatic authorities to mostly rational and legal ones.

Critique and Impact on Modern Theories

The early 20th century inaugurated a period of systematic critical examination, and rejection of the sweeping generalisations of the unilineal theories of sociocultural evolution. Cultural anthropologists such as Franz Boas, along with his students, including Ruth Benedict and Margaret Mead, are regarded as the leaders of anthropology's rejection of classical social evolutionism.

They used sophisticated ethnography and more rigorous empirical methods to argue that Spencer, Tylor, and Morgan's theories were speculative and systematically misrepresented ethnographic data. Theories regarding 'stages' of evolution were especially criticised as illusions. Additionally, they rejected the distinction between 'primitive' and 'civilized' (or 'modern'), pointing out that so-called primitive contemporary societies have just as much history, and were just as evolved, as so-called civilized societies. They therefore argued that any attempt to use this theory to reconstruct the histories of non-literate (i.e. leaving no historical documents) peoples is entirely speculative and unscientific.

They observed that the postulated progression, which typically ended with a stage of civilization identical to that of modern Europe, is ethnocentric. They also pointed out that the theory assumes that societies are clearly bounded and distinct, when in fact cultural traits and forms often cross social boundaries and diffuse among many different societies (and is thus an important mechanism of change). Boas in his culture history approach focused on anthropological fieldwork in an attempt to identify factual processes instead of what he criticized as speculative stages of growth. His approach was a major influence on the American anthropology in the first half of the 20th century, and marked a retreat from high-level generalization and 'systems building'.

Later critics observed that this assumption of firmly bounded societies was proposed precisely at the time when European powers were colonising non-Western societies, and was thus self-serving. Many anthropologists and social theorists now consider unilineal cultural and social evolution a Western myth seldom based on solid empirical grounds. Critical theorists argue that notions of social evolution are simply justifications for power by the elites of society. Finally, the devastating World Wars that occurred between 1914 and 1945 crippled Europe's self-confidence. After millions of deaths, genocide, and the destruction of Europe's industrial infrastructure, the idea of progress seemed dubious at best.

Thus modern socio-cultural evolutionism rejects most of classical social evolutionism due to various theoretical problems:

- The theory was deeply ethnocentric—it makes heavy value judgements on different societies; with Western civilization seen as the most valuable.
- It assumed all cultures follow the same path or progression and have the same goals.
- It equated civilization with material culture (technology, cities, etc.)
- It equated evolution with progress or *fitness,* based on deep misunderstandings of evolutionary theory.

Because social evolution was posited as a scientific theory, it was often used to support unjust and often racist social practices—particularly colonialism, slavery, and the unequal economic conditions present within industrialized Europe. Social Darwinism is especially criticised, as it led to some philosophies used by the Nazis.

Max Weber, Disenchantment, and Critical Theory

Weber's major works in economic sociology and the sociology of religion dealt with the rationalization, secularisation, and so called 'disenchantment' which he associated with the rise of capitalism and modernity. In sociology, rationalization is the process whereby an increasing number of social actions become based on considerations of teleological efficiency or calculation rather than on motivations derived from morality, emotion, custom, or tradition. Rather than referring to what is genuinely 'rational' or 'logical', rationalization refers to a relentless quest for goals that might actually function to the *detriment* of a society. Rationalization is an ambivalent aspect of modernity, manifested especially in Western society; as a behaviour of the capitalist market; of rational administration in the state and bureaucracy; of the extension of modern science; and of the expansion of modern technology.

Weber's thought regarding the rationalizing and secularizing tendencies of modern Western society (sometimes described as the 'Weber Thesis') would blend with Marxism to facilitate critical theory, particularly in the work of thinkers such as Jürgen Habermas. Critical theorists, as antipositivists, are critical of the idea of a hierarchy of sciences or societies, particularly with respect to the sociological positivism originally set forth by Comte. Jürgen Habermas has critiqued the concept of pure instrumental rationality as meaning that scientific-thinking becomes something akin to ideology itself. For theorists such as Zygmunt Bauman, rationalization as a manifestation of modernity may be most closely and regrettably associated with the events of the Holocaust.

Modern Theories

Composite image of the Earth at night, created by NASA and NOAA. The brightest areas of the Earth are the most urbanized, but not necessarily the most populated. Even more than 100 years after the invention of the electric light, most regions remain thinly populated or unlit.

When the critique of classical social evolutionism became widely accepted, modern anthropological and sociological approaches changed respectively. Modern theories are careful to avoid unsourced, ethnocentric speculation, comparisons, or value judgements; more or less regarding individual societies as existing within their own historical contexts. These conditions provided the context for new theories such as cultural relativism and multilineal evolution.

In the 1920s and 30s, Gordon Childe revolutionized the study of cultural evolutionism. He conducted a comprehensive pre-history account that provided scholars with evidence for African and Asian cultural transmission into Europe. He combated scientific racism by finding the tools and artifacts of the indigenous people from Africa and Asia and showed how they influenced the technology of European culture. Evidence from his excavations countered the idea of Aryan supremacy and superiority. Childe explained cultural evolution by his theory of divergence with modifications of convergence. He postulated that different cultures form separate methods that meet different needs, but when two cultures were in contact they developed similar adaptations, solving similar problems. Rejecting Spencer's theory of parallel cultural evolution, Childe found that interactions between cultures contributed to the convergence of similar aspects most often attributed to one culture. Childe placed emphasis on human culture as a social construct rather than products of environmental or technological contexts. Childe coined the terms 'Neolithic Revolution', and 'Urban Revolution' which are still used today in the branch of pre-historic anthropology.

In 1941 anthropologist Robert Redfield wrote about a shift from 'folk society' to 'urban society'. By the 1940s cultural anthropologists such as Leslie White and Julian Steward sought to revive an evolutionary model on a more scientific basis, and succeeded in establishing an approach known as neoevolutionism. White rejected the opposition between 'primitive' and 'modern' societies but did argue that societies could be distinguished based on the amount of energy they harnessed, and that increased energy allowed for greater social differentiation (White's law). Steward on the other hand rejected the 19th-century notion of progress, and instead called attention to the Darwinian notion of 'adaptation', arguing that all societies had to adapt to their environment in some way.

The anthropologists Marshall Sahlins and Elman Service prepared an edited volume, *Evolution and Culture*, in which they attempted to synthesise White's and Steward's approaches. Other anthropologists, building on or responding to work by White and Steward, developed theories of cultural ecology and ecological anthropology. The most prominent examples are Peter Vayda and Roy Rappaport. By the late 1950s, students of Steward such as Eric Wolf and Sidney Mintz turned away from cultural ecology to Marxism, World Systems Theory, Dependency theory and Marvin Harris's Cultural materialism.

Today most anthropologists reject 19th-century notions of progress and the three assumptions of unilineal evolution. Following Steward, they take seriously the relationship between a culture and its environment to explain different aspects of a culture. But most modern cultural anthropologists have adopted a general systems approach, examining cultures as emergent systems and argue that one must consider the whole social environment, which includes political and economic relations among cultures. There are still others who continue to reject the entirety of the evolutionary thinking and look instead at historical contingencies, contacts with other cultures, and the operation of cultural symbol systems. As a result, the simplistic notion of 'cultural evolution' has grown less useful and given way to an entire series of more nuanced approaches to the relationship of culture and environment. In the area of development studies, authors such as Amartya Sen have developed an understanding of 'development' and 'human flourishing' that also question more simplistic notions of progress, while retaining much of their original inspiration.

Neoevolutionism

Neoevolutionism was the first in a series of modern multilineal evolution theories. It emerged in the 1930s and extensively developed in the period following the Second World War and was incorporated into both anthropology and sociology in the 1960s. It bases its theories on empirical evidence from areas of archaeology, palaeontology and historiography and tries to eliminate any references to systems of values, be it moral or cultural, instead trying to remain objective and simply descriptive.

While 19th-century evolutionism explained how culture develops by giving general principles of its evolutionary process, it was dismissed by the Historical Particularists as unscientific in the early 20th century. It was the neoevolutionary thinkers who brought back evolutionary thought and developed it to be acceptable to contemporary anthropology.

Neoevolutionism discards many ideas of classical social evolutionism, namely that of social progress, so dominant in previous sociology evolution-related theories. Then neoevolutionism discards the determinism argument and introduces probability, arguing that accidents and free will greatly affect the process of social evolution. It also supports counterfactual history—asking 'what if' and considering different possible paths that social evolution may take or might have taken, and thus allows for the fact that various cultures may develop in different ways, some skipping entire stages others have passed through. Neoevolutionism stresses the importance of empirical evidence. While 19th-century evolutionism used value judgments and assumptions for interpreting data, neoevolutionism relied on measurable information for analysing the process of socio-cultural evolution.

Leslie White, author of *The Evolution of Culture: The Development of Civilization to the Fall of Rome* (1959), attempted to create a theory explaining the entire history of humanity. The most important factor in his theory is technology. *Social systems are determined by technological systems*, wrote White in his book, echoing the earlier theory of Lewis Henry Morgan. He proposes a society's energy consumption as a measure of its advancement. He differentiates between five stages of human development. In the first, people use the energy of their own muscles. In the second, they use the energy of domesticated animals. In the third, they use the energy of plants (so White refers to agricultural revolution here). In the fourth, they learn to use the energy of natural resources: coal, oil, gas. In the fifth, they harness nuclear energy. White introduced a formula, P=E*T, where E is a measure of energy consumed, and T is the measure of efficiency of technical factors utilising the energy. This theory is similar to Russian astronomer Nikolai Kardashev's later theory of the Kardashev scale.

Julian Steward, author of *Theory of Culture Change: The Methodology of Multilinear Evolution* created the theory of 'multilinear' evolution which examined the way in which societies adapted to their environment. This approach was more nuanced than White's theory of 'unilinear evolution'. Steward rejected the 19th-century notion of progress, and instead called attention to the Darwinian notion of 'adaptation', arguing that all societies had to adapt to their environment in some way. He argued that different adaptations could be studied through the examination of the specific resources a society exploited, the technology the society relied on to exploit these resources, and the organization of human labour. He further argued that different environments and technologies would require different kinds of adaptations, and that as the resource base or technology changed, so too would a culture. In other words, cultures do not change according to some inner logic, but rather in terms of a changing relationship with a changing environment. Cultures therefore would not pass through the same stages in the same order as they changed—rather, they would change in varying ways and directions. He called his theory 'multilineal evolution'. He questioned the possibility of creating a social theory encompassing the entire evolution of humanity; however, he argued that anthropologists are not limited to describing specific existing cultures. He believed that it is possible to create theories analysing typical common culture, representative of specific eras or regions. As the decisive factors determining the development of given culture he pointed to technology and economics, but noted that there are secondary factors, like political system, ideologies and religion. All those factors push the evolution of a given society in several directions at the same time; hence the application of the term 'multilinear' to his theory of evolution.

Marshall Sahlins, co-editor with Elman Service of *Evolution and Culture* (1960), divided the evolution of societies into 'general' and 'specific'. General evolution is the tendency of cultural and social systems to increase in complexity, organization and adaptiveness to environment. However, as the various cultures are not isolated, there is interaction and a diffusion of their qualities (like technological inventions). This leads cultures to develop in different ways (specific evolution), as various elements are introduced to them in different combinations and at different stages of evolution.

In his *Power and Prestige* (1966) and *Human Societies: An Introduction to Macrosociology* (1974), Gerhard Lenski expands on the works of Leslie White and Lewis Henry Morgan. He views technological progress as the most basic factor in the evolution of societies and cultures. Unlike White, who defined technology as the ability to create and utilise energy, Lenski focuses on information—its amount and uses. The more information and knowledge (especially allowing the shaping of natural environment) a given society has, the more advanced it is. He distinguishes four stages of human development, based on advances in the history of communication. In the first stage, information is passed by genes. In the second, when humans gain sentience, they can learn and pass information through by experience. In the third, humans start using signs and develop logic. In the fourth, they can create symbols and develop language and writing. Advancements in the technology of communication translate into advancements in the economic system and political system, distribution of goods, social inequality and other spheres of social life. He also differentiates societies based on their level of technology, communication and economy:

1. hunters and gatherers;
2. agricultural;
3. industrial; and
4. special (like fishing societies).

Talcott Parsons, author of *Societies: Evolutionary and Comparative Perspectives* (1966) and *The System of Modern Societies* (1971) divided evolution into four subprocesses:

1. division, which creates functional subsystems from the main system;
2. adaptation, where those systems evolve into more efficient versions;
3. inclusion of elements previously excluded from the given systems; and
4. generalization of values, increasing the legitimization of the ever more complex system. He shows those processes on 4 stages of evolution:
   (i) primitive or foraging;
   (ii) archaic agricultural;
   (iii) classical or "historic" in his terminology, using formalized and universalizing theories about reality; and
   (iv) modern empirical cultures.

However, these divisions in Parsons theory is the more formal ways in which the evolutionary process is conceptualized and should not be mistaken for with Parsons' actual theory. Parsons develops a theory, where he tries to reveal the complexity of the processes which take form between two points of necessity, the first is the cultural 'necessity', which is given through the values-system of each evolving community; the other is the environmental necessities, which most directly is reflected in the material realities of the basic production system and reflected in the relative capacity of each industrial-economical level at each window of time. Generally, Parsons highlights that the dynamics and directions of these process is shaped by the cultural imperative embodied in the cultural heritage and more secondary an outcome of sheer 'economic' conditions.

Socio-biology

Socio-biology departs perhaps the furthest from classical social evolutionism. It was introduced by Edward Wilson in his 1975 book *Sociobiology: The New Synthesis* and followed his adaptation of evolutionary theory to the field of social sciences. Wilson pioneered the attempt to explain the evolutionary mechanics behind social behaviours such as altruism, aggression, and nurturance. In doing so, Wilson sparked one of the greatest scientific controversies of the 20th century.

Socio-biologists have argued for a dual inheritance theory, which posits that humans are products of both biological evolution and socio-cultural evolution, each subject to their own selective mechanisms and forms of transmission (i.e. in the case of biology, genes, and cultural evolutionary units are often called memes). This approach focuses on both the mechanisms of cultural transmission and the selective pressures that influence cultural change. This version of socio-cultural evolution shares little in common with the stadial evolutionary models of the early and mid-20th century. This approach has been embraced by many psychologists and some cultural anthropologists, but very few physical anthropologists.

The current theory of evolution, the modern evolutionary synthesis (or neo-darwinism), explains that evolution of species occurs through a combination of Darwin's mechanism of natural selection and Gregor Mendel's theory of genetics as the basis for biological inheritance and mathematical population genetics. Essentially, the modern synthesis introduced the connection between two important discoveries; the units of evolution (genes) with the main mechanism of evolution (selection).

Due to its close reliance on biology, socio-biology is often considered a branch of the biology and sociology disciplines, although it uses techniques from a plethora of sciences, including ethology, evolution, zoology, archaeology, population genetics, and many others. Within the study of human societies, socio-biology is closely related to the fields of human behavioural ecology and evolutionary psychology.

Socio-biology has remained highly controversial as it contends genes explain specific human behaviours, although socio-biologists describe this role as a very complex and often unpredictable interaction between nature and nurture. The most notable critics of the view that genes play a direct role in human behaviour have been biologists Richard Lewontin and Stephen Jay Gould.

Since the rise of evolutionary psychology, another school of thought, Dual Inheritance Theory, has emerged in the past 25 years that applies the mathematical standards of Population genetics to modelling the adaptive and selective principles of culture. This school of thought was pioneered by Robert Boyd at UCLA and Peter Richerson at UC Davis and expanded by William Wimsatt, among others. Boyd and Richerson's book, *Culture and the Evolutionary Process* (1985), was a highly mathematical description of cultural change, later published in a more accessible form in *Not by Genes Alone* (2004). In Boyd and Richerson's view, cultural evolution, operating on socially learned information, exists on a separate ground from genetic evolution, and while the two are related, cultural evolution is more dynamic, rapid, and influential on human society than genetic evolution.

Theory of Modernization

Theories of modernization have been developed and popularized in 1950s and 1960s and are closely related to the dependency theory and development theory. They combine the previous theories of socio-cultural evolution with practical experiences and empirical research, especially those from the era of decolonization. The theory states that:

- Western countries are the most developed, and rest of the world (mostly former colonies) are on the earlier stages of development, and will eventually reach the same level as the Western world.
- Development stages go from the traditional societies to developed ones.
- Third World countries have fallen behind with their social progress and need to be directed on their way to becoming more advanced.

Developing from classical social evolutionism theories, theory of modernization stresses the modernization factor: many societies are simply trying (or need to) emulate the most successful societies and cultures. It also states that it is possible to do so, thus supporting the concepts of social engineering and that the developed countries can and should help those less developed, directly or indirectly.

Among the scientists who contributed much to this theory are Walt Rostow, who in his *The Stages of Economic Growth: A Non-Communist Manifesto* (1960) concentrates on the economic system side of the modernization, trying to show factors needed for a country to reach the path to modernization in his Rostovian take-off model. David Apter concentrated on the political system and history of democracy, researching the connection between democracy, good governance and efficiency and modernization. David McClelland approached this subject from the psychological perspective, with his motivations theory, arguing that modernization cannot happen until given society values innovation, success and free enterprise. Alex Inkeles similarly creates a model of *modern personality*, which needs to be independent, active, interested in public policies and cultural matters, open for new experiences, rational and being able to create long-term plans for the future. Some works of Jürgen Habermas are also connected with this subfield.

Theory of modernization has been subject to some criticism similar to that levied on classical social evolutionism, especially for being too ethnocentric, one-sided and focussed on the Western world and culture.

Prediction for a Stable Cultural and Social Future

Cultural evolution follows punctuated equilibrium which Gould and Eldredge developed for biological evolution. Bloomfield has written that human societies follow punctuated equilibrium which would mean first, a stable society, a transition resulting in a subsequent stable society with greater complexity. Using these guidelines, mankind has had a stable animal society, a transition to a stable tribal society, another transition to a stable peasant society and is currently in a transitional industrial society.

The status of a human society rests on the productivity of food production. Deevey reported on the growth of the number of humans. Deevey also reported on the productivity of food production, noting that productivity changes very little for stable societies, but increases during transitions. When productivity and especially food productivity can no longer be increased, Bloomfield has proposed that man will have achieved a stable automated society. Space is also assumed to allow for the continued growth of the human population, as well as provide a solution to the current pollution problem by providing limitless energy from solar satellite power stations.

Scientists have used the theory of evolution to analyze various trends and to predict the future development of societies. These scientists have created the theories of post-industrial societies, arguing that the current era of industrial society is coming to an end, and services and information are becoming more important than industry and goods.

In 1974, sociologist Daniel Bell, author of *The Coming of Post-Industrial Society*, introduced the concept of post-industrial society. He divided the history of humanity into three eras: pre-industrial, industrial and post-industrial. He predicted that by the end of the 20th century, United States, Japan and Western Europe would reach the post-industrial stage. This 'post-industrial' stage would be demonstrated by:

- ❖ domination of the service sector (administration, banking, trade, transport, healthcare, education, science, mass media, culture) over the traditional industry sector (manufacturing industries, which have surpassed the more traditional, agriculture and mining sector after the 19th-century Industrial Revolution);
- ❖ growing importance of information technologies;
- ❖ increased role of long-term planning, modelling future trends;

- domination of technocracy and pragmatism over traditional ethics and ideologies;
- increasing importance and use of technology and intellect;
- changes in the traditional hierarchy of social classes, with highly educated specialists and scientists overtaking the traditional bourgeois.

From the 1970s many other sociologists and anthropologists, like Alvin Toffler and John Naisbitt have followed in Bell's footsteps and created similar theories. John Naisbitt introduced the concept of megatrends: powerful, global trends that are changing societies on the worldwide scale. Among the megatrends that he mentions was the process of globalization. Another important megatrend was the increase in performance of computers and the development of the World Wide Web. Marshall McLuhan introduced the concept of the global village and this term was soon adapted by the researchers of globalization and the Internet. Naisbitt and many other proponents of the theory of post-industrial societies argues that those megatrends lead to decentralization, weakening of the central government, increasing importance of local initiatives and direct democracy, changes in the hierarchy of the traditional social classes, development of new social movements and increased powers of consumers and number of choices available to them (Toffler even used the term 'overchoice').

Some of the more extreme visions of the post-industrial society are those related to the theory of the technological singularity. This theory refers to a predicted point or period in the development of a civilization at which due to the acceleration of technological progress, the societal, scientific and economic change is so rapid that nothing beyond that time can be reliably comprehended, understood or predicted by the pre-singularity humans. Such a singularity was first discussed in the 1950s, and vastly popularized in the 1980s by Vernor Vinge.

Critics of the post-industrial society theory point out that it is very vague and as any prediction, there is no guarantee that any of the trends visible today will in fact exist in the future or develop in the directions predicted by contemporary researchers. However, no serious sociologist would argue it is possible to predict the future, but only that such theories allow us to gain a better understanding of the changes taking place in the modernised world.

Contemporary Discourse Over Socio-cultural Evolution

The Cold War period was marked by rivalry between two superpowers, both of which considered themselves to be the most highly evolved cultures on the planet. The USSR painted itself as a socialist society which emerged out of class struggle, destined to reach the state of communism, while sociologists in the United States (such as Talcott Parsons) argued that the freedom and prosperity of the United States were a proof of a higher level of socio-cultural evolution of its culture and society. At the same time, decolonization created newly independent countries who sought to become more developed—a model of progress and industrialization which was itself a form of sociocultural evolution.

There is, however, a tradition in European social theory from Rousseau to Max Weber that argues that this progression coincides with a loss of human freedom and dignity. At the height of the Cold War, this tradition merged with an interest in ecology to influence an activist culture in the 1960s. This movement produced a variety of political and philosophical programmes which emphasised the importance of bringing society and the environment into harmony.

Current political theories of the new tribalists consciously mimic ecology and the life-ways of indigenous peoples, augmenting them with modern sciences. Ecoregional Democracy attempts to confine the 'shifting groups', or tribes, within 'more or less clear boundaries' that a society inherits from the surrounding ecology, to the borders of a naturally occurring ecoregion.

Progress can proceed by competition between but not within tribes, and it is limited by ecological borders or by Natural Capitalism incentives which attempt to mimic the pressure of natural selection on a human society by forcing it to adapt consciously to scarce energy or materials. Gaians argue that societies evolve deterministically to play a role in the ecology of their biosphere, or else die off as failures due to competition from more efficient societies exploiting nature's leverage.

Thus, some have appealed to theories of socio-cultural evolution to assert that optimising the ecology and the social harmony of closely knit groups is more desirable or necessary than the progression to 'civilization'. A 2002 poll of experts on Nearctic and Neotropic indigenous peoples (reported in *Harper's* magazine) revealed that *all of them* would have preferred to be a typical New World person in the year 1491, prior to any European contact, rather than a typical European of that time.

This approach has been criticised by pointing out that there are a number of historical examples of indigenous peoples doing severe environmental damage (such as the deforestation of Easter Island and the extinction of mammoths in North America) and that proponents of the goal have been trapped by the European stereotype of the noble savage.

Today, post-modernists question whether the notions of evolution or society have inherent meaning and whether they reveal more about the person doing the description than the thing being described. Observing and observed cultures may lack sufficient cultural similarities (such as a common foundation ontology) to be able to communicate their respective priorities easily. Or, one may impose such a system of belief and judgment upon another, via conquest or colonization. For instance, observation of very different ideas of mathematics and physics in indigenous peoples led indirectly to ideas such as George Lakoff's "cognitive science of mathematics", which asks if measurement systems themselves can be objective.

Unilineal Evolution

Unilineal evolution (also referred to as classical social evolution) is a 19th century social theory about the evolution of societies and cultures. It was composed of many competing theories by various sociologists and anthropologists, who believed that Western culture is the contemporary pinnacle of social evolution. Different social status is aligned in a single line that moves from most primitive to most civilized. This theory is now generally considered obsolete in academic circles.

Theories of social and cultural evolution are common in modern European thought. Prior to the 18th century, Europeans predominantly believed that societies on Earth were in a state of decline. European society held up the world of antiquity as a standard to aspire to, and Ancient Greece and Ancient Rome produced levels of technical accomplishment which Europeans of the Middle Ages sought to emulate. At the same time, Christianity taught that people lived in a debased world fundamentally inferior to the Garden of Eden and Heaven. During the Age of Enlightenment, however, European self-confidence grew and the notion of progress became increasingly popular. It was during this period that what would later become known as 'sociological and cultural evolution' would have its roots.

The Enlightenment thinkers often speculated that societies progressed through stages of increasing development and looked for the logic, order and the set of scientific truths that determined the course of human history. Georg Wilhelm Friedrich Hegel, for example, argued that social development was an inevitable and determined process, similar to an acorn which has no choice but to become an oak tree. Likewise, it was assumed that societies start out primitive, perhaps in a Hobbesian state of nature, and naturally progress toward something resembling industrial Europe.

While earlier authors such as Michel de Montaigne discussed how societies change through time, it was truly the Scottish Enlightenment which proved key in the development of cultural evolution. After Scotland's union with England in 1707, several Scottish thinkers pondered on the relationship between progress and the 'decadence' brought about by increased trade with England and the affluence it produced. The result was a series of 'conjectural histories.' Authors such as Adam Ferguson, John Millar, and Adam Smith argued that all societies pass through a series of four stages: hunting and gathering, pastoralism and nomadism, agricultural, and finally a stage of commerce. These thinkers thus understood the changes Scotland was undergoing as a transition from an agricultural to a mercantile society.

Philosophical concepts of progress (such as those expounded by the German philosopher G.W.F. Hegel) developed as well during this period. In France authors such as Claude Adrien Helvétius and other philosophers were influenced by this Scottish tradition. Later thinkers such as Comte de Saint-Simon developed these ideas. Auguste Comte in particular presented a coherent view of social progress and a new discipline to study it — sociology.

These developments took place in a wider context. The first process was colonialism. Although Imperial powers settled most differences of opinion with their colonial subjects with force, increased awareness of non-Western peoples raised new questions for European scholars about the nature of society and culture. Similarly, effective administration required some degree of understanding of other cultures. Emerging theories of social evolution allowed Europeans to organize their new knowledge in a way that reflected and justified their increasing political and economic domination of others: colonized people were less-evolved, colonizing people were more evolved. The second process was the Industrial Revolution and the rise of capitalism which allowed and promoted continual revolutions in the means of production. Emerging theories of social evolution reflected a belief that the changes in Europe wrought by the Industrial Revolution and capitalism were obvious improvements. Industrialization, combined with the intense political change brought about by the French Revolution, US Constitution and Polish Constitution of the 3 May, which were paving the way for the dominance of democracy, forced European thinkers to reconsider some of their assumptions about how society was organized.

Eventually, in the 19th century three great, classical theories of social and historical change were created: the social evolutionism theory, the social cycle theory and the Marxist historical materialism theory. Those theories had one common factor: they all agreed that the history of humanity is pursuing a certain fixed path, most likely that of the social progress. Thus, each past event is not only chronologically, but causally tied to the present and future events. Those theories postulated that by recreating the sequence of those events, sociology could discover the Laws of history.

While social evolutionists agree that the evolution-like process leads to the social progress, classical social evolutionists have developed many different theories, known as theories of unilineal evolution. Social evolutionism was the prevailing theory of early socio-cultural anthropology and social commentary, and is associated with scholars like Auguste Comte, Edward Burnett Tylor, Lewis Henry Morgan, and Herbert Spencer. Social evolutionism represented an attempt to formalize social thinking along scientific lines, later influenced by the biological theory of evolution. If organisms could develop over time according to discernible, deterministic laws, then it seemed reasonable that societies could as well. This really marks the beginning of Anthropology as a scientific discipline and a departure from traditional religious views of 'primitive' cultures.

The term 'Classical Social Evolutionism' is most closely associated with the 19th century writings of Auguste Comte, Herbert Spencer (who coined the phrase 'survival of the fittest') and William Graham Sumner. In many ways Spencer's theory of 'cosmic evolution' has much more in common with the works of Jean-Baptiste Lamarck and Auguste Comte than with contemporary works of Charles Darwin. Spencer also developed and published his theories several years earlier than Darwin. In regard to social institutions, however, there is a good case that Spencer's writings might be classified as 'Social Evolutionism'. Although he wrote that societies over time progressed, and that progress was accomplished through competition, he stressed that the individual (rather than the collectivity) is the unit of analysis that evolves, that evolution takes place through natural selection and that it affects social as well as biological phenomenon.

Progressivism

Both Spencer and Comte view the society as a kind of organism subject to the process of growth — from simplicity to complexity, from chaos to order, from generalisation to specialisation, from flexibility to organisation. They agreed that the process of societies growth can be divided into certain stages, have their beginning and eventual end, and that this growth is in fact social progress — each newer, more evolved society is better. Thus progressivism became one of the basic ideas underlying the theory of social evolutionism.

Comte

Auguste Comte, known as father of sociology, formulated the law of three stages: human development progresses from the theological stage, in which nature was mythically conceived and man sought the explanation of natural phenomena from supernatural beings, through metaphysical stage in which nature was conceived of as a result of obscure forces and man sought the explanation of natural phenomena from them until the final positive stage in which all abstract and obscure forces are discarded, and natural phenomena are explained by their constant relationship. This progress is forced through the development of human mind, and increasing application of thought, reasoning and logic to the understanding of world.

Spencer

Herbert Spencer, who believed that society was evolving toward increasing freedom for individuals; and so held that government intervention, ought to be minimal in social and political life, differentiated between two phases of development, focussing is on the type of internal regulation within societies. Thus he differentiated between military and industrial societies. The earlier, more primitive military society has a goal of conquest and defence, is centralised, economically self-sufficient, collectivistic, puts the good of a group over the good of an individual, uses compulsion, force and repression, rewards loyalty, obedience and discipline. The industrial society has a goal of production and trade, is decentralised, interconnected with other societies via economic relations, achieves its goals through voluntary cooperation and individual self-restraint, treats the good of individual as the highest value, regulates the social life via voluntary relations, and values initiative, independence and innovation.

Regardless of how scholars of Spencer interpret his relation to Darwin, Spencer proved to be an incredibly popular figure in the 1870s, particularly in the United States. Authors such as Edward L. Youmans, William Graham Sumner, John Fiske, John W. Burgess, Lester Frank Ward, Lewis H. Morgan and other thinkers of the gilded age all developed theories of social evolutionism as a result of their exposure to Spencer as well as Darwin.

Morgan

Lewis H. Morgan, an anthropologist whose ideas have had much impact on sociology, in his 1877 classic '*Ancient Societies*' differentiated between three eras: savagery, barbarism and civilisation, which are divided by technological inventions, like fire, bow, pottery in savage era, domestication of animals, agriculture, metalworking in barbarian era and alphabet and writing in civilisation era. Thus Morgan introduced a link between the social progress and technological progress. Morgan viewed the technological progress as a force behind social progress, and any social change — in social institutions, organisations or ideologies have their beginning in the change of technology. Morgan's theories were popularised by Friedrich Engels, who based his famous work *"The Origin of the Family, Private Property and the State"* on it. For Engels and other marxists, this theory was important as it supported their conviction that materialistic factors — economical and technological — are decisive in shaping the fate of humanity.

Durkheim

Émile Durkheim, another of the 'fathers' of sociology, has developed a similar, dichotomical view of social progress. His key concept was social solidarity, as he defined the social evolution in terms of progressing from mechanical solidarity to organic solidarity. In mechanical solidarity, people are self-sufficient, there is little integration and thus there is the need for use of force and repression to keep society together. In organic solidarity, people are much more integrated and interdependent and specialisation and cooperation is extensive. Progress from mechanical to organic solidarity is based first on population growth and increasing population density, second on increasing 'morality density' (development of more complex social interactions) and thirdly, on the increasing specialisation in workplace. To Durkheim, the most important factor in the social progress is the division of labour.

Tylor and Morgan

Anthropologists Sir E.B. Tylor in England and Lewis Henry Morgan in the United States worked with data from indigenous people, whom they claimed represented earlier stages of cultural evolution that gave insight into the process and progression of cultural evolution. Morgan would later have a significant influence on Karl Marx and Friedrich Engels, who developed a theory of cultural evolution in which the internal contradictions in society created a series of escalating stages that ended in a socialist society . Tylor and Morgan elaborated upon, modified and expanded the theory of unilinear evolution, specifying criteria for categorizing cultures according to their standing within a fixed system of growth of humanity as a whole while examining the modes and mechanisms of this growth.

Their analysis of cross-cultural data was based on three assumptions:

- contemporary societies may be classified and ranked as more 'primitive' or more 'civilized';
- There are a determinate number of stages between 'primitive' and 'civilized' (e.g. band, tribe, chiefdom, and state);
- All societies progress through these stages in the same sequence, but at different rates.

Theorists usually measured progression (that is, the difference between one stage and the next) in terms of increasing social complexity (including class differentiation and a complex division of labor), or an increase in intellectual, theological, and aesthetic sophistication. These 19th century ethnologists used these principles primarily to explain differences in religious beliefs and kinship terminologies among various societies.

Ward

There were however notable differences between the work of Lester Frank Ward's and Tylor's approaches. Lester Frank Ward developed Spencer's theory but unlike Spencer, who considered the evolution to be general process applicable to the entire world, physical and sociological, Ward differentiated sociological evolution from biological evolution. He stressed that humans create goals for themselves and strive to realise them, whereas there is no such intelligence and awareness guiding the non-human world, which develops more or less at random. He created a hierarchy of evolution processes. First, there is cosmogenesis, creation and evolution of the world. Then, after life develops, there is biogenesis. Development of humanity leads to anthropogenesis, which is influenced by the human mind. Finally, when society develops, so does sociogenesis, which is the science of shaping the society to fit with various political, cultural and ideological goals.

Edward Burnett Tylor, pioneer of anthropology, focussed on the evolution of culture worldwide, noting that culture is an important part of every society and that it is also subject to the process of evolution. He believed that societies were at different stages of cultural development and that the purpose of anthropology was to reconstruct the evolution of culture, from primitive beginnings to the modern state.

Tönnies

Ferdinand Tönnies describes the evolution as the development from informal society, where people have many liberties and there are few laws and obligations, to modern, formal rational society, dominated by traditions and laws and are restricted from acting as they wish. He also notes that there is a tendency of standardization and unification, when all smaller societies are absorbed into the single, large, modern society. Thus Torbes can be said to describe part of the process known today as the globalisation. Torbes was also one of the first sociologists to claim that the evolution of society is not necessarily going in the right direction, that the social progress is not perfect, it can even be called a regress as the newer, more evolved societies are obtained only after paying a high costs, resulting in decreasing satisfaction of individuals making up that society. Tönnies' work became the foundation of neo-evolutionism.

Boas

The early 20th century inaugurated a period of systematic critical examination, and rejection of unilineal theories of cultural evolution. Cultural anthropologists such as Franz Boas, typically regarded as the leader of anthropology's rejection of classical social evolutionism, used sophisticated ethnography and more rigorous empirical methods to argue that Spencer, Tylor, and Morgan's theories were speculative and systematically misrepresented ethnographic data. Additionally, they rejected the distinction between 'primitive' and 'civilized' (or 'modern'), pointing out that so-called primitive contemporary societies have just as much history, and were just as evolved, as so-called civilized societies. They therefore argued that any attempt to use this theory to reconstruct the histories of non-literate (i.e. leaving no historical documents) peoples is entirely speculative and unscientific. They observed that the postulated progression, which typically ended with a stage of civilization identical to that of modern Europe, is ethnocentric. They also pointed out that the theory assumes that societies are clearly bounded and distinct, when in fact cultural traits and forms often cross social boundaries and diffuse among many different societies (and is thus an important mechanism of change).Boas in his culture history approach focused on anthropological fieldwork in an attempt to identify factual processes instead of what he criticized as speculative stages of growth. His approach was a major influence on the American anthropology in the first half of the 20th century, and marked a retreat from high-level generalization and 'systems building'. The contribution to cultural anthropology by Boas is extraordinary, if not controversial.

Global Change

Later critics observed that this assumption of firmly bounded societies was proposed precisely at the time when European powers were colonizing non-Western societies, and was thus self-serving. Many anthropologists and social theorists now consider unilineal cultural and social evolution a Western myth seldom based on solid empirical grounds. Critical theorists argue that notions of social evolution are simply justifications for power by the elites of society. Finally, the devastating World Wars that occurred between 1914 and 1945 crippled Europe's self-confidence. After millions of deaths, genocide, and the destruction of Europe's industrial infrastructure, the idea of progress seemed dubious at best.

15 Speciation

Speciation is the evolutionary process by which new biological species arise. The biologist Orator F. Cook seems to have been the first to coin the term 'speciation' for the splitting of lineages or 'cladogenesis,' as opposed to 'anagenesis' or 'phyletic evolution' occurring within lineages. Whether genetic drift is a minor or major contributor to speciation is the subject of much ongoing discussion. There are four geographic modes of speciation in nature, based on the extent to which speciating populations are geographically isolated from one another: allopatric, peripatric, parapatric, and sympatric. Speciation may also be induced artificially, through animal husbandry or laboratory experiments. Observed examples of each kind of speciation are provided throughout.

All forms of natural speciation have taken place over the course of evolution; however it still remains a subject of debate as to the relative importance of each mechanism in driving biodiversity.

One example of natural speciation is the diversity of the three-spined stickleback, a marine fish that, after the last ice age, has undergone speciation into new freshwater colonies in isolated lakes and streams. Over an estimated 10,000 generations, the sticklebacks show structural differences that are greater than those seen between different genera of fish including variations in fins, changes in the number or size of their bony plates, variable jaw structure, and colour differences.

There is debate as to the rate at which speciation events occur over geologic time. While some evolutionary biologists claim that speciation events have remained relatively constant over time, some palaeontologists such as Niles Eldredge and Stephen Jay Gould have argued that species usually remain unchanged over long stretches of time, and that speciation occurs only over relatively brief intervals, a view known as *punctuated equilibrium*.

Allopatric

During allopatric (from the ancient Greek *allos*, 'other' + Greek *patra*, 'fatherland') speciation, a population splits into two geographically isolated populations (for example, by habitat fragmentation due to geographical change such as mountain building or social change such as emigration). The isolated populations then undergo genotypic and/or phenotypic divergence as:

(a) they become subjected to dissimilar selective pressures;

(b) they independently undergo genetic drift;

(c) different mutations arise in the two populations.

When the populations come back into contact, they have evolved such that they are reproductively isolated and are no longer capable of exchanging genes.

Island genetics, the tendency of small, isolated genetic pools to produce unusual traits, has been observed in many circumstances, including insular dwarfism and the radical changes among certain famous island chains, for example on Komodo. The Galápagos islands are particularly famous for their influence on Charles Darwin. During his five weeks there he heard that Galápagos tortoises could be identified by island, and noticed that Mockingbirds differed from one island to another, but it was only nine months later that he reflected that such facts could show that species were changeable. When he returned to England, his speculation on evolution deepened after experts informed him that these were separate species, not just varieties, and famously that other differing Galápagos birds were all species of finches. Though the finches were less important for Darwin, more recent research has shown the birds now known as Darwin's finches to be a classic case of adaptive evolutionary radiation.

Peripatric

In peripatric speciation, new species are formed in isolated, smaller peripheral populations that are prevented from exchanging genes with the main population. It is related to the concept of a founder effect, since small populations often undergo bottlenecks. Genetic drift is often proposed to play a significant role in peripatric speciation.

Observed Instances

- ❖ Mayr bird fauna

- The Australian bird *Petroica multicolour*
- Reproductive isolation occurs in populations of *Drosophila* subject to population bottlenecking

The London Underground mosquito is a variant of the mosquito *Culex pipiens* that entered in the London Underground in the nineteenth century. Evidence for its speciation include genetic divergence, behavioural differences, and difficulty in mating.

Parapatric

In parapatric speciation, there is only partial separation of the zones of two diverging populations afforded by geography; individuals of each species may come in contact or cross habitats from time to time, but reduced fitness of the heterozygote leads to selection for behaviours or mechanisms that prevent their inter-breeding. Parapatric speciation is modelled on continuous variation within a 'single', connected habitat acting as a source of natural selection rather than the effects of isolation of habitats produced in peripatric and allopatric speciation.

Ecologists refer to parapatric and peripatric speciation in terms of ecological niches. A niche must be available in order for a new species to be successful.

Sympatric

Sympatric speciation refers to the formation of two or more descendant species from a single ancestral species all occupying the same geographic location.

In sympatric speciation, species diverge while inhabiting the same place. Often-cited examples of sympatric speciation are found in insects that become dependent on different host plants in the same area. However, the existence of sympatric speciation as a mechanism of speciation is still hotly contested. People have argued that the evidences of sympatric speciation are in fact examples of micro-allopatric, or heteropatric speciation. The most widely accepted example of sympatric speciation is that of the cichlids of Lake Nabugabo in East Africa, which is thought to be due to *sexual selection*.

Until recently, there has a been a dearth of hard evidence that supports this form of speciation, with a general feeling that interbreeding would soon eliminate any genetic differences that might appear. But there has been at least one recent study that suggests that sympatric speciation has occurred in Tennessee cave salamanders.

The three-spined sticklebacks, freshwater fishes, that have been studied by Dolph Schluter (who received his Ph.D. for his work on Darwin's finches with Peter J. Grant) and his current colleagues in British Columbia, were once thought to provide an intriguing example best explained by sympatric speciation. Schluter and colleagues found:

- Two different species of three-spined sticklebacks in each of five different lakes.
- A large benthic species with a large mouth that feeds on large prey in the littoral zone.
- A smaller limnetic species — with a smaller mouth — that feeds on the small plankton in open water.
- DNA analysis indicates that each lake was colonized independently, presumably by a marine ancestor, after the last ice age.
- DNA analysis also shows that the two species in each lake are more closely related to each other than they are to any of the species in the other lakes.
- The two species in each lake are reproductively isolated; neither mates with the other.

However, aquarium tests showed:

- the benthic species from one lake will spawn with the benthic species from the other lakes;
- likewise the limnetic species from the different lakes will spawn with each other;
- these benthic and limnetic species even display their mating preferences when presented with sticklebacks from Japanese lakes; that is, a Canadian benthic prefers a Japanese benthic over its close limnetic cousin from its own lake.

Their conclusion in each lake, what began as a single population faced such competition for limited resources that:

- disruptive selection — competition favouring fishes at either extreme of body size and mouth size over those nearer the mean — coupled with:
  - assortative mating – each size preferred mates like it — favoured a divergence into two subpopulations exploiting different food in different parts of the lake.
  - The fact that this pattern of speciation occurred the same way on three separate occasions suggests strongly that ecological factors in a sympatric population can cause speciation.

However, the DNA evidence cited above is from mitochondrial DNA (mtDNA), which can often move easily between closely related species ('introgression') when they hybridize. A more recent study, using genetic markers from the nuclear genome, shows that limnetic forms in different lakes are more closely related to each other (and to marine lineages) than to benthic forms in the same lake. The three-spine stickleback is now usually considered an example of 'double invasion' (a form of allopatric speciation) in which repeated invasions of marine forms have subsequently differentiated into benthic and limnetic forms. The three-spine stickleback provides an example of how molecular biogeographic studies that rely solely on mtDNA can be misleading, and that consideration of the genealogical history of alleles from multiple unlinked markers (i.e. nuclear genes) is necessary to infer speciation histories.

Sympatric speciation driven by ecological factors may also account for the extraordinary diversity of crustaceans living in the depths of Siberia's Lake Baikal.

Speciation via Polyploidization

Speciation via polyploidy: A diploid cell undergoes failed meiosis, producing diploid gametes, which self-fertilize to produce a tetraploid zygote.

Polyploidy is a mechanism often attributed to causing some speciation events in sympatry. Not all polyploids are reproductively isolated from their parental plants, so an increase in chromosome number may not result in the complete cessation of gene flow between the incipient polyploids and their parental diploids.

Polyploidy is observed in many species of both plants and animals, and results in rapid speciation since offspring of, for example, tetraploid x diploid matings result in triploid sterile progeny. It has been proposed that many of the existing plant and most animal species have undergone an event of polyploidization in their evolutionary history. However, reproduction is often by parthenogenesis since polyploid animals are often sterile. [needs further editing—not true in plants]. Rare instances of polyploid mammals are known, but most often result in prenatal death.

Hawthorn Fly

One example of evolution at work is the case of the hawthorn fly, *Rhagoletis pomonella*, also known as the apple maggot fly, which appears to be undergoing sympatric speciation. Different populations of hawthorn fly feed on different fruits. A distinct population emerged in North America in the 19th century some time after apples, a non-native species, were introduced. This apple-feeding population normally feeds only on apples and not on the historically preferred fruit of hawthorns. The current hawthorn feeding population does not normally feed on apples. Some evidence, such as the fact that six out of thirteen allozyme loci are different, that hawthorn flies mature later in the season and take longer to mature than apple flies; and that there is little evidence of interbreeding (researchers have documented a 4-6% hybridization rate) suggests that sympatric speciation is occurring. The emergence of the new hawthorn fly is an example of evolution in progress.

SPECIATION VIA HYBRID FORMATION

Reinforcement (Wallace effect)

Reinforcement is the process by which natural selection increases reproductive isolation. It may occur after two populations of the same species are separated and then come back into contact. If their reproductive isolation was complete, then they will have already developed into two separate incompatible species. If their reproductive isolation is incomplete, then further mating between the populations will produce hybrids, which may or may not be fertile. If the hybrids are infertile, or fertile but less fit than their ancestors, then there will be no further reproductive isolation and speciation has essentially occurred (e.g., as in horses and donkeys.) The reasoning behind this is that if the parents of the hybrid offspring each have naturally selected traits for their own certain environments, the hybrid offspring will bear traits from both, therefore would not fit either ecological niche as well as either parent. The low fitness of the hybrids would cause selection to favour assortative mating, which would control hybridization. This is sometimes called the Wallace effect after the evolutionary biologist Alfred Russel Wallace who suggested in the late 19th century that it might be an important factor in speciation. If the hybrid offspring are more fit than their ancestors, then the populations will merge back into the same species within the area they are in contact.

Reinforcement is required for both parapatric and sympatric speciation. Without reinforcement, the geographic area of contact between different forms of the same species, called their 'hybrid zone', will not develop into a boundary between the different species. Hybrid zones are regions where diverged populations meet and interbreed. Hybrid offspring are very common in these regions, which are usually created by diverged species coming into secondary contact. Without reinforcement the two species would have uncontrollable inbreeding. Reinforcement may be induced in artificial selection experiments as described below.

Artificial Speciation

New species have been created by domesticated animal husbandry, but the initial dates and methods of the initiation of such species are not clear. For example, domestic sheep were created by hybridisation, and no longer produce viable offspring with *Ovis orientalis*, one species from which they are descended. Domestic cattle, on the other hand, can be considered the same species as several varieties of wild ox, gaur, yak, etc., as they readily produce fertile offspring with them.

The best-documented creations of new species in the laboratory were performed in the late 1980s. William Rice and G.W. Salt bred fruit flies, *Drosophila melanogaster,* using a maze with three different choices of habitat such as light/dark and wet/dry. Each generation was placed into the maze, and the groups of flies that came out of two of the eight exits were set apart to breed with each other in their respective groups. After thirty-five generations, the two groups and their offspring were isolated reproductively because of their strong habitat preferences: they mated only within the areas they preferred, and so did not mate with flies that preferred the other areas. The history of such attempts is described in Rice and Hostert (1993).

Hybrid Speciation

Hybridization between two different species sometimes leads to a distinct phenotype. This phenotype can also be fitter than the parental lineage and as such natural selection may then favour these individuals. Eventually, if reproductive isolation is achieved, it may lead to a separate species. However, reproductive isolation between hybrids and their parents is particularly difficult to achieve and thus hybrid speciation is considered an extremely rare event. The Mariana Mallard is known to have arisen from hybrid speciation.

Hybridization without change in chromosome number is called homoploid hybrid speciation. It is considered very rare but has been shown in *Heliconius* butterflies and sunflowers. Polyploid speciation, which involves changes in chromosome number, is a more common phenomenon, especially in plant species.

Gene Transposition As a Cause

Theodosius Dobzhansky, who studied fruit flies in the early days of genetic research in 1930s, speculated that parts of chromosomes that switch from one location to another might cause a species to split into two different species. He mapped out how it might be possible for sections of chromosomes to relocate themselves in a genome. Those mobile sections can cause sterility in inter-species hybrids, which can act as a speciation pressure. In theory, his idea was sound, but scientists long debated whether it actually happened in nature. Eventually a competing theory involving the gradual accumulation of mutations was shown to occur in nature so often that geneticists largely dismissed the moving gene hypothesis.

However, 2006 research shows that jumping of a gene from one chromosome to another can contribute to the birth of new species. This validates the reproductive isolation mechanism, a key component of speciation.

Interspersed Repeats

Interspersed repetitive DNA sequences function as isolating mechanisms. These repeats protect newly evolving gene sequences from being overwritten by gene conversion, due to the creation of non-homologies between otherwise homologous DNA sequences. The non-homologies create barriers to gene conversion. This barrier allows nascent novel genes to evolve without being overwritten by the progenitors of these genes. This uncoupling allows the evolution of new genes, both within gene families and also allelic forms of a gene. The importance is that this allows the splitting of a gene pool without requiring physical isolation of the organisms harbouring those gene sequences.

16 Evolutionary History of Life

The evolutionary history of life on Earth traces the processes by which living and fossil organisms evolved. It stretches from the origin of life on Earth, thought to be over 3,500 million years ago, to the present day. The similarities between all present day organisms indicate the presence of a common ancestor from which all known species have diverged through the process of evolution.

Microbial mats of coexisting bacteria and archaea were the dominant form of life in the early Archean and many of the major steps in early evolution are thought to have taken place within them. The evolution of oxygenic photosynthesis, around 3,500 million years ago, eventually led to the oxygenation of the atmosphere, beginning around 2,400 million years ago. The earliest evidence of eukaryotes (complex cells with organelles), dates from 1,850 million years ago, and while they may have been present earlier, their diversification accelerated when they started using oxygen in their metabolism. Later, around 1,700 million years ago, multicellular organisms began to appear, with differentiated cells performing specialised functions.

The earliest land plants date back to around 450 million years ago, though evidence suggests that algal scum formed on the land as early as 1,200 million years ago. Land plants were so successful that they are thought to have contributed to the late Devonian extinction event. Invertebrate animals appear during the Vendian period, while vertebrates originated about 525 million years ago during the Cambrian explosion.

During the Permian period, synapsids, including the ancestors of mammals, dominated the land, but the Permian–Triassic extinction event 251 million years ago came close to wiping out all complex life. During the recovery from this catastrophe, archosaurs became the most abundant land vertebrates, displacing therapsids in the mid-Triassic.] One archosaur group, the dinosaurs, dominated the Jurassic and Cretaceous periods, with the ancestors of mammals surviving only as small insectivores. After the Cretaceous—Tertiary extinction event 65 million years ago killed off the non-avian dinosaurs mammals increased rapidly in size and diversity. Such mass extinctions may have accelerated evolution by providing opportunities for new groups of organisms to diversify.

Fossil evidence indicates that flowering plants appeared and rapidly diversified in the Early Cretaceous, between 130 million years ago and 90 million years ago, probably helped by coevolution with pollinating insects. Flowering plants and marine phytoplankton are still the dominant producers of organic matter. Social insects appeared around the same time as flowering plants. Although they occupy only small parts of the insect 'family tree', they now form over half the total mass of insects. Humans evolved from a lineage of upright-walking apes whose earliest fossils date from over 6 million years ago. Although early members of this lineage had chimp-sized brains, there are signs of a steady increase in brain size after about 3 million years ago.

The oldest meteorite fragments found on Earth are about 4,540 million years old, this, coupled primarily with the dating of ancient lead deposits, has put the estimated age of Earth at around that time. About 40 million years later a planetoid struck the Earth, throwing into orbit the material that formed the Moon.

Until recently the oldest rocks found on Earth were about 3,800 million years old, leading scientists to believe for decades that Earth's surface had been molten until then. Accordingly, they named this part of Earth's history the Hadean eon, whose name means 'hellish'. However analysis of zircons formed 4,400 to 4,000 million years ago indicates that Earth's crust solidified about 100 million years after the planet's formation and that the planet quickly acquired oceans and an atmosphere, which may have been capable of supporting life.

Evidence from the Moon indicates that from 4,000 to 3,800 million years ago it suffered a Late Heavy Bombardment by debris that was left over from the formation of the Solar system, and the Earth should have experienced an even heavier bombardment due to its stronger gravity. While there is no direct evidence of conditions on Earth 4,000 to 3,800 million years ago, there is no reason to think that the Earth was not also affected by this late heavy bombardment. This event may well have stripped away any previous atmosphere and oceans; in this case gases and water from comet impacts may have contributed to their replacement, although volcanic outgassing on Earth would have contributed at least half.

The earliest identified organisms were minute and relatively featureless, their fossils look like small rods, which are very difficult to tell apart from structures that arise through abiotic physical processes. The oldest undisputed evidence of life on Earth, interpreted as fossilized bacteria, dates to 3,000 million years ago. Other finds in rocks dated to about 3,500 million years ago have been interpreted as bacteria, with geochemical evidence also seeming to show the presence of life 3,800 million years ago. However these analyses were closely scrutinized, and non-biological processes were found which could produce all of the 'signatures of life' that had been reported. While this does not prove that the structures found had a non-biological origin, they cannot be taken as clear evidence for the presence of life. Currently, the oldest unchallenged evidence for life is geochemical signatures from rocks deposited 3,400 million years ago, although these statements have not been thoroughly examined by critics.

Biologists reason that all living organisms on Earth must share a single last universal ancestor, because it would be virtually impossible that two or more separate lineages could have independently developed the many complex biochemical mechanisms common to all living organisms. As previously mentioned the earliest organisms for which fossil evidence is available are bacteria, cells far too complex to have arisen directly from non-living materials. The lack of fossil or geochemical evidence for earlier organisms has left plenty of scope for hypotheses, which fall into two main groups:

1. that life arose spontaneously on Earth; or
2. that it was 'seeded' from elsewhere in the universe.

The idea that life on Earth was 'seeded' from elsewhere in the universe dates back at least to the fifth century BCE. In the twentieth century it was proposed by the physical chemist Svante Arrhenius, by the astronomers Fred Hoyle and Chandra Wickramasinghe, and by molecular biologist Francis Crick and chemist Leslie Orgel. There are three main versions of the 'seeded from elsewhere' hypothesis: from elsewhere in our Solar system via fragments knocked into space by a large meteor impact, in which case the only credible source is Mars; by alien visitors, possibly as a result of accidental contamination by micro-organisms that they brought with them; and from outside the Solar system but by natural means. Experiments suggest that some micro-organisms can survive the shock of being catapulted into space and some can survive exposure to radiation for several days, but there is no proof that they can survive in space for much longer periods. Scientists are divided over the likelihood of life arising independently on Mars, or on other planets in our galaxy.

Independent Emergence on Earth

Life on earth is based on carbon and water. Carbon provides stable frameworks for complex chemicals and can be easily extracted from the environment, especially from carbon dioxide. The only other element with similar chemical properties, silicon, forms much less stable structures and, because most of its compounds are solids, would be more difficult for organisms to extract. Water is an excellent solvent and has two other useful properties: the fact that ice floats enables aquatic organisms to survive beneath it in winter; and its molecules have electrically negative and positive ends, which enables it to form a wider range of compounds than other solvents can. Other good solvents, such as ammonia, are liquid only at such low temperatures that chemical reactions may be too slow to sustain life, and lack water's other advantages. Organisms based on alternative biochemistry may however be possible on other planets.

Research on how life might have emerged unaided from non-living chemicals focuses on three possible starting points: self-replication, an organism's ability to produce offspring that are very similar to itself; metabolism, its ability to feed and repair itself; and external cell membranes, which allow food to enter and waste products to leave, but exclude unwanted substances. Research on abiogenesis still has a long way to go, since theoretical and empirical approaches are only beginning to make contact with each other.

REPLICATION FIRST: RNA WORLD

Membranes First: Lipid World

It has been suggested that double-walled 'bubbles' of lipids like those that form the external membranes of cells may have been an essential first step. Experiments that simulated the conditions of the early Earth have reported the formation of lipids, and these can spontaneously form liposomes, double-walled 'bubbles', and then reproduce themselves. Although they are not intrinsically information-carriers as nucleic acids are, they would be subject to natural selection for longevity and reproduction. Nucleic acids such as RNA might then have formed more easily within the liposomes than they would have outside.

The Clay Theory

RNA is complex and there are doubts about whether it can be produced non-biologically in the wild. Some clays, notably montmorillonite, have properties that make them plausible accelerators for the emergence of an RNA world: they grow by self-replication of their crystalline pattern; they are subject to an analog of natural selection, as the clay 'species' that grows fastest in a particular environment rapidly becomes dominant; and they can catalyze the formation of RNA molecules. Although this idea has not become the scientific consensus, it still has active supporters.

Research in 2003 reported that montmorillonite could also accelerate the conversion of fatty acids into 'bubbles', and that the 'bubbles' could encapsulate RNA attached to the clay. These 'bubbles' can then grow by absorbing additional lipids and then divide. The formation of the earliest cells may have been aided by similar processes.

A similar hypothesis presents self-replicating iron-rich clays as the progenitors of nucleotides, lipids and amino acids.

The replicator in virtually all known life is deoxyribonucleic acid. DNA's structure and replication systems are far more complex than those of the original replicator.

Even the simplest members of the three modern domains of life use DNA to record their 'recipes' and a complex array of RNA and protein molecules to 'read' these instructions and use them for growth, maintenance and self-replication. This system is far too complex to have emerged directly from non-living materials. The discovery that some RNA molecules can catalyze both their own replication and the construction of proteins led to the hypothesis of earlier life-forms based entirely on RNA. These ribozymes could have formed an RNA world in which there were individuals but no species, as mutations and horizontal gene transfers would have meant that the offspring in each generation were quite likely to have different genomes from those that their parents started with. RNA would later have been replaced by DNA, which is more stable and therefore can build longer genomes, expanding the range of capabilities a single organism can have. Ribozymes remain as the main components of ribosomes, modern cells' 'protein factories'.

Although short self-replicating RNA molecules have been artificially produced in laboratories, doubts have been raised about where natural non-biological synthesis of RNA is possible. The earliest 'ribozymes' may have been formed of simpler nucleic acids such as PNA, TNA or GNA, which would have been replaced later by RNA.

Environmental and Evolutionary Impact of Microbial Mats

Microbial mats are multi-layered, multi-species colonies of bacteria and other organisms that are generally only a few millimeters thick, but still contain a wide range of chemical environments, each of which favours a different set of micro-organisms. To some extent each mat forms its own food chain, as the by-products of each group of micro-organisms generally serve as 'food' for adjacent groups.

Stromatolites are stubby pillars built as microbes in mats slowly migrate upwards to avoid being smothered by sediment deposited on them by water. There has been vigorous debate about the validity of alleged fossils from before 3,000 million years ago, with critics arguing that so-called stromatolites could have been formed by non-biological processes. In 2006 another find of stromatolites was reported from the same part of Australia as previous ones, in rocks dated to 3,500 million years ago.

In modern underwater mats the top layer often consists of photosynthesizing cyanobacteria which create an oxygen-rich environment, while the bottom layer is oxygen-free and often dominated by hydrogen sulfide emitted by the organisms living there. It is estimated that the appearance of oxygenic photosynthesis by bacteria in mats increased biological productivity by a factor of between 100 and 1,000. The reducing agent used by oxygenic photosynthesis is water, which is much more plentiful than the geologically-produced reducing agents required by the earlier non-oxygenic photosynthesis. From this point onwards life itself produced significantly more of the resources it needed than did geochemical processes. Oxygen is toxic to organisms that are not adapted to it, but greatly increases the metabolic efficiency of oxygen-adapted organisms. Oxygen became a significant component of Earth's atmosphere about 2,400 million years ago. Although eukaryotes may have been present much earlier, the oxygenation of the atmosphere was a prerequisite for the evolution of the most complex eukaryotic cells, from which all multicellular organisms are built. The boundary between oxygen-rich and oxygen-free layers in microbial mats would have moved upwards when photosynthesis shut down overnight, and then downwards as it resumed on the next day. This would have created selection pressure for organisms in this intermediate zone to acquire the ability to tolerate and then to use oxygen, possibly via endosymbiosis, where one organism lives inside another and both of them benefit from their association.

Cyanobacteria have the most complete biochemical 'toolkits' of all the mat-forming organisms. Hence they are the most self-sufficient of the mat organisms and were well-adapted to strike out on their own both as floating mats and as the first of the phytoplankton, providing the basis of most marine food chains.

Diversification of Eukaryotes

Eukaryotes may have been present long before the oxygenation of the atmosphere, but most modern eukaryotes require oxygen, which their mitochondria use to fuel the production of ATP, the internal energy supply of all known cells. In the 1970s it was proposed and, after much debate, widely accepted that eukaryotes emerged as a result of a sequence of endosymbioses between 'procaryotes'. For example: a predatory micro-organism invaded a large procaryote, probably an archaean, but the attack was neutralized, and the attacker took up residence and evolved into the first of the mitochondria; one of these chimeras later tried to swallow a photosynthesizing cyanobacterium, but the victim survived inside the attacker and the new combination became the ancestor of plants; and so on. After each endosymbiosis began, the partners would have eliminated unproductive duplication of genetic functions by re-arranging their genomes, a process which sometimes involved transfer of genes between them. Another hypothesis proposes that mitochondria were originally sulfur or hydrogen metabolising endosymbionts, and became oxygen-consumers later. On the other hand mitochondria might have been part of eukaryotes' original equipment.

There is a debate about when eukaryotes first appeared: the presence of steranes in Australian shales may indicate that eukaryotes were present 2,700 million years ago; however an analysis in 2008 concluded that these chemicals infiltrated the rocks less than 2,200 million years ago and prove nothing about the origins of eukaryotes. Fossils of the alga *Grypania* have been reported in 1,850 million-year-old rocks (originally dated to 2,100 million years ago but later revised), and indicates that eukaryotes with organelles had already evolved. A diverse collection of fossil algae were found in rocks dated between 1,500 million years ago and 1,400 million years ago The earliest known fossils of fungi date from 1,430 million years ago.

Multicellularity

The simplest definitions of 'multicellular', for example 'having multiple cells', could include colonial cyanobacteria like Nostoc. Even a professional biologist's definition such as 'having the same genome but different types of cell' would still include some genera of the green alga Volvox, which have cells that specialize in reproduction. Multicellularity evolved independently in organisms as diverse as sponges and other animals, fungi, plants, brown algae, cyanobacteria, slime moulds and myxobacteria. For the sake of brevity this article focuses on the organisms that show the greatest specialization of cells and variety of cell types, although this approach to the evolution of complexity could be regarded as 'rather anthropocentric'.

The initial advantages of multicellularity may have included: increased resistance to predators, many of which attacked by engulfing;

the ability to resist currents by attaching to a firm surface; the ability to reach upwards to filter-feed or to obtain sunlight for photosynthesis; the ability to create an internal environment that gives protection against the external one; and even the opportunity for a group of cells to behave 'intelligently' by sharing information. These features would also have provided opportunities for other organisms to diversify, by creating more varied environments than flat microbial mats could.

Multicellularity with differentiated cells is beneficial to the organism as a whole but disadvantageous from the point of view of individual cells, most of which lose the opportunity to reproduce themselves. In an asexual multicellular organism, rogue cells which retain the ability to reproduce may take over and reduce the organism to a mass of undifferentiated cells. Sexual reproduction eliminates such rogue cells from the next generation and therefore appears to be a prerequisite for complex multicellularity.

The available evidence indicates that eukaryotes evolved much earlier but remained inconspicuous until a rapid diversification around 1,000 million years ago. The only respect in which eukaryotes clearly surpass bacteria and archaea is their capacity for variety of forms, and sexual reproduction enabled eukaryotes to exploit that advantage by producing organisms with multiple cells that differed in form and function.

Evolution of Sexual Reproduction

The defining characteristic of sexual reproduction is recombination, in which each of the offspring receives 50 per cent of its genetic inheritance from each of the parents. Bacteria also exchange DNA by bacterial conjugation, the benefits of which include resistance to antibiotics and other toxins, and the ability to utilize new metabolites. However conjugation is not a means of reproduction, and is not limited to members of the same species — there are cases where bacteria transfer DNA to plants and animals.

The disadvantages of sexual reproduction are well-known: the genetic reshuffle of recombination may break up favourable combinations of genes; and since males do not directly increase the number of offspring in the next generation, an asexual population can out-breed and displace in as little as 50 generations a sexual population that is equal in every other respect. Nevertheless the great majority of animals, plants, fungi and protists reproduce sexually. There is strong evidence that sexual reproduction arose early in the history of eukaryotes and that the genes controlling it have changed very little since then. How sexual reproduction evolved and survived is an unsolved puzzle.

The Red Queen Hypothesis suggests that sexual reproduction provides protection against parasites, because it is easier for parasites to evolve means of overcoming the defences of genetically identical clones than those of sexual species that present moving targets, and there is some experimental evidence for this. However there is still doubt about whether it would explain the survival of sexual species if multiple similar clone species were present, as one of the clones may survive the attacks of parasites for long enough to out-breed the sexual species.

The Mutation Deterministic Hypothesis assumes that each organism has more than one harmful mutation and the combined effects of these mutations are more harmful than the sum of the harm done by each individual mutation. If so, sexual recombination of genes will reduce the harm that bad mutations do to offspring and at the same time eliminate some bad mutations from the gene pool by isolating them in individuals that perish quickly because they have an above-average number of bad mutations. However the evidence suggests that the MDH's assumptions are shaky, because many species have on average less than one harmful mutation per individual and no species that has been investigated shows evidence of synergy.

The random nature of recombination causes the relative abundance of alternative traits to vary from one generation to another. This genetic drift is insufficient on its own to make sexual reproduction advantageous, but a combination of genetic drift and natural selection may be sufficient. When chance produces combinations of good traits, natural selection gives a large advantage to lineages in which these traits become genetically linked. On the other hand the benefits of good traits are neutralized if they appear along with bad traits. Sexual recombination gives good traits the opportunities to become linked with other good traits, and mathematical models suggest this may be more than enough to offset the disadvantages of sexual reproduction. Other combinations of hypotheses that are inadequate on their own are also being examined.

The following hypotheses attempt to explain how and why sex evolved:

- It may have enabled organisms to repair genetic damage. The most primitive form of sex may have been one organism repairing damaged DNA by replicating an undamaged strand from a similar organism.
- Sexual reproduction may have originated from selfish parasitic genetic elements propagating themselves by transfer to new hosts.
- It may have evolved from cannibalism, where some of the victim's DNA was incorporated into the cannibal organism.
- Sexual reproduction may have evolved from ancient haloarchaea through a combination of jumping genes, and swapping plasmids.

- Or it may have evolved as a form of vaccination in which infected hosts exchanged weakened symbiotic copies of parasitic DNA as protection against more virulent versions. The meiosis stage of sexual reproduction may then have evolved as a way of removing the symbiotes.

Bacteria also exchange DNA by bacterial conjugation, the benefits of which include resistance to antibiotics and other toxins, and the ability to utilize new metabolites. However conjugation is not a means of reproduction and is not limited to members of the same species, and there are cases where bacteria transfer DNA to plants and animals. Nevertheless it may be an example of the 'selfish genetic element' hypothesis, as it transfers DNA by means of such a 'selfish gene', the F-plasmid.

Fossil Evidence for Multicellularity and Sexual Reproduction

The Francevillian Group Fossil, dated to 2,100 million years ago, is the earliest known fossil organism that is clearly multicellular. They may have had differentiated cells. Another early multicellular fossil, *Qingshania*, dated to 1,700 million years ago, appears to consist of virtually identical cells. The red alga called *Bangiomorpha*, dated at 1,200 million years ago, is the earliest known organism which certainly has differentiated, specialized cells, and is also the oldest known sexually-reproducing organism. The 1,430 million-year-old fossils interpreted as fungi appear to have been multicellular with differentiated cells. The 'string of beads' organism *Horodyskia*, found in rocks dated from 1,500 million years ago to 900 million years ago, may have been an early metazoan; however it has also been interpreted as a colonial foraminiferan.

Animals are multicellular eukaryotes, and are distinguished from plants, algae, and fungi by lacking cell walls. All animals are motile, if only at certain life stages. All animals except sponges have bodies differentiated into separate tissues, including muscles, which move parts of the animal by contracting, and nerve tissue, which transmits and processes signals.

The earliest widely-accepted animal fossils are rather modern-looking cnidarians (the group that includes jellyfish, sea anemones and hydras), possibly from around 580 million years ago, although fossils from the Doushantuo Formation can only be dated approximately. Their presence implies that the cnidarian and bilaterian lineages had already diverged.

The Ediacara biota, which flourished for the last 40 million years before the start of the Cambrian, were the first animals more than a very few centimetres long. Many were flat and had a 'quilted' appearance, and seemed so strange that there was a proposal to classify them as a separate kingdom, Vendozoa. Others, however, been interpreted as early molluscs (*Kimberella*), echinoderms, and arthropods (*Spriggina*, *Parvancorina*). There is still debate about the classification of these specimens, mainly because the diagnostic features which allow taxonomists to classify more recent organisms, such as similarities to living organisms, are generally absent in the Ediacarans. However there seems little doubt that *Kimberella* was at least a triploblastic bilaterian animal, in other words significantly more complex than cnidarians.

The small shelly fauna are a very mixed collection of fossils found between the Late Ediacaran and Mid Cambrian periods. The earliest, *Cloudina*, shows signs of successful defence against predation and may indicate the start of an evolutionary arms race. Some tiny Early Cambrian shells almost certainly belonged to molluscs, while the owners of some 'armor plates', *Halkieria* and *Microdictyon*, were eventually identified when more complete specimens were found in Cambrian lagerstätten that preserved soft-bodied animals.

In the 1970s there was already a debate about whether the emergence of the modern phyla was 'explosive' or gradual but hidden by the shortage of Pre-Cambrian animal fossils. A re-analysis of fossils from the Burgess Shale lagerstätte increased interest in the issue when it revealed animals, such as *Opabinia*, which did not fit into any known phylum. At the time these were interpreted as evidence that the modern phyla had evolved very rapidly in the 'Cambrian explosion' and that the Burgess Shale's 'weird wonders' showed that the Early Cambrian was a uniquely experimental period of animal evolution. Later discoveries of similar animals and the development of new theoretical approaches led to the conclusion that many of the 'weird wonders' were evolutionary 'aunts' or 'cousins' of modern groups – for example that *Opabinia* was a member of the lobopods, a group which includes the ancestors of the arthropods, and that it may have been closely related to the modern tardigrades. Nevertheless there is still much debate about whether the Cambrian explosion was really explosive and, if so, how and why it happened and why it appears unique in the history of animals.

Most of the animals at the heart of the Cambrian explosion debate are protostomes, one of the two main groups of complex animals. One deuterostome group, the echinoderms, many of which have hard calcite 'shells', are fairly common from the Early Cambrian small shelly fauna onwards. Other deuterostome groups are soft-bodied, and most of the significant Cambrian deuterostome fossils come from the Chengjiang fauna, a lagerstätte in China. The Chengjiang fossils *Haikouichthys* and *Myllokunmingia* appear to be true vertebrates, and *Haikouichthys* had distinct vertebrae, which may have been slightly mineralized. Vertebrates with jaws, such as the Acanthodians, first appeared in the Late Ordovician.

Evolution of Soil

Before the colonization of land, soil, a combination of mineral particles and decomposed organic matter, did not exist. Land surfaces would have been either bare rock or unstable sand produced by weathering. Water and any nutrients in it would have drained away very quickly.

Films of cyanobacteria, which are not plants but use the same photosynthesis mechanisms, have been found in modern deserts, and only in areas that are unsuitable for vascular plants. This suggests that microbial mats may have been the first organisms to colonize dry land, possibly in the Precambrian. Mat-forming cyanobacteria could have gradually evolved resistance to desiccation as they spread from the seas to tidal zones and then to land. Lichens, which are symbiotic combinations of a fungus (almost always an ascomycete) and one or more photosynthesizers (green algae or cyanobacteria), are also important colonizers of lifeless environments, and their ability to break down rocks contributes to soil formation in situations where plants cannot survive. The earliest known ascomycete fossils date from 423 to 419 million years ago in the Silurian.

Soil formation would have been very slow until the appearance of burrowing animals, which mix the mineral and organic components of soil and whose feces are a major source of the organic components. Burrows have been found in Ordovician sediments, and are attributed to annelids ('worms') or arthropods.

Social Insects

The social insects are remarkable because the great majority of individuals in each colony are sterile. This appears contrary to basic concepts of evolution such as natural selection and the selfish gene. In fact there are very few eusocial insect species: only 15 out of approximately 2,600 living families of insects contain eusocial species, and it seems that eusociality has evolved independently only 12 times among arthropods, although some eusocial lineages have diversified into several families. Nevertheless social insects have been spectacularly successful; for example although ants and termites account for only about 2 per cent of known insect species, they form over 50 per cent of the total mass of insects. Their ability to control a territory appears to be the foundation of their success.

Humans

Modern humans evolved from a lineage of upright-walking apes that has been traced back over 6 million years ago to *Sahelanthropus*. The first known stone tools were made about 2.5 million years ago, apparently by *Australopithecus garhi*, and were found near animal bones that bear scratches made by these tools. The earliest hominines had chimp-sized brains, but there has been a four-fold increase in the last 3 million years; a statistical analysis suggests that hominine brain sizes depend almost completely on the date of the fossils, while the species to which they are assigned has only slight influence. There is a long-running debate about whether modern humans evolved all over the world simultaneously from existing advanced hominines or are descendants of a single small population in Africa, which then migrated all over the world less than 200,000 years ago and replaced previous hominine species. There is also debate about whether anatomically-modern humans had an intellectual, cultural and technological 'Great Leap Forward' under 100,000 years ago and, if so, whether this was due to neurological changes that are not visible in fossils.

The sacrifice of breeding opportunities by most individuals has long been explained as a consequence of these species' unusual haplodiploid method of sex determination, which has the paradoxical consequence that two sterile worker daughters of the same queen share more genes with each other than they would with their offspring if they could breed. However Wilson and Hölldobler argue that this explanation is faulty: for example, it is based on kin selection, but there is no evidence of nepotism in colonies that have multiple queens. Instead, they write, eusociality evolves only in species that are under strong pressure from predators and competitors, but in environments where it is possible to build 'fortresses'; after colonies have established this security, they gain other advantages though co-operative foraging. In support of this explanation they cite the appearance of eusociality in bathyergid mole rats, which are not haplodiploid.

The earliest fossils of insects have been found in Early Devonian rocks from about 400 million years ago, which preserve only a few varieties of flightless insect. The Mazon Creek lagerstätten from the Late Carboniferous, about 300 million years ago, include about 200 species, some gigantic by modern standards, and indicate that insects had occupied their main modern ecological niches as herbivores, detritivores and insectivores. Social termites and ants first appear in the Early Cretaceous, and advanced social bees have been found in Late Cretaceous rocks but did not become abundant until the Mid Cenozoic.

Land Vertebrates

Tetrapods, vertebrates with four limbs, evolved from other rhipidistians over a relatively short timespan during the Late Devonian, between 370 million years ago and 360 million years ago. From the 1950s to the early 1980s it was thought that tetrapods evolved from fish that had already acquired the ability to crawl on land, possibly in order to go from a pool that was drying out to one that was deeper. However in 1987 nearly-complete fossils of *Acanthostega* from about 363 million years ago showed that this Late Devonian transitional animal had legs and both lungs and gills, but could never have survived on land: its limbs and its wrist and ankle joints were too weak to bear its weight; its ribs were too short to prevent its lungs from being squeezed flat by its weight; its fish-like tail fin would have been damaged by dragging on the ground. The current hypothesis is that *Acanthostega*, which was about 1 metre (3.3 ft) long, was a wholly aquatic predator that hunted in shallow water. Its skeleton differed from that of most fish, in ways that enabled it to raise its head to breathe air while its body remained submerged, including: its jaws show modifications that would have enabled it to gulp air; the bones at the back of its skull are locked together, providing strong attachment points for muscles that raised its head; the head is not joined to the shoulder girdle and it has a distinct neck.

The Devonian proliferation of land plants may help to explain why air-breathing would have been an advantage: leaves falling into streams and rivers would have encouraged the growth of aquatic vegetation; this would have attracted grazing invertebrates and small fish that preyed on them; they would have been attractive prey but the environment was unsuitable for the big marine predatory fish; air-breathing would have been necessary because these waters would have been short of oxygen, since warm water holds less dissolved oxygen than cooler marine water and since the decomposition of vegetation would have used some of the oxygen.

Later discoveries revealed earlier transitional forms between *Acanthostega* and completely fish-like animals. Unfortunately there is then a gap of about 30 million years between the fossils of ancestral tetrapods and Mid Carboniferous fossils of vertebrates that look well-adapted for life on land. Some of these look like early relatives of modern amphibians, most of which need to keep their skins moist and to lay their eggs in water, while others are accepted as early relatives of the amniotes, whose water-proof skins and eggs enable them to live and breed far from water.

Land Invertebrates

Animals had to change their feeding and excretory systems, and most land animals developed internal fertilization of their eggs. The difference in refractive index between water and air required changes in their eyes. On the other hand in some ways movement and breathing became easier, and the better transmission of high-frequency sounds in air encouraged the development of hearing.

Some trace fossils from the Cambrian-Ordovician boundary about 490 million years ago are interpreted as the tracks of large amphibious arthropods on coastal sand dunes, and may have been made by euthycarcinoids, which are thought to be evolutionary 'aunts' of myriapods. Other trace fossils from the Late Ordovician a little over 445 million years ago probably represent land invertebrates, and there is clear evidence of numerous arthropods on coasts and alluvial plains shortly before the Silurian-Devonian boundary, about 415 million years ago, including signs that some arthropods ate plants. Arthropods were well pre-adapted to colonise land, because their existing jointed exoskeletons provided protection against desiccation, support against gravity and a means of locomotion that was not dependent on water.

The fossil record of other major invertebrate groups on land is poor: none at all for non-parasitic flatworms, nematodes or nemerteans; some parasitic nematodes have been fossilized in amber; annelid worm fossils are known from the Carboniferous, but they may still have been aquatic animals; the earliest fossils of gastropods on land date from the Late Carboniferous, and this group may have had to wait until leaf litter became abundant enough to provide the moist conditions they need.

The earliest confirmed fossils of flying insects date from the Late Carboniferous, but it is thought that insects developed the ability to fly in the Early Carboniferous or even Late Devonian. This gave them a wider range of ecological niches for feeding and breeding, and a means of escape from predators and from unfavourable changes in the environment. About 99 per cent of modern insect species fly or are descendants of flying species.

Oxygenic photosynthesis accounts for virtually all of the production of organic matter from non-organic ingredients. Production is split about evenly between land and marine plants, and phytoplankton are the dominant marine producers.

The processes that drive evolution are still operating. Well-known examples include the changes in colouration of the peppered moth over the last 200 years and the more recent appearance of pathogens that are resistant to antibiotics. There is even evidence that humans are still evolving, and possibly at an accelerating rate over the last 40,000 years.

17 Modern Evolutionary Synthesis

The modern evolutionary synthesis is also referred to as the new synthesis, the modern synthesis, the evolutionary synthesis and the neo-darwinian synthesis. It is a union of ideas from several biological specialties which provides a widely accepted account of evolution. The synthesis reflects the current overwhelming consensus. The synthesis was produced over a decade (1936-1947). The previous development of population genetics (1918-1932) was a stimulus, as it showed that Mendelian genetics was consistent with natural selection and gradual evolution. The synthesis is still, to a large extent, the current paradigm in evolutionary biology.

Julian Huxley invented the term, when he produced his book, *Evolution: The Modern Synthesis* (1942). Other major figures in the modern synthesis include R. A. Fisher, Theodosius Dobzhansky, J.B.S. Haldane, Sewall Wright, E.B. Ford, Ernst Mayr, Bernhard Rensch, Sergei Chetverikov, George Gaylord Simpson, and G. Ledyard Stebbins.

The modern synthesis solved difficulties and confusions caused by the specialisation and poor communication between biologists in the early years of the 20th century. Discoveries of early geneticists were difficult to reconcile with gradual evolution and the mechanism of natural selection. The synthesis reconciled the two schools of thought, while providing evidence that studies of populations in the field were crucial to evolutionary theory. It drew together ideas from several branches of biology that had become separated, particularly genetics, cytology, systematics, botany, morphology, ecology and paleontology.

The modern synthesis bridged the gap between experimental geneticists and naturalists, and between both and palaeontologists. It states that:

All evolutionary phenomena can be explained in a way consistent with known genetic mechanisms and the observational evidence of naturalists.

Evolution is gradual: small genetic changes, recombination ordered by natural selection. Discontinuities amongst species (or other taxa) are explained as originating gradually through geographical separation and extinction (not saltation).

Natural selection is by far the main mechanism of change; even slight advantages are important when continued. The object of selection is the phenotype in its surrounding environment.

The role of genetic drift is equivocal. Though strongly supported initially by Dobzhansky, it was downgraded later as results from ecological genetics were obtained.

Thinking in terms of populations, rather than individuals, is primary: the genetic diversity existing in natural populations is a key factor in evolution. The strength of natural selection in the wild is greater than previously expected; the effect of ecological factors such as niche occupation and the significance of barriers to gene flow are all important.

In palaeontology, the ability to explain historical observations by extrapolation from microevolution to macroevolution is proposed. Historical contingency means explanations at different levels may exist. Gradualism does not mean constant rate of change.

The idea that speciation occurs after populations are reproductively isolated has been much debated. In plants, polyploidy must be included in any view of speciation. Formulations such as 'evolution consists primarily of changes in the frequencies of alleles between one generation and another' were proposed rather later. The traditional view is that developmental biology ('evo-devo') played little part in the synthesis, but an account of Gavin de Beer's work by Stephen J. Gould suggests he may be an exception.

Charles Darwin's *The Origin of Species* was successful in convincing most biologists that evolution had occurred, but was less successful in convincing them that natural selection was its primary mechanism. In the 19th and early 20th centuries, variations of Lamarckism, orthogenesis ('progressive' evolution), and saltationism (evolution by jumps) were discussed as alternatives. Also, Darwin did not offer a precise explanation of how new species arise. As part of the disagreement about whether natural selection alone was sufficient to explain speciation, George Romanes coined the term neo-Darwinism to refer to the version of evolution advocated by Alfred Russel Wallace and August Weismann with its heavy dependence on natural selection. Weismann and Wallace rejected the Lamarckian idea of inheritance of acquired characteristics, something that Darwin had not ruled out.

Weismann's idea was that the relationship between the hereditary material, which he called the germ plasm (de: *Keimplasma*), and the rest of the body (the soma) was a one-way relationship: the germ-plasm formed the body, but the body did not influence the germ-plasm, except indirectly in its participation in a population subject to natural selection. Weismann was translated into English, and though he was influential, it took many years for the full significance of his work to be appreciated. Later, after the completion of the modern synthesis, the term neo-Darwinism came to be associated with its core concept: evolution, driven by natural selection acting on variation produced by genetic mutation, and genetic recombination (chromosomal crossovers).

Gregor Mendel's work was re-discovered by Hugo de Vries and Carl Correns in 1900. News of this reached William Bateson in England, who reported on the paper during a presentation to the Royal Horticultural Society in May 1900. It showed that the contributions of each parent retained their integrity rather than blending with the contribution of the other parent. This reinforced a division of thought, which was already present in the 1890s. The two schools were:

- Saltationism (large mutations or jumps), favored by early Mendelians who viewed hard inheritance as incompatible with natural selection
- Biometric school: led by Karl Pearson and Walter Weldon, argued vigorously against it, saying that empirical evidence indicated that variation was continuous in most organisms, not discrete as Mendelism predicted.

The relevance of Mendelism to evolution was unclear and hotly debated, especially by Bateson, who opposed the biometric ideas of his former teacher Weldon. Many scientists believed the two theories substantially contradicted each other. This debate between the biometricians and the Mendelians continued for some 20 years and was only solved by the development of population genetics.

T.H. Morgan began his career in genetics as a saltationist, and started out trying to demonstrate that mutations could produce new species in fruit flies. However, the experimental work at his lab with *Drosophila melanogaster*, which helped establish the link between Mendelian genetics and the chromosomal theory of inheritance, demonstrated that rather than creating new species in a single step, mutations increased the genetic variation in the population.

The Foundation of Population Genetics

The first step towards the synthesis was the development of population genetics. R.A. Fisher, J.B.S. Haldane, and Sewall Wright provided critical contributions. In 1918, Fisher produced the paper 'The Correlation Between Relatives on the Supposition of Mendelian Inheritance', which showed how the continuous variation measured by the biometricians could be the result of the action of many discrete genetic loci. In this and subsequent papers culminating in his 1930 book *The Genetical Theory of Natural Selection,* Fisher was able to show how Mendelian genetics was, contrary to the thinking of many early geneticists, completely consistent with the idea of evolution driven by natural selection. During the 1920s, a series of papers by J.B.S. Haldane applied mathematical analysis to real world examples of natural selection such as the evolution of industrial melanism in peppered moths. Haldane established that natural selection could work in the real world at a faster rate than even Fisher had assumed.

Sewall Wright focussed on combinations of genes that interacted as complexes, and the effects of inbreeding on small relatively isolated populations, which could exhibit genetic drift. In a 1932 paper he introduced the concept of an adaptive landscape in which phenomena such as cross breeding and genetic drift in small populations could push them away from adaptive peaks, which would in turn allow natural selection to push them towards new adaptive peaks. Wright's model would appeal to field naturalists such as Theodosius Dobzhansky and Ernst Mayr who were becoming aware of the importance of geographical isolation in real world populations. The work of Fisher, Haldane and Wright founded the discipline of population genetics. This is the precursor of the modern synthesis, which is an even broader coalition of ideas.

The Modern Synthesis

Theodosius Dobzhansky, a Ukrainian emigrant, who had been a postdoctoral worker in Morgan's fruit fly lab, was one of the first to apply genetics to natural populations. He worked mostly with *Drosophila pseudoobscura.* He says pointedly: "Russia has a variety of climates from the Arctic to sub-tropical . . . Exclusively laboratory workers who neither possess nor wish to have any knowledge of living beings in nature were and are in a minority". Not surprisingly, there were other Russian geneticists with similar ideas, though for some time their work was known to only a few in the West. His 1937 work *Genetics and the Origin of Species* was a key step in bridging the gap between population geneticists and field naturalists. It presented the conclusions reached by Fisher, Haldane, and especially Wright in their highly mathematical papers in a form that was easily accessible to others. It also emphasized that real world populations had far more genetic variability than the early population geneticists had assumed in their models, and that genetically distinct sub-populations were important. Dobzhansky argued that natural selection worked to maintain genetic diversity as well as driving change. Dobzhansky had been influenced by his exposure in the 1920s to the work of a Russian geneticist named Sergei Chetverikov who had looked at the role of recessive genes in maintaining a reservoir of genetic variability in a population before his work was shut down by the rise of Lysenkoism in the Soviet Union.

Edmund Brisco Ford's work complemented that of Dobzhansky. It was as a result of Ford's work, as well as his own, that Dobzhansky changed the emphasis in the third edition of his famous text from drift to selection. Ford was an experimental naturalist who wanted to test natural selection in nature. He virtually invented the field of research known as ecological genetics. His work on natural selection in wild populations of butterflies and moths was the first to show that predictions made by R.A. Fisher were correct. He was the first to describe and define genetic polymorphism, and to predict that human blood group polymorphisms might be maintained in the population by providing some protection against disease.

Ernst Mayr's key contribution to the synthesis was *Systematics and the Origin of Species*, published in 1942. Mayr emphasized the importance of allopatric speciation, where geographically isolated sub-populations diverge so far that reproductive isolation occurs. He was sceptical of the reality of sympatric speciation believing that geographical isolation was a prerequisite for building up intrinsic (reproductive) isolating mechanisms. Mayr also introduced the biological species concept that defined a species as a group of interbreeding or potentially interbreeding populations that were reproductively isolated from all other populations. Before he left Germany for the United States in 1930, Mayr had been influenced by the work of German biologist Bernhard Rensch. In the 1920s Rensch, who like Mayr did field work in Indonesia, analyzed the geographic distribution of polytypic species and complexes of closely related species paying particular attention to how variations between different populations correlated with local environmental factors such as differences in climate. In 1947, Rensch published *Neuere Probleme der Abstammungslehre: die Transspezifische Evolution* (English translation 1959: *Evolution above the Species level*). This looked at how the same evolutionary mechanisms involved in speciation might be extended to explain the origins of the differences between the higher level taxa. His writings contributed to the rapid acceptance of the synthesis in Germany.

George Gaylord Simpson was responsible for showing that the modern synthesis was compatible with paleontology in his book *Tempo and Mode in Evolution* published in 1944. Simpson's work was crucial because so many paleontologists had disagreed, in some cases vigorously, with the idea that natural selection was the main mechanism of evolution. It showed that the trends of linear progression (in for example the evolution of the horse) that earlier paleontologists had used as support for neo-Lamarckism and orthogenesis did not hold up under careful examination. Instead the fossil record was consistent with the irregular, branching, and non-directional pattern predicted by the modern synthesis.

The modern evolutionary synthesis continued to be developed and refined after the initial establishment in the 1930s and 1940s. The work of W. D. Hamilton, George C. Williams, John Maynard Smith and others led to the development of a gene-centric view of evolution in the 1960s. The synthesis as it exists now has extended the scope of the Darwinian idea of natural selection to include subsequent scientific discoveries and concepts unknown to Darwin, such as DNA and genetics, which allow rigorous, in many cases mathematical, analyses of phenomena such as kin selection, altruism, and speciation.

A particular interpretation most commonly associated with Richard Dawkins, author of *The Selfish Gene*, asserts that the gene is the only true unit of selection. Dawkins further extended the Darwinian idea to include non-biological systems exhibiting the same type of selective behaviour of the 'fittest' such as memes in culture. The synthesis continues to undergo regular review.

After the synthesis the history and causes of evolution are subject to various subdisciplines of evolutionary biology. The areas of segments give an impression of the contributions of subdisciplines to the literature of evolutionary biology.

There are a number of discoveries in earth sciences and biology which have arisen since the synthesis. Listed here are some of those topics which are relevant to the evolutionary synthesis, and which seem soundly based.

Understanding of Earth History

The Earth is the stage on which the evolutionary play is performed. Darwin studied evolution in the context of Charles Lyell's geology, but our present understanding of Earth history includes some critical advances made during the last half-century.

The age of the Earth has been revised upwards. It is now estimated at 4.56 billion years, about one-third of the age of the universe. It is worth noting that the Phanerozoic only occupies the last 1/9th of this period of time.

The triumph of Alfred Wegener's idea of continental drift came around 1960. The key principle of plate tectonics is that the lithosphere exists as separate and distinct tectonic plates, which ride on the fluid-like (visco-elastic solid) asthenosphere. This discovery provides a unifying theory for geology, linking phenomena such as volcanos, earthquakes, orogeny, and providing data for many paleogeographical questions. One major question is still unclear: when did plate tectonics begin?

Our understanding of the evolution of the Earth's atmosphere has progressed. The substitution of oxygen for carbon dioxide in the atmosphere, which occurred in the Proterozoic, caused probably by cyanobacteria in the form of stromatolites, caused changes leading to the evolution of aerobic organisms.

The identification of the first generally accepted fossils of microbial life was made by geologists. These rocks have been dated as about 3.465 billion years ago. Walcott was the first geologist to identify pre-Cambrian fossil bacteria from microscopic examination of thin rock slices. He also thought stromatolites were organic in origin. His ideas were not accepted at the time, but may now be appreciated as great discoveries.

Information about paleoclimates is increasingly available, and being used in paleontology. One example: the discovery of massive ice ages in the Proterozoic, following the great reduction of CO_2 in the atmosphere. These ice ages were immensely long, and led to a crash in microflora.

Catastrophism and mass extinctions. A partial reintegration of catastrophism has occurred, and the importance of mass extinctions in large-scale evolution is now apparent. Extinction events disturb relationships between many forms of life and may remove dominant forms and release a flow of adaptive radiation amongst groups that remain. Causes include meteorite strikes K–T junction; Upper Devonian); flood basalt provinces (Deccan traps at K/T junction; Siberian traps at P-T junction); and other less dramatic processes.

Our present knowledge of earth history strongly suggests that large-scale geophysical events influenced macroevolution and megaevolution. These terms refer to evolution above the species level, including such events as mass extinctions, adaptive radiation, and the major transitions in evolution.

Symbiotic Origin of Eukaryotic Cell Structures

Once symbiosis was discovered in lichen and in plant roots (rhizobia in root nodules) in the 19th century, the idea arose that the process might have occurred more widely, and might be important in evolution. Anton de Bary invented the concept of *symbiosis*; several Russian biologists promoted the idea; Edwin Wilson mentioned it in his epic text *The Cell*; a book was published in the U.S.A. in 1927 with the title *Symbionticism and the origin of species*; and there was a brief mention by Julian Huxley in 1930; all in vain because sufficient evidence was lacking. Symbiosis as a major evolutionary force was not discussed at all in the evolutionary synthesis.

The role of symbiosis in cell evolution was revived partly by Joshua Lederberg, and finally brought to light by Lynn Margulis in a series of papers and books. It turns out that some cell organelles are of microbial origin: mitochondria and chloroplasts definitely, cilia, flagella and centrioles possibly, and perhaps the nuclear membrane and much of the chromosome structure as well. What is now clear is that the evolution of eukaryote cells is either caused by, or at least profoundly influenced by, symbiosis with bacterial and archaean cells in the Proterozoic.

The origin of the eukaryote cell by symbiosis in several stages was not part of the evolutionary synthesis. It is, at least on first sight, an example of megaevolution by big jumps. However, what symbiosis provided was a copious supply of heritable variation from microorganisms, which was fine-tuned over a long period to produce the cell structure we see today. This part of the process is consistent with evolution by natural selection.

The ability to analyse sequence in macromolecules (protein, DNA, RNA) provides evidence of descent, and permits us to work out genealogical trees covering the whole of life, since now there are data on every major group of living organisms. This project, begun in a tentative way in the 1960s, has become a search for the universal tree or the universal ancestor, a phrase of Carl Woese. The tree that results has some unusual features, especially in its roots. There are two kingdoms of prokaryotes: bacteria and archaea, both of which contributed genetic material to the eukaryotes, mainly by means of symbiosis. Also, since bacteria can pass genetic material to other bacteria, their relationships look more like a web than a tree. Once eukaryotes were established, their sexual reproduction produced the traditional branching tree-like pattern, the only diagram Darwin put in the *Origin*. The last universal ancestor (LUA) would be a prokaryotic cell before the split between the bacteria and archaea. LUA is defined as most recent organism from which all organisms now living on Earth descend (some 3.5 to 3.8 billion years ago, in the Archean era).

This technique may be used to clarify relationships within any group of related organisms. It is now a standard procedure, and examples are published regularly. April 2009 sees the publication of a tree covering all the animal phyla, derived from sequences from 150 genes in 77 taxa.

Early attempts to identify relationships between major groups were made in the 19th century by Ernst Haeckel, and by comparative anatomists such as Thomas Henry Huxley and E. Ray Lankester. Enthusiasm waned: it was often difficult to find evidence to adjudicate between different opinions. Perhaps for that reason, the evolutionary synthesis paid surprisingly little attention to this activity. It is certainly a lively field of research today.

Evo-devo

What once was called embryology played a modest role in the evolutionary synthesis, mostly about evolution by changes in developmental timing (allometry and heterochrony). Man himself was, according to Bolk, a typical case of evolution by retention of juvenile characteristics (neoteny). He listed many characters where "Man, in his bodily development, is a primate foetus that has become sexually mature". Unfortunately, his interpretation of these ideas was non-Darwinian, but his list of characters is both interesting and convincing.

Modern interest in Evo-devo springs from clear proof that development is closely controlled by special genetic systems, and the hope that comparison of these systems will tell us much about the evolutionary history of different groups. In a series of experiments with the fruit-fly *Drosophila*, Edward B. Lewis was able to identify a complex of genes whose proteins bind to the cis-regulatory regions of target genes. The latter then activate or repress systems of cellular processes that accomplish the final development of the organism. Furthermore, the sequence of these control genes show *co-linearity*: the order of the loci in the chromosome parallels the order in which the loci are expressed along the anterior-posterior axis of the body. Not only that, but this cluster of master control genes programmes the development of all higher organisms. Each of the genes contains a homeobox, a remarkably conserved DNA sequence. This suggests the complex itself arose by gene duplication. In his Nobel lecture, Lewis said "Ultimately, comparisons of the [control complexes] throughout the animal kingdom should provide a picture of how the organisms, as well as the [control genes] have evolved".

The term *deep homology* was coined to describe the common origin of genetic regulatory apparatus used to build morphologically and phylogenetically disparate animal features. It applies when a complex genetic regulatory system is inherited from a common ancestor, as it is in the evolution of vertebrate and invertebrate eyes. The phenomenon is implicated in many cases of parallel evolution.

A great deal of evolution may take place by changes in the control of development. This may be relevant to punctuated equilibrium theory, for in development a few changes to the control system could make a significant difference to the adult organism. An example is the giant panda, whose place in the Carnivora was long uncertain. Apparently, the giant panda's evolution required the change of only a few genetic messages (5 or 6 perhaps), yet the phenotypic and lifestyle change from a standard bear is considerable. The transition could therefore be effected relatively swiftly.

Fossil Discoveries

In the past thirty or so years there have been excavations in parts of the world which had scarcely been investigated before. Also, there is fresh appreciation of fossils discovered in the 19th century, but then denied or deprecated: the classic example is the Ediacaran biota from the immediate pre-Cambrian, after the Cryogenian period. These soft-bodied fossils are the first record of multicellular life. The interpretation of this fauna is still in flux.

Many outstanding discoveries have been made, and some of these have implications for evolutionary theory. The discovery of feathered dinosaurs and early birds from the Lower Cretaceous of Liaoning, N.E. China have convinced most students that birds did evolve from coelurosaurian theropod dinosaurs. Less well known, but perhaps of equal evolutionary significance, are the studies on early insect flight, on stem tetrapods from the Upper Devonian, and the early stages of whale evolution.

A shaft of light has been thrown on the evolution of flatfish (pleuronectiformes), such as plaice, sole, turbot and halibut, by recent work. Flatfish are interesting because they are one of the few vertebrate groups with external asymmetry. Their young are perfectly symmetrical, but the head is remodelled during a metamorphosis, which entails the migration of one eye to the other side, close to the other eye. Some species have both eyes on the left (turbot), some on the right (halibut, sole); all living and fossil flatfish to date show an 'eyed' side and a 'blind' side. The lack of an intermediate condition in living and fossil flatfish species had led to debate about the origin of such a striking adaptation. The case was considered by Lamark, who thought flatfish precursors would have lived in shallow water for a long period, and by Darwin, who predicted a gradual migration of the eye, mirroring the metamorphosis of the living forms. Darwin's long-time critic St. George Mivart thought that the intermediate stages could have no selective value, and in the 6th edition of the *Origin*, Darwin made a concession to the possibility of acquired traits. Many years later the geneticist Richard Goldschmidt put the case forward as an example of evolution by saltation, bypassing intermediate forms.

A recent examination of two fossil species from the Eocene has provided the first clear picture of flatfish evolution. The discovery of stem flatfish with incomplete orbital migration refutes Goldschmidt's ideas, and demonstrates that "the assembly of the flatfish bodyplan occurred in a gradual, step-wise fashion". There are no grounds for thinking that incomplete orbital migration was maladaptive, because stem forms with this condition ranged over two geological stages, and are found in localities which also yield flatfish with the full cranial asymmetry. The evolution of flatfish falls squarely within the evolutionary synthesis.

Index

N